The World in Canada

Diaspora, Demography, and Domestic Politics

Edited by

DAVID CARMENT AND
DAVID BERCUSON

McGill-Queen's University Press
Montreal & Kingston · London · Ithaca

Legal deposit first quarter 2008
Bibliothèque nationale du Québec

Printed in Canada on acid-free paper that is 100% ancient forest free
(100% post-consumer recycled), processed chlorine free.

This book has been published with the aid of a grant from the Canadian
Defence and Foreign Affairs Institute (CDFAI) which was also the main
sponsor of the "World in Canada" conference in Ottawa in 2005.

McGill-Queen's University Press acknowledges the support of the Canada
Council for the Arts for our publishing program. We also acknowledge the
financial support of the Government of Canada through the Book
Publishing Industry Development Program (BPIDP) for our publishing
activities.

Library and Archives Canada Cataloguing in Publication

The world in Canada: diaspora, demography, and domestic
   politics / edited by David Carment and David Bercuson.

   Includes bibliographical references and index.
   ISBN 978-0-7735-3296-0
   ISBN 978-0-7735-3297-7

   1. Canada – Foreign relations –1945-   . 2. Multiculturalism –
Canada. 3. Canada – Emigration and immigration – Political
aspects. 4. Canada – Politics and government – 21st century.
I. Carment, David, 1959- II. Bercuson, David Jay, 1945-

FC104.W67 2007   327.71009'049   C2007-906671-2

This book was typeset by Interscript in 10.5/13 Baskerville.

THE WORLD IN CANADA

Contents

For Madeleine

Acknowledgments

The authors would like to thank Sonia Bouffard and Sara Michel for their research support and Souleima El Achkar for her translation work. We are grateful to the Canadian Defence and Foreign Affairs Institute for their support.

THE WORLD IN CANADA

Introduction

DAVID CARMENT AND DAVID BERCUSON

2007 marks the 140th anniversary of the Canadian Confederation. The Canada of 2007 is a very different nation than the one that celebrated the Centennial of Confederation in 1967. In the last thirty-nine years the nation's demographics have changed dramatically. The most important and most obvious shift has come in the ethnic makeup of Canada. The nation's chief source of immigrants are nations and regions far removed from the homelands of Canada's traditional two founding peoples, French and English-speaking. To observe the students crowding into almost any public school in the nation today is to see that the peoples of Africa, Latin America, Southeast Asia, China, the Middle East, and the Indian subcontinent are coming to Canada literally by the millions. Every now and then a survey will announce that by year so and so the majority of the population in British Columbia's lower mainland or Toronto will not count English as its first language. Visible minorities from North Africa, Haiti, the Middle East, and member nations of La Francophonie are transforming the face of Montreal. The European-based culture, so all-pervasive even as late as 1967, is being replaced by a multicultural milieu that is a positive and exciting development for some Canadians but a troubling and challenging one for others.

The nation has changed in other significant ways. The "war" babies or "boomers" as they have more recently been called have been working their way through the stages of life in a manner likened to the way anacondas swallow their prey. Once the student radicals of the 1960s, they are now the retirees of the 2000s; their needs and desires are radically different from what they have been over the past forty years. At one time, changing the world for the better was their top goal in life, now it is to keep their health as they enter old age and, perhaps, to change medicare for the better.

Canada is also undergoing a rapid shift in population. Outmigration of non-Francophones and a declining birthrate have lowered Quebec's share of the overall population to less than 30 percent, and forecasts project that that number will go lower still in the next decade. Ontario, especially Metropolitan Toronto, continues to grow more rapidly than any other province or region, giving it – and the Greater Toronto Area (GTA) – major clout in the House of Commons, but a growing split between the more conservative, rural areas of Ontario and the teeming GTA is increasingly evident in voting patterns and social attitudes. British Columbia and Alberta are also growing rapidly, not as much as Ontario, but enough so that the populations of these two westernmost provinces are, today, virtually equal to all of Quebec. By the same token, Atlantic Canada's share of the population continues to shrink.

Canadian democracy is just starting to reflect the ongoing changes that have taken place over the last forty years. The distribution of seats in the House of Commons lags badly when compared to population shifts due to a number of deliberate limitations placed on "representation by population" by politicians of past generations. And immigrant communities are almost always late to political activism. Earliest generations have traditionally been too busy establishing themselves, learning English, earning a living, or seeing to the future of their children to get deeply involved in politics. It is only now, in the last decade and a half, that immigration-based electoral politics has emerged so strongly in a large number of Canada's cities. That new activism can be readily seen in the changing nature of Parliamentary representatives.

THE WORLD IN CANADA: OUTLINE

Just as we might see Canada at home in the world, we cannot be blind to the fact that the world is at home in Canada. Accordingly, contributors to this volume trace changes in Canada's demographic makeup explore the relationship between domestic politics and Canadian foreign policy across the fields of diplomacy, development, defense, and security, and immigration. Some chapters show that Quebec has different sensibilities to international issues, and this has been historically the case.

The underlying theme of this volume is set forth in the first chapter, "A Question of Degree: The Prime Minister, Political Leadership, and Canadian Foreign Policy," by Adam Chapnick. He argues that foreign-policymaking and leadership are heavily constrained by a complex combination of motivations, coalitions, and linkages at the domestic level. Canada's successful political leaders are ones who adapt their strategies to these constraints. Only after these characteristics have been assessed carefully and balanced in relation to each other can it be determined how and why domestic factors influence Canadian foreign policy.

This theme reflects several assumptions. The first is that Canada's foreign-policymakers must consider the dispersion of preferences among their constituents. In turn, Canadians should be able to separate a foreign policy that legitimately reflects their interests and values from one that does not. Thus, the second assumption is consistent with the first: a Canadian foreign policy cannot be considered viable if it contradicts the preferences of ordinary Canadians. The third assumption is that Canada's leaders must retain some minimal degree of support among their constituency to stay in power. These assumptions emphasize important linkages between and among structural conditions, normative constraints, and strategic opportunities that are conducive to successful foreign-policymaking. In brief, under certain conditions, the motivation to pursue certain foreign policy choices arises as much from domestic considerations as from the international structural conditions associated with them.

This interpretation of linkage politics portrays elites as essentially non-self-sufficient individuals who respond to their environment and adapt, with varying degrees of success, to the influence of mass sentiments. Elites will seek to optimize results in light of other actors' interests. Sometimes, due to international and domestic constraints, which can work at cross-purposes, the choices made may be sub-optimal and relatively unsuccessful. The credibility of a foreign policy depends in part on the likelihood that it will be carried out, which increases with domestic support for such a commitment. Conversely, the more powerful the domestic groups that anticipate a resulting disadvantage, the less credible and sustainable will be any presumed policy.

Minority governments are particularly vulnerable. A wait-and-see game of doing just enough to ensure support for non-controversial foreign policies would be the preferred option for any leader wanting to stay in power. Given the inherent complexity of such a process, the difficulty in managing multiple working relationships with individual MPs from across the political and the ideological spectrums, and above all the need to avoid premature collapse, minority governments generally choose to accomplish very little and avoid controversy. It should come as no surprise that minority governments have toppled because of their failure to generate the necessary support for controversial defense policies (Diefenbaker's contentious turn at government comes to mind). But when properly managed a minority government can withstand both disagreement and challenge when it stands on principle. Lester B. Pearson, for example, not only survived a minority government situation but produced some of Canada's most enduring policies because of it. Minority government or not, effective foreign policies depend on finding the right coalitions to support them. In short, as Chapnick reminds us, domestic constraints can generate opportunities for creative statecraft. They need not be an excuse for inaction.

The balance of the chapters in this volume confront three questions as they relate to the constraints and opportunities of diasporas, demography, and domestic politics. First, what are the implications of the dramatic and sustained shift in the Canadian ethnic mosaic for foreign policy? More specifically, in what ways do diasporas influence Canadian foreign policy and what impact will and should Canada's demographic changes have on Canadian foreign and security policy in the long term?

As chapter 2, "Assessing the Impact of Recent Immigration Trends on Canadian Foreign Policy," by Elizabeth Riddell-Dixon, argues, when Canada takes action in a certain part of the world, or concentrates on a particular foreign-policy issue, it may often be the case that this is due to pressure from interest groups lobbying for their own particular cause. Today, there is an increasing openness to invite such groups to lobby on foreign-policy issues and it is expected that there will be an increase in their influence on the foreign-policy agenda even though these diasporas are very distinct and heterogeneous and may not yet be capable of influencing the policymaking process. The term diaspora has come to be widely used in the past few years beyond its original narrow association with Greek, Jewish, and Armenian ethnic communities. Members of a diaspora may include ethnic migrants, first-, second-, or even third-generation immigrants, as well as expatriates, students, guest workers, and refugees. The term reflects the rise of truly transnational populations, people who can be thought of as almost literally living in two places, playing an active role in two communities simultaneously.

The connections that today's diasporas retain with their communities of origin differ substantially from those held by previous generations of ethnic migrants. Technological advances in the late twentieth century – the rise of cheap and ubiquitous telecommunications and travel coupled with financial liberalization – have created a new type of "hyper-connectivity" between diasporas and their home communities. Remittances are central to this connectivity.

For most of Canada's history, more than 90 percent of its immigrants came from Western Europe. From the 1970s onward, Canada saw a remarkable change in its patterns of immigration with 33 percent of immigrants coming from Asia, rising to 58 percent in 1990, while European immigration declined. In recent years, more than 50 percent of new immigrants to Canada have come from Asia, mostly from China and India, making successful relations with Asia-Pacific key to Canada's foreign-policy objectives. As the world population increases from 6.5 billion to 9.1 billion, an increase in Canadian immigration will become necessary to sustain our public institutions. The levels of net migration from emerging and developing economies will be very high.

In line with the transformation in Canada's demography, Riddell-Dixon's chapter, the second of the volume, suggests that the emergence of Canadian political parties allied with ethnic groups and diaspora communities could become acceptable practice. Today transnational but informal knowledge and financial networks established by immigrant communities play a role in Canada's development and diplomatic programming. However, the risks of such networking, especially the role of remittances in fuelling conflict, should be closely evaluated. The active participation of diaspora groups in diplomacy, development, and trade clearly has positive as well as negative consequences that have to be examined.

Should Canada regulate the remittance market? Obviously, there is a call for a balance between the need of destination countries who benefit from financial flows and those remittances used to finance conflict. In this regard, the Government of Canada requires improved intelligence capabilities to study the impact of remittances in Canada but also in countries that receive them. The total amount of remittances from Canada's diaspora groups significantly dwarfs Canada's official development assistance (ODA) of slightly over 2 billion dollars. The remittance figure, which is hard to pinpoint, is much higher. Taken together with the ODA, the total amount of money as a percentage of our GNP that moves to developing countries from Canada is much higher than the much touted 0.7 percent development assistance benchmark, used to rank OECD countries. No one knows what the total figure is, but it is most likely higher than that of the Scandinavian countries, who lack the demographic diversity that make diaspora remittances possible. Of course there are some regions, specifically sub-Saharan Africa, where foreign investment is low to begin with, and these countries are fragile in part for that reason. In sum, we need to better understand how to harness the positive aspects of diaspora remittances and mitigate the negative impact they have on sustaining conflicts abroad.

Consider the cases of Haiti and Jamaica as examined in chapter 3 by Stewart Prest, Andrew Harrington, and Per Unheim. Canada has long claimed to have a "special" relationship with both these countries; language, geography, economics, and political considerations have all played a role in the formation and evolution of these relationships. Canada has repeatedly taken a lead role in international efforts to intervene in Haiti, providing financial, military, and humanitarian support to the island on numerous occasions. Canada has made Jamaica the second largest recipient of its development assistance in the region. In many ways, Montreal is the fulcrum of the Haiti relationship, just as Toronto is for the Jamaican relationship. These are the points at which the countries physically intersect. As the dominant Francophone metropolis in the Americas, Montreal has become home to a thriving, vibrant Haitian-Canadian community. With roots extending back more than half a century, Haitian-Canadians have become an integral part of the city. Similarly Toronto has become the home of a thriving Jamaican community.

As this chapter shows, both countries have troubles. Both Jamaica and Haiti's instability have implications for security in Canada. Though the relationship is indeed a complex one, the way in which Canada's immigration patterns have evolved over time to favour both countries often means that some of the less savoury dimensions of conflict in the homeland are having an impact on Canada, including the increasing presence of organized crime, gangland murders, and drug trafficking.

Chapter 4, "Multiculturalism and Canadian Foreign Policy," by Jack Granatstein, demonstrates that not only does Canada's current ethnic configuration impact on foreign-policymaking but this has historically been the case as well. As Canada's ethnic mosaic becomes more fragmented, there is the possibility that so, too, will our foreign policy, until as Granatstein points out, our national self-interest will have succumbed to a dizzying array of competing and contradictory parochial values.

Granatstein's chapter is a wake-up call for many countries that, like Canada, will be looking for answers on how to solve demographic shifts. For example, the Europeans could look to Canada regarding its immigration system, including how it recruits potential immigrants, how it deals with integration, how it repatriates criminals to their homelands, and how it has managed the bilingual aspect of its society. Granatstein's argument that Canada's core interests – security, unity, economics, democracy, and freedom – can and should be separated from soft values is provocative and probably the correct one. On the one hand, it is true that astute political leaders will never forego the opportunity to play the value card. On the other hand, Canada's political system obliges our leaders to retain at least a plurality of popular support in order to maintain political power. Canada's leaders therefore should not pursue any policy that serves the interests of one group at a real expense to others. In sum, value-driven adventurism that impinges on Canada's core interests should be discouraged.

In chapter 5, "The Parizeau-Chrétien Version: Ethnicity and Canadian Grand Strategy," David Haglund takes up the challenge of untangling the intricate and complex relationship between demography, Quebec, and Canadian foreign policy. Haglund sets out to alert us to the fact that Canada's decision-makers are strategic in their thinking, opting for short- to medium-term policy choices that will assure them of re-election and forestall long-terms structural transformation in the Canadian and Quebec political scene that would adversely affect their power base. Haglund refers to this as the "Pettigrew perspective"; a prudent, essentially realpolitik approach that reflects calculations about power at home and abroad and results in caution in the face of multiple constraints.

Value-driven foreign policies can be expected to occur only when there are strong, even overwhelming preferences and where a broad general consensus exists. Haglund draws on the Liberal

Party's efforts to tap into "anti-Americanism" both outside and in Quebec as an example of this strategy and suggests that the approach stood the Liberals in good stead during the Chrétien era, especially when it was channelled toward their own defense spending objectives. Within Quebec and among separatists specifically, Haglund argues that realpolitik strategies remain in play on important matters of defense and security. This is troubling to say the least because it quite clearly indicates that a "Canadian" grand strategy has not been an essential part of Canadian foreign policy for at least the last decade or so.

In chapter 6, "Muslim Communities: The Pitfalls of Decision-Making in Canadian Foreign Policy," Sami Aoun examines the sociopolitical perceptions of Arab Muslim communities in Canada and the reasons why these diaspora communities are thus far limited in influencing the political agenda in Canada. Aoun argues that, while the Arab Muslim community represents one of the biggest ethnocultural communities in Canada with strong ties to the homeland, this community is also very heterogeneous in nature. Cohesion is weak among community members mainly because the Arab Muslim community is diluted through cross-cutting class structures and regions.

Aoun identifies the attacks on the World Trade Center and the war in Iraq as two events that divided the Arab Muslim community even further. In particular, the war in Iraq deepened the growing lack of cohesion within the Arab Muslim community by dividing their views according to their ethnocultural group (Shiite vs Sunni). To a lesser extent, other events such as the Zahra Khazemi case in Iran, Darfur, and Rafiq Hariri's assassination in Lebanon increased rivalry between the various ethnocultural diasporas who compose the Arab Muslim community in Canada. Aoun's argument is important because it suggests that changes in Canada's demography toward politically mobilized and potentially contentious groups is likely to continue apace and that, more importantly perhaps, some aspects of Canadian foreign policy may be inherently incommensurable with some parts of its new population base, especially in the important areas of security and defense.

We turn now to the second question this volume seeks to answer: namely, how responsive is Canadian foreign policy to shifts in Canadian demography? Does foreign-policy formulation and execution take into account the needs and concerns of the diverse segments

of the Canadian population? Or is Canadian foreign policy the purview of a cloistered and monochromatic elite, insulated and isolated from cosmopolitan and transnational issues?

In chapter 7, "Just How Liberal-Democratic Is Canadian Foreign
Policy?: A Pluralist Test," Christian Leuprecht and Todd Hataley review the extant theoretical literature in order to evaluate the operational premise of the Liberal Government's International Policy
Statement that Canada should and can be a leader in the world. In
their careful and detailed juxtaposition of public opinion polls
against government actions they find an overwhelming bias among
elites to pursue a foreign policy that enhances Canada's economic
performance over and above other objectives. This elite bias flies in
the face of some fundamental realities regarding Canada's changing demography and geo-strategic position in North America. As
Leuprecht and Hataley argue, as do other chapters in this volume,
Canada's shifting demography and its relationship to the United
States will always ensure a Canadian foreign policy that is about
more than advancing economic interests.

How can the sensitive topic of Canada-US relations be handled?
Even before Jean Chrétien retired and Paul Martin was ousted, it was
long viewed that this special relationship required special handling
and its own minister to go along with it. The Harper Government
has clearly chosen to develop similar means to handle the US-Canada
relationship while at the same time deflecting criticism that it is either doing too much or not enough in its relationship with Canada's
southern partner.

That recent past governments and the bureaucratic elite have an
essentially conservative, trade-oriented, pro-US agenda is echoed in
chapter 8, "Public Perceptions of Canada-US Relations: Regional-
ism and Diversity," by Evan Potter. The idea that Canadians and especially new Canadians and Quebecers are somewhat at odds with
this agenda is also reinforced in this chapter. Potter's analysis of the
polls suggests that there may be an emerging democratic malaise in
this country. The combination of the increasing power of political
appointees, the lack of real and effective public consultation, and
the absence of political leadership to engage the public have all
contributed to this malaise. More specifically, Potter finds essential
differences of opinion on foreign policy in a number of important
areas. First there are essential differences of opinion between new
Canadians and Quebecers. He believes the two are interrelated.

New Canadians from Eastern Europe, Asia, and Africa are, to a certain extent, adopting opinions about foreign policy that reflect the established English communities versus those opinions that are professed by the French demographic in the country.

Second, he finds that government policies have not yet embraced the values that new Canadians hold. Indeed such an approach may be undesirable because there are so many different values at play. For example, governmental institutions perceive the Cold War, the fall of the Berlin Wall, and the 1991 Gulf War as important international events that influence their mandate. Indeed, "established Canadians" cling to the belief that Canada is still a middle power internationally. They believe that Canada can still lead the world in norm setting, big ideas, and soft-power concepts like human security. Yet, many new Canadians do not closely identify with these events, values, and ideas. In this regard, according to Potter, the ideas and interests of "established Canadians" seem to dominate the political agenda as it is the largest voting group in Canada. Yet Canada needs to be more forward-thinking in terms of its foreign policy by being more aware of the changes that are occurring in China and India, Latin America, Eastern Europe, and Africa and draft comprehensive policies to respond to these changes.

Potter's chapter is significant because it shows that foreign policy is important to all Canadians, but pinpointing an explicit set of values upon which to base a foreign policy may be near impossible. The Government of Canada's challenge is to demonstrate how governmental decisions concerning international affairs *impacts the interests* of the Canadian public.

For example, since the mid-1990s, Canada has staked its international reputation on the development of "soft power" tools, strategies, and ideas. The Canadian-sponsored International Commission on Intervention and State Sovereignty and human security agendas serve as examples of how Canada has tried to develop a values-based approach to foreign policy. Such ideas, while important for agenda setting, norm development, and multilateralism matter little to Canadians if they do not have a more clearly defined set of actionable policies defined by Canadian national interests.

There is some movement in this regard. Canada has chosen to work with far fewer countries through its bilateral development assistance programs, which are set to put in place operational tools that heretofore have not been part of its "soft power" agenda, and has decided to extend its defense capabilities far deeper and far wider than it ever did during the latter half of the twentieth century. With a concentration of efforts on an operational approach (as opposed to an idea-based approach) to foreign policy – whether it be in aid, diplomacy, or defense – the Canadian Government will be expected to demonstrate to the Canadian public that Canada's actions are contributing to a more stable and prosperous international environment. Precision, focus, and, above all, a clearly defined national interest that sets out priority countries, regions, and issues is now more essential than ever before.

The third question this volume seeks to answer is, how does domestic politics influence foreign-policymaking in Canada? More specifically, how does the relationship between Quebec and the rest of Canada shape foreign policy choices? Chapter 9, "Defense Policy Distorted by the Sovereignist Prism? The Bloc Québécois on Security and Defense Questions (1990–2005)," by Stéphane Roussel and Charles-Alexandre Théorêt, shows that there is a difference in opinion among Quebecers on matters of defense compared to other Canadians. The problem, they argue, lies in the qualification of this difference.

Conventional wisdom argues that this distinction is premised on Quebecers as being essentially pacifist, anti-militarist, and isolationist. Nevertheless, the authors argue, Quebecer attitudes are changing. Quebecers are becoming more and more "Pearsonian" in their outlook. In particular, sovereignists do not conform to the traditional model. They stress participation in the UN, the maintenance of peace, development aid, and support for international law. This tendency is made obvious when one considers the program of the Bloc Québécois. Indeed, the Bloc proposes an internationalist position.

However, certain contradictions persist. These contradictions emanate from the nature of the Bloc itself. In particular, one of the major contradictions of the sovereignists' position relates to Canadian participation in NORAD. Indeed, NORAD is perceived as an institution of safety and security. Roussel and Théorêt's chapter points out the basic incongruities between the Bloc's opposition to the anti-ballistic missile defense program and its support fro NORAD.

Some of these points are reinforced in the volume's final chapter, "Interpreting Quebec's International Relations: Whim or Necessity?" by Nelson Michaud. According to Michaud, Quebec actively seeks to promote its economic interests and cultural independence on the international scene, but the major obstacle to establishing an independent international presence is the absence of international recognition of Quebec as an independent legal entity. Indeed, Quebec is perceived as forming part of the Canadian confederation, of which the federal government is seen as the sole de facto international actor. In this context, the international role sought by Quebec remains limited by virtue of its inclusion within Canada.

In drawing comparisons to similar cases, Michaud finds that several federal states have found mutually beneficial arrangements that are encased within the constitutions of these countries. The Belgian constitution, for example, makes it possible for the provinces to play a part in foreign politics. Building on these insights, Michaud offers up some possibilities for federal-provincial international relations. He suggests that a negotiated solution that moderates the sensitivities of both Quebec and Ottawa will be best. Moreover, this option would also be beneficial to other Canadian provinces. Thus far, the Canada-Quebec international relations scene has been dominated by moderation on both sides to the extent that Quebec's and Canada's federal politicians continue to voluntarily abide by agreed upon rules of the game. As long as this basic level of mutual trust exists within Canada's elites, then the long-term viability of Quebec's place in Canada remains intact and the need for an independent Quebec foreign policy is minimized.

In comparing the findings of these chapters, we conclude that there is both continuity and transformation in Canadian foreign policy. First, with respect to transformation, Canada's rapidly changing demography may well be its defining feature into the foreseeable future, shaping the choices of where and how policymakers will engage the world. The increasing role of diaspora communities – whether it be in the form of remittance flows, the influence they bring to bear on Canada's engagement in conflicts abroad, or the impact they have on domestic security – is a key issue within this transformation and needs to be better understood. Various chapters in this volume suggest that managing this transformation could be difficult and often antagonistic. For example, first-generation Canadians are apt to interpret Canadian values and interests in ways that are distinct from previous generations. Canada's foreign policy should more accurately reflect these interests and values.

Second, with respect to continuity, we note that the differences in foreign-policy orientation between Quebec and the rest of Canada will not become less muted with time. Rather, chapters in this volume suggest that, if anything, there has been a sharpening of these differences in a post-9/11 world. Canada's political leadership has always had to fine-tune its foreign-policy choices in relation to these perceived differences, even when there is broad general consensus on fundamental issues such as support for the United Nations, intervention in failed states, or establishing stronger ties with the US or Europe.

In examining these continuities and transformations there is still room for optimism, however. Regardless of how dysfunctional and idiosyncratic it may appear to an outsider, Canada's foreign policy will, by virtue of its demography, diaspora, and domestic politics, continue to reflect a diversity of viewpoints, interests, and values.

1

A Question of Degree: The Prime Minister, Political Leadership, and Canadian Foreign Policy

ADAM CHAPNICK

Does the prime minister control Canadian foreign policy? In a country caught in the midst of a profound demographic and cultural transformation, are the personalities and leadership styles in Ottawa important contributors to the political direction of the nation on the world stage? A quick glance at recent headlines would suggest yes. In 2004, the journalist and commentator Andrew Cohen (A12) called external affairs "the area which could offer the prime minister the best chance to make a difference." Only days after the Conservatives won the 2006 election, the *Toronto Star* ran the line "Harper's Latin American Challenge" across the top of their front page (Harper 2006: A1). And in a 2006 national poll the marketing firm POLLARA was asked by the Canadian Institute of International Affairs to measure "Canadians' Expectations for Stephen Harper's Foreign Policy."

Academic analyses of the impact of personality and leadership styles on the general political process are consistent with this assumption of the dominance of the political leader, typically finding that heads of government will directly affect the way that foreign policy is made. Whether an individual leader's impact on the process will affect policy outcomes, however, is less clear. Indeed, in Canada it is rare to find cases of policies having been made predominantly by a single actor. It is even rarer to note instances where those policies have had a measurable impact on world affairs. This is not to suggest that Canadian prime ministers have been incapable or incompetent; rather, Canada's international position and the sociocultural dynamics of its domestic polity have restricted the opportunities for even the most ambitious leaders to effect change. Historically, Canadian heads of government have made their limited impact on global foreign-policy outcomes by affecting international norms, a result typically only evident years after they have left office.

POLITICAL LEADERSHIP IN HISTORY

For historians, political scientists, and analysts of public-policy administration, it is difficult, if not impossible, to minimize the importance of individual perceptions, memories, choices, and management techniques.[1] "It is people, after all, who make policy," writes Leslie Pal (16), "people with different personalities and talents ... their efforts must invariably have some effect." Moreover, in an international crisis – such as the immediate threat of war – even the smallest variations among political actors can have significant ramifications, particularly when the individuals are in positions of leadership (Brecher and Wilkenfeld; Greenstein; Richardson).

In the case of Canadian external relations, the impact of personality is enhanced by the centrality of the prime minister to the policy process. In his pioneering work of 1961, James Eayrs observed that the pre-eminence of the prime minister in the parliamentary system made the leader's responsibility for foreign affairs inevitable. Ten years later, when Thomas Hockin assembled a group of analysts and policymakers to discuss the unique responsibilities of the prime minister in Canadian society, his participants concluded that the leader had a marked ability to shape public thinking on international issues and to manipulate the policy agenda (Hockin; Fletcher). A decade later Kim Richard Nossal provided the most thorough evidence of the importance of the prime minister. For all intents and purposes, he explained, Canadian heads of government were constitutionally responsible for treaty-making, diplomacy, and leading the country to war. They were the primary conduits between their state and other international political leaders. They made the key domestic appointments that affected, if not determined, how foreign policy was planned and pursued. An even more contemporary assessment by political scientist Paul Gecelovsky has concurred.[2]

In the early 2000s, Prime Minister Martin's experience supported these observations. Journalists who praised his foreign policy decisions noted that he was "emerging as his own foreign affairs minister" and described members of his Cabinet as implementers of his ideas instead of innovators of their own (Travers). Critics similarly pointed to Martin himself as the cause of his government's "dismal record" in world affairs. It was Martin, wrote Mary Janigan (2005: 18) in *Maclean's*, who single-handedly derailed the release of the Canadian international policy statement with the simple proclamation, "I don't like it." When a much-revised version was finally published, those who had been directly involved largely agreed that the prime minister had made a significant difference. Martin's L-20 was given prominent treatment, for example, regardless of whatever skepticism might have been felt within Foreign Affairs Canada. There was also money available to pursue a "Big Canada" approach to world affairs, an idea that had come directly from the prime minister's office. It was Martin's statement, and the drafters were therefore confident that it would be supported with action.[3]

To this point, however, that statement has had little real impact on world affairs; with the defeat of the Liberals, it is unlikely that it ever will. Prime Minister Martin seems to have affected the domestic policy process, but the outcomes of that process are, at best, unclear. This result is neither surprising nor entirely his own doing. Political leaders, both in Canada and more generally, face what Andrew Cooper (75) calls "the conditioning effect of domestic and international constraints as well as the circumstances and timing of engagement (or lack of engagement)." At the systemic level, the hierarchical structure of the world order severely limits the ability of the leader of a smaller power to exert influence in international affairs (Chapnick 2000). Regardless of the strength or commitment of its leadership, a country like Canada will not necessarily be included at the highest stage of global discussions and therefore "cannot be full master of its own destiny" (Farrell: 167). While it has often been argued that the personality of a political leader will have its most significant impact on the country's foreign policy in a time of crisis and ambiguity (Hermann 1984; Hudson), in the Canadian case, these moments have generally only highlighted the relative powerlessness of the national leadership to effect global change.

Domestic constraints also play a significant role. Empirical studies have shown that leaders in democratic states like Canada, who are forced to maintain national unity to keep power, will naturally be more risk-averse on the world stage (Hermann 2003; Edinger; Hockin). This caution is often politically advantageous, but it generally diffuses a policy's impact. Conservative leaders are also more likely to display less interest in foreign affairs and to solicit others' opinions before making decisions, once again negating their own personal effect on the results. Only those who are either utterly obsessed with foreign policy, or completely ignorant of its importance, tend to make decisions on their own (Dyson; Greenstein; Hermann 1980).

Considering these overwhelming restrictions and limitations, it is understandable that, even in cases when Canada has played a notable role on the world stage, the history of Canadian external relations provides few examples of political leaders leaving a personal mark. Canada's military and economic contribution to the Second World War, for example, was impressive. After the fall of France, and before the formal entrance of the United States, Canada was the second most important military power on the Allied side. The combination of its billion-dollar gift to Great Britain in 1942 and its 1943 commitment to Mutual Aid prevented the British economy from collapsing. These initiatives, however, can hardly be credited to Prime Minister Mackenzie King alone. C.D. Howe's Ministry of Munitions and Supply, the contributions of the Canadian business community, and the ability of the federal government to convince French Canada of the legitimacy of depleting the national treasury to support Great Britain all played important roles.

Canada was the third most important participant in the North Atlantic Treaty negotiations of 1947 through 1949 and deserves much of the credit for enshrining Article 2 in the charter of the organization, but again, the accomplishments here – carried out under two different prime ministers – were hardly individual efforts. Hume Wrong's ability to communicate effectively in Washington, for example, and the United States' lack of interest in the socioeconomic implications of the article also played a part.

Canada contributed significantly to the reinvention of the Commonwealth as a multicultural institution in the immediate postwar period and to the admission of new members to the United Nations in the 1940s and 1950s. In neither case was the prime minister, or any other national leader for that matter, ultimately crucial to the changes. They were largely negotiated multilaterally at the official level. In these instances, the flexibility of the international institutions themselves deserve much of the credit for the results.

The Canadian contribution to the temporary end of the Suez Crisis has been attributed primarily to Nobel Prize-winning Canadian Secretary of State for External Affairs Lester Pearson. Pearson, however, was one of many members of the Liberal Cabinet and could not have succeeded without the support of his prime minister, Louis St. Laurent, and the intervention of US Representative to the United Nations Henry Cabot Lodge and Secretary of State John Foster Dulles. In the end, Pearson's vision of UN peacekeeping was not even implemented in 1956.

While it is more difficult to assess the impact of actions that were never taken, it is reasonable to assume that domestic constraints have also restricted the influence of Canadian leaders on the international order. Had Mackenzie King not feared incurring the wrath of French-Canadian nationalists as a result of Canada's generous support of Great Britain during the Second World War, he might have been better able to leverage his country's contribution into greater influence in plotting Allied strategy both during the battles and in preparation for the peace to follow. Twenty years later, John Diefenbaker's instincts told him to keep Canada away from a peacekeeping mission in the Congo. It was a civil war, he figured, and one in which neither side seemed welcoming of an international intervention. Moreover, the Canadian army was overextended, and the economy was not strong. Had Diefenbaker followed his initial thinking, perhaps the impact of a Canadian decision to stay out of the Congo might have halted the evolution of UN peacekeeping toward peacemaking. Instead, he submitted to public pressure to maintain Canada's perfect peacekeeping record and participated in what was a hopeless mission.

Under Diefenbaker's Liberal successors, Lester Pearson and Pierre Trudeau, Canada began to expand its foreign aid program into French-speaking Africa. The decision was not involuntary, but it was a direct response to domestic political pressures that had been building in Quebec since the onset of the Quiet Revolution. As a result, the assistance was spread over a large number of states in the hopes of demonstrating to Quebecers how important each individual French-speaking former colony in Africa was to the federal government. These smaller contributions could only have a limited

impact, leading one to wonder whether, without the domestic constraints, Canadian official development assistance might have been
more strategically concentrated and, by extension, influential.

Even when Canada's leaders seem to have made a distinct impact
at the domestic policy level, the results have rarely provoked real
change globally. One might credit Mackenzie King and his personal relationship with Franklin Roosevelt, for example, for the
Ogdensburg Agreement – a 1940 pact that created a Permanent
Joint Board on Defence between the two countries and led almost
inevitably to NORAD seventeen years later – but the US attitude toward the defense of Canada did not change because of it. For
Roosevelt, Ogdensburg merely affirmed something that was already
true. The United States would not tolerate attacks on the continent
that came from the north.

Similarly, defenders of John Diefenbaker have claimed that his
courageous decision to become the only white head of government
to denounce apartheid at the Commonwealth heads of government meeting in March 1961 forced South Africa to withdraw from
the organization. This contention, however, ignores the prime minister's reliance on India's decision to take a hard line against South
Africa to shield him from any blame if something had gone wrong.
Diefenbaker did play "the dominant role in formulating the Canadian position throughout" (Hilliker and Barry: 165), but were it
not for India's aggressiveness, he might just have likely taken the
same noncommittal position he had taken at the previous heads of
government meeting in 1960. South Africa's exclusion from the
Commonwealth was a result of Indian pressure as much as it was
Diefenbaker's initiative.

As prime minister in 1965, rejecting the counsel of nearly all of
his advisers, Lester Pearson spoke out boldly against Lyndon
Johnson's policy in Vietnam, generating newspaper headlines
across North America. But his comments did not change Washington's approach to the war. Pearson's advocacy of a temporary cease-
fire went unheeded, and the wrath that the prime minister
incurred from the US president restricted Canadian influence on
subsequent US foreign-policy decisions.

Just before he announced his retirement from politics (for the second time), Pierre Trudeau decided to travel the world to promote an
end to the Cold War. The decision was opposed by members of the

civil service as well as by members of his Cabinet. Nevertheless, as one source close to Trudeau reported to historians Jack Granatstein and Robert Bothwell (366, 372), the prime minister "couldn't be stopped despite the best efforts of External Affairs and others. [He] was going to do what he believed in." This peace mission, which saw Trudeau make over ten stops in Western Europe, Asia, the Soviet Union, and the United States, resonated among some Canadians. The prime minister also spoke with a number of prominent world leaders. Once again, though, the impact was negligible. As one US official recalled, after Trudeau left Washington "We never heard much more about the initiative." Nor will one find references to it in international histories of the end of the Cold War.

Finally, Brian Mulroney might justifiably take significant credit for dramatically accelerating the process that led to the Canada-United States Free Trade Agreement. Free trade was not part of his original election platform, and he made the decision to pursue it on his own. Mulroney's independent decision-making during a crisis in the 1988 election campaign was also crucial to his party's victory and the agreement's passage. Nevertheless, in the grander scheme of global economic relations, the increased integration of the two North American economies that resulted from the agreement did not represent a significant departure from the developments of the previous one hundred years.

Perhaps it is unfair to focus exclusively on positive actions. One could argue that leaders of a non-great power like Canada might exert greater international influence when they choose *not* to commit their country to a particular policy. In January 1948, nearing the end of his long political career, Mackenzie King spoke to his minister of finance about a new reciprocity agreement with the United States. "My own approval strongly given," he wrote at the end of a memorandum summarizing their conversation. The prime minister made encouraging references to the potential agreement in his diary in February as his officials continued negotiations with their US counterparts. By March, however, with the details of the deal nearly in place, King began to have second thoughts. The issue would have caused controversy in the House of Commons and might have led to accusations that he had abandoned Great Britain. The following month he called off the discussions. "But for taking this step, I am sure real trouble would arise in the future," he wrote in his diary (Pickersgill and Förster: 261, 273). Clearly, King's personal thoughts and feelings controlled the policy process. His decision upset members of his civil service and seemed to conflict with the advice of his senior ministers. At the more practical level, however, the prime minister had much less of an impact. Trade between Canada and the United States continued to increase. The Americanization of the Canadian economy was not deterred. And Canada's relationship with Great Britain did not get stronger.

The Cuban Missile Crisis provides another example of the power of the prime minister to influence process through inaction. At the same time, though, it reinforces the limits of this power beyond the national borders. In 1962 John Diefenbaker embraced an opportunity to deny the request of a colleague he detested, US President John F. Kennedy. When the Americans placed their NORAD forces on a level of alert technically known as Defcon 3 to defend against a possible war with the Soviet Union, it was Diefenbaker alone who refused to allow Canadian forces to immediately do the same. In spite of a "ground swell of Canadian support for the leadership of President Kennedy," in the press and among the national public, along with pressures from his military advisers and members of his Cabinet, Diefenbaker held fast for two days. In the end, however, his inaction had no impact on the crisis. The United States disregarded the Canadian delay, proving that "at the moment of any nuclear confrontation, the authority of the Prime Minister of Canada [would] count for little" (Lyon: 304, 306).

While admittedly selective, these examples are much more the rule than the exception. The history of Canadian external relations has been dominated largely by conservative policy choices, reflective of the restrictions placed upon the country and its leaders by history, geography, democracy, and the national polity (Chapnick 2005b; Stairs 1982). Certainly, prime ministers have attempted to create personal legacies through foreign-policy initiatives designed to proclaim their differences from their predecessors, but as David Malone and William Hogg have both shown, in spite of the rhetoric and the endless reviews, there has been little real change in Canadian foreign policy at the operational level since 1945. On the whole it is rare to see Canada's national leaders differ significantly in their attitudes toward the rest world, making their individual impact difficult to quantify (Stairs 2001).

In 1988, in his broad review of Canadian public policy, Leslie Pal (21, 24) concluded, "leadership is necessary but impossible. Leaders cannot, in most circumstances, make events; they lack the necessary power and face too many constraints." Nevertheless, Pal refused to dismiss prime ministers as inconsequential. Rather, he proposed that "the problem lies not with how we conceive of leadership, but in the assumptions we make about the nature of power." The latter had to be reconceived to reflect whether or not individuals could "set the terms by which actors in different arenas will orient themselves in the policy process." This conclusion can be applied to foreign policy specifically: to recognize the power of the Canadian prime minister abroad, one might have to stop focusing so intently on concrete state-level actions that have attracted significant worldwide attention and to consider instead the historical impact of the political leadership on the shaping of international norms. In this case, there is some evidence to suggest that an individual prime minister can have a long-term effect both at home and abroad.

Until recently, traditional assessments of Canada's contribution to the founding of the United Nations have made only limited mention of Prime Minister William Lyon Mackenzie King. Himself more interested in an upcoming national election at home, and having spent much of the war dealing with controversies surrounding conscription, King appears to have had little to do with the shaping of the new world structure in 1945. It was King, after all, who ordered his representatives at the San Francisco Conference not to press the great powers on the question of their veto. Nor was he particularly concerned with a special position for the so-called middle powers on the Security Council.

It would be misleading, however, to argue that King was therefore uninterested in world affairs or in international order. Early in his life, he had been an engaged student of labour negotiation and social reform. In his only significant scholarly work, *Industry and Humanity*, the future Canadian prime minister recognized the similarities between industrial conflict and traditional global power struggles, noting that just as representatives of labour and business could settle their disputes most effectively through peaceful negotiation, "the acceptance of nations of the principle of investigation before the resort to hostilities would mark the dawn of a new era in the history of the world" ([1918] 1973: 335). For King, international relations were about people; their safety, security, and willingness to compromise formed the basis of a stable, functioning world order.

This attitude shaped his approach to what became the United Nations Organization (UN). King was hardly interested in the UN as a structure and cared only minimally about Canada's specific powers within it. When his government learned, for example, that what became known as the United Nations Declaration of 1942 was going to include a formal distinction between the great powers – in this case the United States, the United Kingdom, the Soviet Union, and China – and the rest of the allies, a differentiation that hardly made sense given Canada's significant contribution to the war (particularly relative to China), the prime minister hardly noticed. As the war continued, King took virtually no part in the Allies' military decision-making process and only stood up for Canadian interests in any meaningful way on issues relating to the so-called "softer" side of security, such as supplies, relief, and rehabilitation.

Historians traditionally recount that during the war, and throughout the negotiations to create the UN, King's Liberal Government promoted the concept of functional representation, the idea that a state's influence in the world should be determined on an issue-by-issue basis, commensurate with its contribution to the particular situation in question. For King himself, however, functionalism meant something somewhat different. When he spoke to the House of Commons in 1943 he noted that the principle was particularly applicable "in economic matters" (1943: 4558). There was a difference between traditional, military conceptions of international security and general global well-being. The former was the responsibility of the great powers; the latter was a duty shared by all people. King foresaw Canada as a potentially significant world actor on socioeconomic, or what might well have been called industrial, issues. It was here that he believed Canadian foreign-policy planners should focus. This less popular but certainly more realistic thinking originally frustrated officials in the Department of External Affairs. Eventually, most of them came to support the idea.

By late 1943 King's behaviour in international discussions of the future world order had fallen into a pattern. Questions of war, or of traditional conceptions of global security, could be left to the major allies, "but the same conditions," he told his Cabinet War Committee, "would not obtain in times of peace" (Cabinet War Committee). As he explained to the House of Commons in August 1944, peace meant more than just military might: "The concentration on security, and on the need to marshal overwhelming force to meet threats to security, is not enough. Security from war is indeed essential, but real security requires international action and organization in many other fields – in social welfare, in trade, in technical progress, in transportation, and in economic development." If Canada were to play a significant role in the postwar world, he implied, it would have to be in these other areas (King 1944: 5909).

This attitude – which meant downplaying the exciting questions at the UN negotiations such as the reach of the great power veto or the right of the so-called middle powers to preferential treatment in elections to the Security Council – upset some of Canada's more idealistic civil servants, but the more practical came to adopt King's views as their own. By early January 1945 Canada's associate undersecretary for external affairs, Hume Wrong, had realized that – considering the unwillingness of the great powers to relinquish control over security issues, and his minister and prime minister's reluctance to push them in this area – if Canada were to make a difference in the new world security organization it would have to be in the economic and social fields. Over the next four months, as Wrong became a vocal champion of the non-military issues, Mackenzie King uncharacteristically did nothing to interfere (Chapnick 2005a).

In March 1945 Wrong's emphasis on the economic and social side of security received a public endorsement from his usually cautious prime minister. King (1945a: 26) promised the House of Commons that Canada would be "prominent" and "useful" in the non-military discussions: "The humanitarian tradition which has played so worthy a part in our national life should give us a special interest in worldwide social betterment which the assembly and social and economic council will seek to foster." He was not nearly as specific when it came to traditional security issues. At the San Francisco Conference to found the UN, King was true to his word. He ordered his delegation to pursue a policy of caution throughout the negotiations, to rarely take the lead, and to ensure that the great powers remained committed to the new world body. The key for Canada, it seemed, was the success of the conference overall, as opposed to any specific national achievements. "The years of war," he told the delegates to the second plenary session, "have surely taught the supreme lesson that men and nations should not be made to serve selfish national ends ... Nations everywhere must unite to save and serve humanity" (King 1945b: 194).

For King, all of humanity would also be served by strong economic and social provisions in the Charter, and he therefore allowed his officials to be more aggressive in their negotiations on
these issues. Lester Pearson, then the ambassador to the United
States, who had earlier shown little interest himself in the non-
military side of the UN, became a prime advocate, telling the Canadian Broadcasting Corporation that the new organization would
have to "come to think and act less and less in terms of force and
more and more in terms of forces ... the forces that create or destroy international unity and goodwill; the forces that create poverty or promote well-being" (1945). The Canadian delegation went
on to play a particularly active and forthright role in strengthening
the Charter's economic and social provisions, noting as often as
possible the linkages between military security and social stability.

What resulted was an Economic and Social Council that looked
nothing like the shell of a deliberative body proposed by the great
powers. This was a testament to Mackenzie King. It was his idea, not
his officials'. The Canadian delegation pursued the ECOSOC initiative with passion because King allowed it to, something he was un-
willing to do when it came, for example, to a campaign to restrict
the great power veto. Critics might certainly suggest that ECOSOC
has been relatively insignificant over the last sixty years, that once
again the impact of the Canadian prime minister was more evident
in terms of process than outcomes, but in this case there is reason
to think differently. Certainly, the Council's practical influence has
been less than noteworthy. Its normative importance, however, remains evident today. Strengthening the provisions of the Economic
and Social Council made a statement to the international community that security had to be conceptualized more broadly than in
purely military terms. Ensuring that the Council was part of the
new world organization's principal machinery, as opposed to
merely becoming an unimportant appendage, made it easier for individuals in later years to gain an audience when they argued for
the importance of international development to global stability.
King can take significant credit for the increasing relevance of human security to contemporary discourse, even if it remains difficult
to quantify its impact.

Ironically, considering his personal frustrations with King while
serving under him in the Department of External Affairs, Lester
Pearson was the prime minister who added the most to his legacy in

terms of worldwide impact. Between 1963 and 1968 Pearson pre-
sided over governments that increased Canada's commitment to development assistance by close to 300 percent. The prime minister's
motivations were certainly mixed, but he clearly did believe in the
role of financial aid in promoting and maintaining global security.
The tangible national contribution made during his term, combined
with his worldwide reputation, later gained Pearson an invitation
from World Bank President Robert McNamara to chair a commission on international development that would recommend improve-
ments to the condition of assistance programs across the world.

Among what became known as the Pearson Commission's recommendations was what one analyst aptly described as "a new target [in] the lexicon" of international development (Morrison: 85).
The former Canadian prime minister called for developed countries to increase their foreign aid budgets to 0.7 percent of their
gross national product by no later than 1980. The target seems to
have been set with Ottawa's prior commitments (made during the
Pearson administration) in mind, since the Commission referred
to Canada as one of six developed countries that would have the
least difficulty meeting it (Pearson 1969). Admittedly, Pearson had
already retired from his domestic political duties when he wrote
the report, and indeed under his successor Canada failed to commit to the 0.7 percent number by a specific date as the Commission
had requested, but the figure was subsequently endorsed by the
United Nations General Assembly in 1970 and became a long-term
Canadian goal. More than thirty-five years later, it remains the standard by which proponents of development assistance evaluate the
contributions of UN member-states to global security.

King and Pearson were both able to have such long-lasting impacts
for a number of similar reasons. In neither case did the cause merit
front-page international headlines. ECOSOC was eclipsed in the media by the rest of the UN, and Pearson's report was published in the
midst of the Vietnam War. These issues were also not taken particularly seriously by the most powerful states. Domestically, the Canadian economy was strong, and the idea of investing in the social
betterment of international society appealed to a then left-leaning
national public. Both initiatives lent themselves well to nationalist
rhetoric. King could tell Canadians that their accomplishment improved the state of all of humanity, while Pearson could argue that
foreign aid directed toward democratic countries reflected Canada's

commitment to the Cold War. King's opposition in the 1940s was weak and disorganized. Pearson's in the 1960s was no better. In both cases, moreover, the Conservatives would have struggled to find flaws in the federal government's policy. Finally, neither initiative was contingent on an immediate national commitment.

If there is a recipe for a Canadian prime minister to follow to achieve international influence through foreign policy it might be something like: select a relatively innocuous issue with multilateral implications; promote it passionately but carefully; do so during a period of economic prosperity; leave the opposition little to criticize; demand nothing from the Canadian public; do not expect the results to be evident until long after you have retired from politics; and perhaps most important, do not dare to take credit for your achievement.

Is there hope, then, for current and future Canadian federal leaders? History would counsel caution. No matter how cooperative the international community, how passionate the prime minister, how united the national public, and how healthy the national economy, the ability of a Canadian head of government to shape international events remains limited. There are simply too many practical, political, and normative restrictions that deny the prime minister the chance to develop and implement a foreign policy that is not only new and unique in its outlook but also measurably significant in its global impact. At the same time, however, it is possible for an influential leader with a personal interest in what is commonly perceived as a less noteworthy global issue to have a long-term effect on how the international community thinks about concepts like security. One might even go so far as to suggest that the recent successful prime-ministerial diplomatic initiative to keep what has been referred to as "tough wording" (Harper 2005: A6) in the recent UN declaration about the so-called "responsibility to protect" might eventually be judged as further evidence of this underrecognized power.

In 1976, Bruce Thordarson (691) observed that comprehensive solutions to the growing international dependence on energy and the increasing global tendency to destroy the environment would never be reached until individual states had developed their own proactive policies. "Heads of government," he predicted, "who alone possess an internal mandate and yet are aware of external ramifications, may ironically find in the future that their foreign policy leadership can best be exercised in the pursuit of appropriate policies in the domestic sphere." His thinking remains equally appropriate today, particularly in Ottawa. Regardless of its leader, Canada is unlikely to play a crucial role in the international security debate any time soon; however, on the more obscure issues, such as perhaps water conservation, for example, on which the most significant powers have yet to develop firm, explicit, and effective policies, there might well be space for a smaller state, led by a committed leader, to shape a future global norm in the image of its own policies at home. In the words of historian Sidney Hook (8), heroic leadership is always possible, it is merely "a question of degree."

NOTES

The author would like to thank Erin Baldwin for her research assistance and the editors and anonymous reviewers for their helpful suggestions.

1 On the influences on foreign policy behaviour, see Chan and Sylvan; Ravenhill; and Keller.
2 See also Michaud.
3 Confidential interviews with members of Foreign Affairs Canada. The author thanks them for their candour.

2

Assessing the Impact of Recent Immigration Trends on Canadian Foreign Policy

ELIZABETH RIDDELL-DIXON

INTRODUCTION

Data from the 2001 Census reveals that Canada is increasingly multiethnic and multicultural. In 2001, more than 18 percent of the population was foreign born – the highest percentage in seventy years.[1] On a per capita basis, Canada accepts significantly more immigrants than any other G8 country.[2] Today most immigrants are from Asia, whereas Europe was the main source fifty years ago. The trends are clear: Canada's ethnic composition is increasingly diverse, much of our foreign-born population comprises very recent arrivals, and our newcomers of the past decade have been drawn from areas of the globe very different from the major sources of half a century ago. These trends prompt the question: what are the implications of our increasingly diverse ethnicity for the makers of Canadian foreign policy?

The chapter begins by examining recent trends in legal migration into Canada. In considering the implications of these demographic changes for Canadian foreign policy, it is important to answer two broad questions. What are the foreign policy priorities for newcomers? What is their potential for exerting influence in the policymaking process? These questions are addressed sequentially.

Assessing influence is extremely difficult. There are so many factors to consider and most of the important consultations take place behind closed doors and hence off the public record. There are thousands of ethnic groups in Canada; they differ enormously in their goals, memberships, resources, tactics, and access to government officials – all of which affect their ability to exert influence in the political system. Few of these groups have been studied in depth; hence the empirical data required to make generalizations about their efficacy do not exist. Furthermore, it is very difficult to establish cause and effect. For example, Canada's trade with China has increased dramatically in the past ten years. How much of this increase is due to the actions of recent Chinese immigrants and how much is due to the fact that Canada, like other northern countries, has been working hard to establish trade connections with the world's fastest growing economy?

RECENT TRENDS IN MIGRATION TO CANADA

The past forty-five years have seen significant increases in the numbers of newcomers admitted to Canada and dramatic changes in the primary sources of immigrants. In 2001, 5.4 million people, or 18.4 percent of the Canadian population, were foreign born.[3] Between 1991 and 2001, 1.8 million people, or 6.2 percent of the total population, immigrated to Canada.[4] This number represented a significant increase over the 1.2 million who had been admitted during the 1980s and who, by 1991, comprised only 4.3 percent of the total population.[5] Prior to 1960, 90 percent of all immigrants to Canada came from Europe and only 3 percent were born in Asia.[6] Today 58 percent of our immigrants come from Asia and the Middle East, with the People's Republic of China being the leading country of birth.[7] More than 40 percent of our newcomers emanated from one of seven Asian countries: the People's Republic of China, India, the Philippines, Hong Kong, Sri Lanka, Pakistan, and Taiwan.[8] In contrast, only 20 percent came from Europe and the percentages from other geographic regions were relatively small: the Caribbean and Central and South America accounted for 11 percent; Africa was the birthplace of 8 percent; and 3 percent were born in the US.[9]

There are three main categories of migrants to Canada: the economic class, which comprised 57 percent of immigrants in 2004 (up from 50 percent in 1995); the family class, which constituted 26 percent of immigrants in 2004 (down from 36 percent in 1995);

and refugees, who comprised only 14 percent of all migrants in 2004 (up from 13 percent in 1995).[10] Not only are economic immigrants most numerous but the proportion of economic-class immigrants has been increasing over the past decade, while the numbers of family-class immigrants have declined and the figures for refugees have shown little change. The economic class aims to attract people who will contribute to making the Canadian economy strong and prosperous by bringing in large scale investments and/or starting businesses here. Privileging this category of immigrant supports the contention of the dominant-class approach that public policies reflect the long-term interests of the capitalist class.[11]

Although similar numbers of men and women were admitted to Canada, the former are overrepresented in the business class, while women are more likely to enter under the family class. This trend lends credence to feminist contentions that public policies are not gender neutral, regardless of their intent.

In light of the changing composition of Canadian society, it is not surprising that Canadians identified more than two hundred different ethnic origins when asked to give their ancestry in the 2001 Census.[12] The demographic shifts are due in part to changes in Canada's immigration policies, but they are also the result of deteriorating social conditions and increased outbreaks of violence and social unrest in many parts of the world.

FOREIGN POLICY PRIORITIES FOR THE NEWCOMERS

There is no doubt that recent immigrants and refugees, like Canadians in general, are more interested in domestic issues that in matters of foreign policy. The Canadian Ethnocultural Council, a coalition of thirty-three national ethnocultural umbrella organizations, focuses on political advocacy and educational activities to promote multiculturalism in Canada and to ensure that all can participate fully and equally in Canadian society. Most of its briefs to government focus on domestic issues, such as education, labour, health, and preserving cultural heritage.[13] International migration is the only area of foreign policy that it addresses consistently. While ethnic groups vary enormously in terms of the range and nature of their goals, some broad observations can be made about their foreign-policy objectives.

The first point of note is that ethnic groups do have foreign-policy interests. A variety of concerns are regularly raised before the House of Commons Standing Committee on Citizenship and Immigration, and the Standing Committee on Foreign Affairs and its subcommittees. For example, the criteria for citizenship are considered unnecessarily stringent. The government's decision to give greater priority to business immigrants than to family-class immigrants is criticized for hindering family reunification and containing a built-in gender bias. Concerns are raised about the treatment of domestic workers and permanent residents. Complaints are made about the understaffing in visa/immigration offices both within and outside Canada and about the backlog in processing applications. The government is urged to ensure that national standards are maintained when the provinces take over responsibility for matters pertaining to immigration. There are demands for greater protection for the political rights, mobility rights, and constitutional rights of immigrants. A further concern is Canada's failure to recognize credentials earned abroad, which often results in immigrants and refugees having to pursue further training in Canada, which can be expensive and time-consuming. Moreover, the need to find employment to support themselves and their families prevents many from taking the necessary courses to upgrade their qualifications; hence the skills and knowledge that they bring are not fully utilized.

Newcomers to Canada have several sets of foreign-policy interests: liberalizing Canada's immigration and refugee laws, expanding trade links with their countries of origin, securing increased Canadian aid for their places of birth, and getting Canada to take sides on political issues involving their countries of origin. Each is discussed below.

As the numbers of newcomers increase, the pressure to liberalize Canada's immigration and refugee laws will intensify. Immigrants are usually keen to bring relatives and friends to Canada; hence they pressure the Canadian Government to amend its immigration and refugee laws to allow more people into the country, especially from countries that are already the leading sources of newcomers.[14] Yet at the same time that the pressure to liberalize immigration and refugee laws is increasing, the Canadian Government is facing counter-pressure from the US to tighten its immigration and refugee laws. The US considers Canadian immigration and refugee laws too lax and a threat to US security. Neither set of pressures is likely to abate in the near future; hence Ottawa will face the tough challenge of finding an appropriate balance between competing domestic and external demands.

Business immigrants increase the pressure for more extensive trade links with their countries of origin. Within the business class, there are three categories: investors, entrepreneurs, and self-employed persons. To qualify for the first two categories, an individual must be able to demonstrate substantial business experience. In addition, an investor must have "a minimum net worth of CDN $800,000 and make an investment of CDN $400,000," while an entrepreneur needs to invest at least $300,000 in a Canadian business.[15] Self-employed persons must create their own employment. Anyone meeting these criteria, especially the requirements for investors and entrepreneurs, brings not only financial resources but also extensive business contacts as well as a knowledge of the language and culture of their countries of origin – all of which facilitate trade relations between that country and Canada.

China is the leading country of origin for business immigrants. Trade and investment between Canada and China have increased dramatically in the past fifteen years. Between 1990 and 2002, exports to China increased by 136 percent, imports from China rose by 1,046 percent, Canadian direct investment in China grew by a whopping 11,017 percent, and China's direct investment in Canada increased by 315 percent.[16] In 2004, Canada's exports to China increased by a further 38.8 percent, while its imports rose 29.7 percent.[17] According to Statistics Canada, "Canada was one of the few nations whose growth in exports to China last year surpassed the growth in imports."[18] No doubt these increases reflect Canada's longer-term efforts, which date back to the early 1970s, to capitalize on China's enormous domestic market. Yet such trends have no doubt been encouraged by the recent influx of business immigrants from China. After the United States, China is Canada's largest trading partner.

A wide range of ethnically based business groups already appear regularly before the Standing Committee on Foreign Affairs and its subcommittees. In many cases, they argue that the Canadian Government is not doing enough to support their economic enterprises abroad. For example, in hearings before the Subcommittee on International Trade, Trade Disputes and Investment, the Hong

Kong-Canada Business Association – the largest bilateral trade association in Canada – asserted "we don't have enough support from and interaction with Canadian officials. We have excellent support from and communications with the Hong Kong officials."[19] As new Canadians become more numerous and more established, the pressure on the Canadian Government to actively promote closer bilateral trade arrangements with countries that are the leading sources of our newcomers should intensify.

Having such ethnic diversity can enhance Canada's competitive position in expanding its trade, especially in the burgeoning Asian markets. The rapidly growing Chinese market, for example, is not easy to penetrate. To do so requires long-term engagement and offers relatively few short-term economic returns, which is tough on Canadian firms. Chinese Canadians with intimate knowledge of the Chinese economy and extensive business contacts in China may help Canada to overcome problems of access and provide a kind of "fast track" entry to Chinese markets. There is definitely a complementarity between Canada's official trade missions, which often involve politicians at the highest level as well as business people, and the pattern of recruiting business-class immigrants.

Immigrants and refugees come with strong emotional ties to their countries of birth. Once here, advances in communications technologies enable them to stay informed about developments in their countries of origin. Such information may prompt them to seek higher levels of Canadian short- and long-term development assistance. When the tsunami struck South Asia in 2004, Asian groups in Canada were quick to lobby the government for aid to the afflicted region. In addition, they worked with the media to generate broad public pressure for government action as well as to solicit individual and corporate donations for relief efforts overseas. In 2005 we saw similar activities undertaken by Canadians of Pakistani extraction in the aftermath of October's devastating earthquake.

Newcomers also pressure the Canadian Government to take particular positions regarding political controversies abroad. On some issues, they are likely to add support to current policy directions. For example, one would expect refugees who have fled their native lands to lobby the Canadian Government to sanction the abusive regime, as was the case with the Haitian community in Montreal. This does not pose a problem when Canada is already highly critical of a foreign government. Sudanese Canadians, with the support of other Canadian NGOs concerned with human rights, have urged the Canadian Government to mobilize diplomatic, political, and financial resources to stop the mass tortures and killings in Darfur.[20] Such demands are consistent with the general direction of Canadian foreign policy. Former Prime Minister Martin not only strongly condemned the human rights atrocities in Darfur and the failure of the international community to put an end to such abuses but Canada provided more material support than most countries. At the April 2005 International Donors' Conference for Sudan, of the total amount committed – US$4.5 billion – Canada pledged US$71 million over two years.[21] A month later, at a pledging conference organized by the African Union to raise money for its peacekeeping mission in Darfur, Canada stood out as the largest contributor, promising US$150 million.[22]

Refugees who have fled crimes of genocide and/or crimes against humanity can be expected to encourage the Canadian Government to vigorously promote efforts to address international impunity. Addressing international impunity has been a priority for the Department of Foreign Affairs since the late 1990s. Canada played a leading role in the establishment of the International Criminal Court, and it continues to work to ensure the Court's efficacy. Likewise, the rise of women's groups, such as the National Organization of Immigrant and Visible Minority Women of Canada, should increase domestic support for the Canadian International Development Agency's commitment to Women in Development programs.

Canadian officials at the most senior levels have identified poverty and intense feelings of marginalization and alienation as root causes of terrorism.[23] Through dialogue with Muslim communities in Canada, the government can gain a better understanding of these problems and of the types of solutions that may be acceptable and practical in Islamic countries. Arab groups have been active in presenting their views on Canada's relations with Muslim countries to the House of Commons Standing Committee on Foreign Affairs.[24]

Canada's intelligence service may benefit from developing closer relations with diverse ethnic communities. The latter can provide valuable insights into changing conditions in various parts of the globe as well as language skills and cultural understanding to aid in the analysis of data from their countries of origin.

There are other areas, however, in which responding to ethnic pressures may have political and economic costs. An independent national homeland is sought by many Sikhs and Tamils living in Canada, but for the Canadian Government to adopt these political objectives would undermine not only its relations with India and Sri Lanka, respectively, but also the credibility of its arguments for maintaining Canada's national unity. Some ethnic groups pressure the Canadian Government to criticize other states, such as China and Turkey, for their human-rights record. Were the Canadian Government to succumb to such pressure for much tougher sanctioning of these countries, it would risk damaging its relations with a major trading partner in the case of the former and a NATO ally in the case of the latter.

Racial profiling has assumed greater prominence in the wake of the 9/11 terrorist attacks on the US. In October 2002, the Bush Administration announced that those born in Iran, Iraq, Libya, Pakistan, Saudi Arabia, Sudan, Syria, or Yemen, who were not immigrants to the US, would be singled out and subjected to extra scrutiny at US borders. The Canadian Ethnocultural Council as well as Arab and Muslim communities in Canada were quick to condemn the US position and to urge the Canadian Government to protest the discriminatory policy. The Canadian Government did lodge a complaint with its neighbour and foremost trading partner. On one hand, the move upheld human rights by speaking out against racial profiling. On the other hand, it did nothing to improve the already strained relations between the Chrétien and Bush Governments or to alleviate the latter's concerns that Canada was responding too slowly and inadequately to the terrorist threats facing the United States.

From the extensive fundraising campaigns that are carried out among many ethnic communities in Canada to secure resources for partisan forces overseas, it is clear that political conflicts back home are profoundly important to at least some newcomers.[25] If violence broke out between India and Pakistan, would those born in these two countries not have strong feelings about the desired outcome? Would there not be strong lobbying efforts to persuade the Canadian Government to take sides?

Our changing demographics may pressure the Canadian Government to become involved with issues on which it has not traditionally taken a stance and from which it might prefer to remain somewhat distant. The changes may also prompt Canada to take positions that contradict its traditional approaches, which may in some cases cause tensions with our traditional allies. The Middle East provides perhaps the best example of an area fraught with conflict, in which Canada's most important trading partner perceives itself having vital interests and where strong and articulate groups (both Arab and Jewish) are vehemently lobbying to promote their objectives. Weighing all these variables presents an enormous challenge for Canadian policymakers. Canada is unlikely to have much influence over the situation in the Middle East. Furthermore, the political costs of increased intervention are significant, since any involvement may be perceived by at least one of the major factions as siding with the enemy. For these reasons, Middle East politics may be an area where the Canadian Government wishes to maintain a low profile. Yet this will prove to be more difficult as competing domestic pressures for action intensifies.

There may be increasing numbers of situations where domestic demands for action do not reflect the best overall interests of the country. Thus the Canadian Government faces an arduous challenge: the need to be receptive to the views of its citizens, including its newcomers, while at the same time formulating and implementing policies that are in the best interests of Canadians as a whole. Having established that recent immigrants and refugees have foreign-policy interests that they seek to promote, it is time to assess their potential for exerting influence in the foreign-policymaking process.

POTENTIAL FOR EXERTING INFLUENCE

There are two principal avenues through which ethnic communities can seek direct influence in the policymaking process: participating in the electoral process and forming a nongovernmental organization (NGO) to lobby the government on behalf of shared objectives. The literature on Canadian foreign policy would not lead us to expect recent immigrants to exert significant influence in either respect. Each of these avenues is examined below.

The Electoral Process

Canadian citizens can participate in the electoral process by voting and, if they want to be even more directly involved, by running for

political office. Recent arrivals tend to settle in geographically concentrated areas; hence their potential for influencing electoral outcomes is increased. Immigrants and refugees are more likely to live
in large urban centres than are Canadians in general. In 2001,
64 percent of Canadians were city dwellers, while 94 percent of those
who came to Canada in the 1990s settled in urban centres.[26] In the
past decade, most immigrants (73 percent) settled in one of three
cities: Toronto, Vancouver, and Montreal – cities that are home to
"just over one-third of Canada's total population."[27] In short, newcomers are proportionately more geographically concentrated in
these three cities than are those born in this country. Furthermore,
the data for 2001 show a marked increase over the statistics for the
previous three decades.[28] In 2004, 42.4 percent of all permanent
residents arriving in Canada settled in Toronto, while Montreal and
Vancouver received 16.1 percent and 13.9 percent respectively.[29]

Of course, newcomers do not instantly become voters, since voting is a privilege reserved for Canadian citizens. The criteria for citizenship include being a permanent resident who has lived in
Canada for three consecutive years before applying and who can
communicate in English or French and pass a citizenship test.[30]
Hence, there is a time lag between arrival in Canada and being eligi-
ble to vote. Over time, however, the members of ethnic minorities
(i.e., those who are not of British and/or French descent) have
swelled the ranks of the electorate, and they will continue to do so.
Since ethnic communities tend to be geographically concentrated,
one may expect them to exert increasing influence over political
choices, most of which are likely to be in the domestic realm but
some of which will relate to the types of foreign-policy objectives discussed earlier (e.g., immigration and refugee policies, trade, foreign
aid, and international politics concerning their countries of origin.)

While geographic concentration may enhance the chances of affecting electoral outcomes, the nature of the Canadian electoral
system militates against fully realizing this potential. Drawing on
the work of Jerome Black, Anver Saloojee outlines a range of structural barriers faced by racial minorities when they try to run for political office:

• The recruitment process works to confer advantages on established
  groups. This is accomplished in two distinct ways: because they dominate among the gatekeepers and because they tend to recruit in their
  own images.

- Those who currently dominate the higher echelons of established political parties are reluctant to share power, "they do not yield their monopoly to new social groups."
- Racial discrimination that subtly acts to exclude members of racialized communities.
- The continual reliance by recruiters on established networks in the British and French communities to recruit prospective candidates.
- Incumbency that "works to preserve the status quo."[31]

As a result of these factors, members of racialized communities are less likely to be chosen as candidates by the main political parties, especially in winnable ridings. There are, of course, other factors to consider. For example, in her study of ethnic groups in Montreal, Miriam Lapp found that some communities – like the Chinese – are less interested in political activism.[32] All these factors may help explain why ethnic minorities are underrepresented in House of Commons.

Although the Canadian Government has been strongly promoting multiculturalism since the mid-1970s, its emphasis on ethnic diversity is not well reflected in the composition of the House of Commons. Ethnic minorities have modestly increased their presence in Parliament from what it was three decades ago, although the growth has not been steady. There was an unprecedented increase in the 1993 election when the representation of ethnic minorities came close to reflecting their proportion of the Canadian population.[33] In the 1997 election, their representation rose by almost 1 percent, but it dropped by 1.3 percent in the 2000 election.[34] Between 1997 and 2000, the proportion of seats held by visible minorities actually decreased from 6.4 percent to 5.6 percent.[35] Of the 307 members of Parliament elected in 2004, thirty-seven (12 percent) were born outside Canada.[36] The geographic origins of these members are as follows: Europe (nineteen), Asia (seven), Africa (five), Latin America (two), the United States (two), and the Caribbean (two). Fourteen of the thirty-seven are visible minorities, and together they comprise only 4.6 percent of the 38th Parliament. Women, in general, and women from minority communities, in particular, remain grossly underrepresented in Parliament. Women's share of seats has remained fairly constant at around 20 percent over the last three elections.[37] Clearly, it is still not an equal playing field in any sense, and women who do manage to get elected tend to have stronger than average credentials.[38]

In short, the election to the House of Commons of visible minorities and especially women of colour has not kept pace with demographic trends. Nonetheless, their numbers have risen from the levels three decades ago as ethnic communities have become sufficiently integrated to be able to mobilize politically and to field candidates more effectively. Numbers, however, tell only part of the story. One must also consider whether members of Parliament are able to champion the foreign policy objectives of their ethnic communities.

The Canadian political system militates against members of Parliament successfully affecting the direction or substance of Canadian foreign policy. While cabinet ministers and bureaucrats are central actors, Parliament plays a relative minor part in foreign-policy formulation. Its role consists largely of criticizing and approving legislation, and of holding the executive responsible to the electorate. The influence of individual members of Parliament is severely limited by institutional constraints, such as party discipline, which, especially under a majority government, ensures that few changes are made to legislation after it is introduced to the House of Commons.[39] Private member's bills receive low priority and usually meet with little success.

Politicians are primarily concerned with domestic affairs, and foreign-policy issues rarely make election agendas. For at least the past decade, the government has been preoccupied with issues of the debt, budgetary constraints, and national unity, which have eclipsed other issues, including the foreign-policy concerns of immigrants and refugees.

Yet, members of Parliament cannot completely ignore the pressing demands of their constituents if they hope for re-election. If immigration trends continue, newcomers will ultimately become more numerous in the House of Commons, and more members will be elected to represent ridings with pronounced ethnic concentrations. As a result, the pressure to have the concerns of ethnic communities reflected in Canadian foreign policy will increase.

NGO Advocacy

Twenty years ago relatively few ethnic groups had an active involvement with foreign-policy issues.[40] Now not only do most ethnic communities have their own lobby groups but there are national umbrella groups, which in turn participate in the work of the macro-level umbrella organization: the Canadian Ethnocultural Council.

NGO efficacy is determined by a wide range of factors: a group's resources, its tactics, the nature of its objectives, its timing, and perceptions of its legitimacy. Paul Pross provides a useful distinction between institutional and issue-oriented groups.[41] The former have established, cohesive organizational structures, permanent offices, paid staff, and stable memberships. They understand the policy-making process, enjoy fairly long-term relationships with relevant sectors of government, and seek long-term benefits from such relationships. Hence, institutionalized groups are well positioned to monitor government policy and to cultivate ongoing relations with key policymakers. These groups are, according to Pross, most likely to realize their lobbying goals. Issue-oriented groups, in contrast, focus on more narrow, short-term goals and generally lack the internal cohesion, focus, organizational structures, stable memberships, and established access to key policymakers enjoyed by the institutional groups. While no group fits either prototype perfectly, ethnic groups are likely to be closer to the issue oriented – rather than the institutionalized – end of the continuum.

Yet as groups become more established, acquire better resources, and gain experience with the foreign-policymaking process, they can move along the continuum toward the institutionalized end. In the early 1980s, the Jewish lobby was effective – it was strong and relatively well resourced, and it spoke with a unified voice in public – while Arab groups were far less well organized and institutionalized and they represented very disparate communities. Today the Jewish lobby remains highly sophisticated and institutionalized; however Arab and Muslim groups have moved a considerable way along the continuum toward institutionalization. They have become much more prominent than they were twenty years ago, and their strong and articulate voices are being heard in the political process. For instance, the Council of American-Islamic Relations Canada, an umbrella group whose membership comprises over 140 local and national Muslim organization, mounted a lobbying campaign to persuade the prime minister to advocate for the release of Canadian Muslims considered to be unjustly imprisoned in Syria and to organize an independent inquiry into the alleged torture of Canadian Muslims by other countries.[42]

Access to key government decision-makers is most readily available to those with the best bargaining chips: those having resources desired by those responsible for formulating and implementing political decisions. Financial resources enable a group to contribute campaign funds or to provide a service to a politician or political party. More importantly, they facilitate hiring professional staff and developing the structures, tools, and commodities to bargain more effectively with government officials. Having the ability to deliver (or withhold) large blocs of geographically concentrated votes may facilitate influence with politicians. Bureaucrats responsible for policy development are more receptive to groups with the expertise required for the effective formulation and implementation of policies and programs. Organizational structures that parallel the state's political structures facilitate the cultivation of key contacts and permit persistent and diverse lobbying efforts.

In addition to its internal resources, a group's potential to exert influence is affected by its goals, the degree to which it is perceived to be credible, its sense of timing, and its ability to court allies. It is easier to get a sympathetic hearing from policymakers when one's goals are compatible with the latter's perception of the national interest. Government officials are more receptive to groups that they consider legitimate and that will be seen as credible allies. Timing is extremely important. As a rule, it is best to start lobbying early in the process rather than waiting until after a policy has been announced as official government policy.

Having support outside government is also advantageous. Ethnic groups often find allies among other Canadian NGOs. Although people born in Africa comprise a small percentage of our population, their concerns about African development are being championed by the Africa Canada Forum – an umbrella group for some forty organizations in Canada – as well as by Canadian development assistance groups working in Africa. It helps to have public opinion on one's side; however, cultivating societal support is very time consuming, and it taxes the resources and the stamina of the group and its leadership. Furthermore, media coverage, which is vital to the process, is not equally accessible to all issues, and even groups that do capture positive media attention are likely to find such support short-lived.

While each of the sets of factors discussed above can enhance an NGO's efficacy, no one factor or even a combination of factors can guarantee success. For a group to be effective, it needs to have a critical mass of support, sufficient homogeneity to have unity of purpose, and leaders who understand how to seek access into the policymaking process. With their rising numbers and their growing sophistication,

ethnic groups are increasingly able to meet these internal requirements, although not all are equally well positioned to do so. The Jewish community has been very effective in speaking with a united voice.
Arab Canadians are much more disparate; hence it can be difficult
for them to agree on policy objectives, especially those toward the
Middle East. Would Lebanese Canadians and Syrian Canadians be
able to agree on a desired outcome to the longstanding animosity between their respective countries? There are, however, issues, such as
racial profiling in the wake of the 9/11 terrorist attacks, on which it is
much easier for them to reach consensus.[43]

An NGO's potential for success is profoundly affected by the political climate at home as well as by developments abroad – something over which NGOs generally have little control. The external
environment, which includes the actions of foreign actors and
events in other parts of the globe, constitutes a major determinant
of Canada's foreign policies and sets the parameters within which
Canadian decision-makers have to operate. Canada exerted little, if
any, influence over the US-led war on Iraq, the UN Security Council's failure to authorize a UN force to stop the killings and torture
in Darfur, the renewal of civil war in Haiti, and the US administration's decision to tighten its border regulations. Yet these are
crucial events to which Canada has had to respond. Some developments abroad work to the advantage of ethnic communities. The
international attention accorded to the earthquake in Pakistan created an atmosphere in which Canadians were more likely to be receptive to Pakistani groups seeking aid for the victims. In other
cases, however, developments abroad do not help ethnic communities. The Bush administration's preoccupation with fighting terrorism has made it harder for Muslim groups concerned with racial
profiling to have their views reflected in policy.

At home, Canada's policies to nurture and promote multiculturalism, which are seen as critical bulwarks for ethnic groups, have received diminished government support in the past decade.[44] The
federal multicultural program is no longer providing ethnic groups
with core funding, which has significantly undermined their financial bases. Increased immigration has been accompanied by a back-
lash from those who see immigrants taking jobs from Canadians
and being a drain on the public purse. The Reform/Alliance
Party's rise to prominence in the House of Commons presented a
tough challenge to government policies in this area.

In the 1993 election, the Reform Party called not only for abandoning the policy of multiculturalism (along with any form of official recognition of ethnic collectivities including bilingualism and Aboriginal self-government) but also called for a reduction in the annual immigration level by at least 50 percent, a position not supported by any other party, i.e., the Liberals, the Progressive Conservatives, the New Democrats, and the Bloc Québécois.[45]

The political climate of the past decade has not been entirely welcoming of newcomers and their demands. Most recent studies of NGO involvement conclude that NGOs exert relatively little influence in the Canadian foreign-policymaking process.[46] As a subcategory of NGOs, ethnic groups are unlikely to fare any better.

CONCLUSIONS

The factors prompting people to leave their countries of origin and seek a new life in Canada will only increase. At the same time, Canada depends on immigrants to maintain its labour force and ensure its prosperity. In response to the country's aging population, its low birth rate, and its chronic shortage of skilled workers, the government is planning to increase immigration levels by 40 percent over the next five years.[47] The result will be newcomers entering our country in larger numbers and comprising ever greater proportions of our population. Their arrival does not create a major change overnight, but it is likely to result in an incremental reorientation that will have profound effects in the long run.

NOTES

The author acknowledges assistance from the Alumni Research Awards program, Faculty of Social Science, The University of Western Ontario.

1 Statistics Canada, "Canada's Ethnocultural Portrait," 2.
2 For Canada, the net international migration rate was .61 percent, while it was .52 percent for the United States – the next highest recipient – and just over .2 percent for Germany, the Russian Federation, and the United Kingdom. Statistics Canada, "The Daily: Demographic Statistics," 1.
3 The percentage in 1996 was 17.4. Statistics Canada, "Canada's Ethnocultural Portrait," 2.

4 Ibid., 4.

5 Ibid.

6 Ibid., 4, 5.

7 Ibid., 4.

8 Ibid.

9 Ibid.

10 Citizenship and Immigration, "Facts and Figures, 2004: Canada – Permanent Residents by Category," 3.

11 For a comprehensive discussion of the approach and its applicability to Canadian foreign policy, see Cranford Pratt, "Competing Perspectives on Canadian Development Assistance Policies."

12 Statistics Canada, "Canada's Ethnocultural Portrait," 12.

13 Audrey Kobayashi, "Advocacy from the Margins: The Role of Minority Ethnocultural Associations in Affecting Public Policy in Canada," 262–6.

14 For example, in 2005 the House of Commons Standing Committee on Citizenship and Immigration heard briefs regarding the admission and integration of newcomers into Canada from a wide variety of ethnic groups, including the Calgary Immigrant Women's Association, Canadian Arab Federation, Canadian Islamic Congress, Canadian Polish Congress, Centre Cultural Islamique du Québec, Centre of Integration for African Immigrants, Chinese Canadian National Council, Chinese Professional Association of Canada, Coalition Against the Deportation of Palestinians, Communauté Catholique Congolaise du Canada, German Canadian Council, Golden Triangle Sikh Association of Canada, Hungarian Cultural Society of Greater Vancouver, India Welfare Association of Canada, National Alliance of Philippine Women in Canada, National Association of Canadians of Origin in India, National Congress of Chinese Canadians, National Indo-Canadian Council, National Organization of Immigrant and Visible Minority Women of Canada, Pakistan Canada Association of Calgary, Portugese Canadian National Congress, Sikh Federation of Edmonton, sos Viet Phi, Ukrainian Canadian Civil Liberties Association, Ukrainian Canadian Congress, and Ukrainian Professional and Business Federation of Canada.

15 Citizenship and Immigration, "Who Is a Business Immigrant," 1.

16 Statistics compiled from Industry Canada, "Canadian Imports (Exports) Year Annual Trend 1990–2002."

17 Statistics Canada, "Study: Canada's Trade and Investment with China."

18 Statistics Canada, "Study," 1.

19 Subcommittee on International Trade, Trade Disputes and Investment, Standing Committee on Foreign Affairs and International Trade,

37th Parliament, 2nd Session, "Presentation by Mitch Kowalski, Vice-President, Hong Kong-Canada Business Association," 2.

20 For example, the Canadian Jewish Congress recently joined the Darfur Association of Canada in calling on the Canadian Government to take further action to prevent the crisis in Darfur from becoming a Rwanda-like genocide. Canadian Jewish Congress, "CJC Pacific Region and Darfur Association Call on Prime Minister to Keep His Commitments."

21 For consistency, the Canadian pledge of CDN$90 million has been converted to US dollars. The original figure was drawn from CBC News, "PM offers $170 M, 100 troops to Sudan." Of Canada's pledge, just over 30 percent was allocated specifically to Darfur.

22 In contrast, the United States promised an additional US$50 million. UN Office for the Coordination of Humanitarian Affairs, "Sudan: Annan calls for support to AU mission in Darfur."

23 Prime Minister's Office, "Address by Prime Minister Jean Chrétien on the Occasion of the United Nations General Assembly High-Level Plenary Debate on the New Partnership for Africa's Development," 2.

24 For example, over the past three years, the Committee has heard briefs on the subject from the Aga Khan Foundation of Canada, BADIL Resource Centre for Palestinian Residency and Refugee Rights, Canadian Arab Federation, Canadian Islamic Congress, Council on American-Islamic Relations-Canada, and National Council on Canada Arab Relations.

25 Stewart Bell, "Blood Money: International Terrorist Fundraising in Canada." Bell notes, however, that newcomers are often coerced into contributing funds under threat of violence; hence it is hard to determine how many contributors actually strongly support the cause.

26 Statistics Canada, "Canada's Ethnocultural Portrait," 5.

27 Ibid.

28 Of all immigrants to Canada in the 1980s and 1970s, 66 percent and 58 percent, respectively, chose to settle in Toronto, Vancouver, or Montréal. Statistics Canada, "Canada's Ethnocultural Portrait," 5.

29 Citizenship and Immigration, "Facts and Figures 2004: Immigration Overview: Permanent and Temporary Residents," 1–3.

30 Citizenship and Immigration, "Becoming a Canadian Citizen," 1.

31 Anver Saloojee, "Inclusion and Exclusion: A Framework of Analysis for Understanding Political Participation by Members of Racialized and Newcomer Communities," 43. Saloojee cites the passages in quotation marks from Jerome Black, "Minority Representation in the Canadian Parliament Following the 1997 Election: Patterns of Continuity and Change."

32 Miriam Lapp, "Ethnic Group Leaders and the Mobilization of Voter Turnout: Evidence from Five Montreal Communities."

33 Jerome H. Black, "Ethnoracial Minorities in the Canadian House of Commons: The Case of the 36th Parliament," 106.

34 Jerome H. Black, "Ethnoracial Minorities in the House of Commons: An Update on the 37th Parliament," 25–6.

35 Black, "Ethnoracial Minorities in the House of Commons," 25–6.

36 Figures compiled from Parliament, "38th Parliament, Members of the House of Commons" and "Members of the House of Commons, 1867 to Date: Born Outside Canada."

37 Nikki Macdonald, "Women Beneath the Electoral Barrier," 26.

38 Jerome H. Black, "Entering the Political Elite in Canada: The Case of Minority Women as Parliamentary Candidates and MPs," 162.

39 John English, "The Member of Parliament and Foreign Policy."

40 Elizabeth Riddell-Dixon, *The Domestic Mosaic: Interest Groups and Canadian Foreign Policy.*

41 *Group Politics and Public Policy*, 114–15, 117.

42 Council on American-Islamic Relations Canada, "Demand Prime Minister Appoint Investigation into Torture of Canadian Muslims Abroad."

43 In response to Bill C-36 – the Liberal Government's anti-terrorism legislation – the Council on American-Islamic Relations Canada presented a detailed brief to the Standing Committee on Justice and Human Rights on behalf of more than 140 Canadian Muslim groups, in which it outlined the ways in which their member could be negatively impacted by the legislation. Council on American-Islamic Relations Canada, "Muslims Must Immediately Urge Parliamentary Committee to Amend Bill C-36."

44 Audrey Kobayashi, "Advocacy from the Margins," 243–5.

45 Yasmeen Abu-Laban, "Welcome/STAY OUT: The Contradiction of Canadian Integration and Immigration Policies at the Millennium," 195.

46 See Mark Neufeld, "Democratization in/of Canadian Foreign Policy: Critical Reflections"; Kim Richard Nossal, "The Democratization of Canadian Foreign Policy: The Elusive Ideal"; Cranford Pratt, "Competing Perspectives on Canadian Development Assistance Policies"; Elizabeth Riddell-Dixon, *Canada and the Beijing Conference on Women: Governmental Politics and NGO Participation*, especially 182–9; and Sandra Whitworth, "Women, and Gender, in the Foreign Policy Review Process." A major exception was the landmines case, which was clearly a unique coming together of factors propitious to NGO efficacy. See Maxwell A. Cameron, Robert J. Lawson, and Brian W. Tomlin (eds), *To Walk without Fear: The Global Movement to Ban Landmines*, and Veronica Kitchen, "From Rhetoric to Reality: Canada, the United States, and the Ottawa Process to Ban Landmines."

47 Alexander Panetta, "Ottawa Plans to Boost Immigrant Intake."

3

Jamaica, Haiti, and the Role
of Diasporas

ANDREW HARRINGTON, STEWART PREST,
AND PER UNHEIM

INTRODUCTION

This chapter presents an analysis of the role that diasporas play in
contributing to and preventing conflict in Jamaica and Haiti. Canada has long claimed to have a "special" relationship with both
countries; language, geography, economics, and political considerations have all played a role in the formation and evolution of these
relationships, while sustained migration from both Caribbean
countries to Canada's largest cities – Toronto and Montreal, in particular – has entrenched them over time.

Both Jamaica and Haiti experience domestic troubles, and instability in each country has implications for Canadian security. Canada
has repeatedly taken a lead role in international interventions in
Haiti, providing financial, military, and humanitarian support on numerous occasions. Jamaica, meanwhile, is the second largest recipient of Canadian development assistance in the region. Both
countries also have large diaspora communities that offer opportunities for political and economic entrepreneurs. In many ways, Montreal is the fulcrum of the Haitian-Canadian relationship, as is
Toronto for the relationship with Jamaica. These are the points at
which the countries physically intersect. As the dominant Francophone metropolis in the Americas, Montreal has become home to a vibrant Haitian-Canadian community. With roots extending back more

than half a century, Haitian-Canadians are an integral part of the city. Similarly, Toronto is home to a thriving Jamaican community. Though the relationships are complex, the way in which Canada's immigration patterns have evolved over time to favour both countries has meant that some of the less savoury dimensions of conflict in the homeland have an impact on Canada, which include an increased presence of organized crime, gangland murders and drug trafficking.

Jamaica suffers persistent low-level civil violence and an exceptionally high crime rate related to inter- and intra-gang violence (Barrera et al.), while Haiti has experienced full collapse and numerous foreign interventions. The fact that both countries are Small Island Developing States (SIDS) provides both countries with partial immunization against certain conventional effects of large-scale conflict and horizontal diffusion but also creates conditions favourable to protracted, low-intensity organized violence. Jamaica and Haiti may be unlikely to engage in direct confrontation with neighbouring states, but they do engage in "safety valve" behaviours whereby internal conflict is allowed to build to a certain level and is then externalized. The capacity to manage this kind of dangerous process has been compromised but contained in the case of Haiti, while in Jamaica the process is manifest in low-intensity violence that often spills over into the diaspora community, with fatal results. A key question is why conflict has been fatal in Haiti but not in Jamaica; does the answer lie in part in the distinct role the diaspora has played in either country?

In answering this question we begin by noting that the linkage between diaspora communities and domestic violence is inherently ambiguous, with both positive and negative dimensions. As a result, thorough analysis requires that all aspects of diaspora activities be properly documented, weighed, and evaluated for their impact. In examining the security dimension, questions include: what roles do Haiti and Jamaica's diaspora communities play in protest, rebellion and other forms of mobilization; is the criminalization of conflict more likely than political mobilization; and are we looking at the diffusion of conflict motivated more by greed than grievance?

In an attempt to answer these questions, we first identify the background conditions as well as proximate political and socioeconomic causes that generate insecurity in Jamaica and Haiti. Treating each country as a separate case study allows us to tease out distinct patterns of conflict, criminality, and cooperation and then draw conclusions based on a comparison of these patterns. In the next section we specify the security linkages between Canada and these countries and examine the ties and potential roles of each country's diaspora as a positive force for change at home. We conclude with a summary of how the security of these two countries and the presence of significant diaspora populations could have considerable implications for Canadian foreign policy.

CASE STUDY: JAMAICA

Background

As with many other SIDS, Jamaica faces specific challenges unlike those encountered in larger, more diverse states. To the extent that conflict-related activities are present, they are manifest in problems and vulnerabilities not necessarily associated with conventional conflict. Consequently, such phenomena may be overlooked in studies employing standard measures of conflict such as the number of battle-related deaths (Carment et al.). As stated above, while Jamaica's domestic problems have not resulted in the wholesale outbreak of conflict, the country has experienced persistent, low-intensity civil violence and a high crime rate, primarily as a result of gang-related activities (Barrera et al.). It should be noted these problems may exist across the island, but the focal point is in the capital, Kingston.

Proximate Causes of Conflict and Crime

POLITICAL FACTORS. Jamaica may be characterized, somewhat paradoxically, as a stable, two-party parliamentary democracy with a tendency for violence in the lead-up to its quadrennial general elections.[1] The centre-left People's Nationalist Party (PNP) has governed Jamaica since 1989. After taking over from former Prime Minister P.J. Patterson in March 2006 in an internal vote, well-known former Minister of Local Government Portia-Simpson Miller became *de facto* prime minister of a government haunted by its reputation for corruption,[2] inefficiency, and "political tribalism" (Kerr); moreover, Jamaica ranked sixty-fourth out of 158 countries in Transparency International's Corruption Perceptions Index in 2005.[3] Acknowledging this, the government recently took steps to crack down on corruption and promote good governance, including the introduction of access to information legislation and the enactment of a *Corruption Prevention Act.*[4] As of late 2006, however, Prime Minister Simpson-Miller was already being criticized for her alleged lack of effective leadership, and new allegations of "governmental sleaze" stemming from the PNP's 2006 annual conference have both decreased the public's faith in genuine reform and buoyed the hopes of the opposition Jamaican Labour Party (JLP) less than ten months before the next general election.[5]

SOCIOECONOMIC FACTORS. Jamaica's economy depends significantly upon primary commodity exports, tourism, and remittances from islanders living and working abroad.[6] The country is highly vulnerable to economic shocks that accompany natural disasters such as Hurricanes Ivan, Emily, and Dennis in 2004 and 2005 (World Bank 2006a, 99).[7] Jamaica's national debt to GDP ratio is extreme,[8] and, as a result, high debt payments have severely limited government spending. A persistent increase in domestic price levels has also been a concern for Jamaican consumers; inflation reached 15.3 percent annually in 2005.

Though these statistics are not encouraging, other trends appear more positive. Unemployment dropped over 3 percentage points between 2002 and October 2005,[9] and the opening of the Caribbean Single Market and Economy (CSME) in January 2006 is hoped to expand economic opportunities within member countries (Barrera et al.). The implementation of the PetroCaribe agreement with Venezuela should reduce the country's vulnerability to volatile petroleum prices, (Barrera et al.), while the Jamaican Government has recently taken steps toward reducing its national debt to sustainable levels through fiscal austerity measures and investment promotion.[10]

CRIMINALITY AND PERSISTENT LOW-INTENSITY VIOLENCE. Like many SIDS, Jamaica has suffered neither international conflict nor open civil war in forty years of independence; instead, various political and economic problems have manifested themselves in persistent low-intensity internal violence and civil unrest (Carment et al.). Arguably, the key factor driving such activity is gang-related violence. Some Jamaican gangs have political dimensions, having served, and in some cases been created to serve, as enforcement wings for political parties. Gangs incubated urban "garrison communities," using coercion and threats of violence to mobilize voters and bring preferred candidates to power (Kerr). By the 1980s, clashes between militant wings of the parties resulted in many fatalities (Erikson and Minson, 159–71). Sporadic riots, intimidation, and police crackdowns on opposition parties continue to characterize general election periods.[11] Previous electoral campaigns have featured allegations of security forces being "hand-picked" to "target and intimidate" opposition groups.[12] Though not verified, these allegations are a strong indicator of the politicization of violence in the small island nation.

Many gangs have turned from politics to the drug trade while still retaining their strong political links.[13] Various other local and international gangs have emerged to capitalize on the illicit drug trade, controlling various neighbourhoods. Grinding "tit for tat" gang violence resulted in a record 1,700 homicides and a high overall crime rate in 2005.[14] Despite a positive trend in Jamaica's unemployment rate and a "youth bulge" (the proportion of the population under fifteen years of age – declining over the past fifteen years) 30 percent of Jamaica's population remains under fifteen and school enrolment beyond the primary level is decreasing (Barrera et al.). Increased gang participation among disenchanted youth seems probable in light of the paucity of available opportunities (Barrera et al.).

Gang activity in foreign cities with large Jamaican diaspora communities is often connected with gang activity in Jamaica, and vice versa. Jamaicans deported from the United States, the United Kingdom, and Canada often re-assimilate into gangs in Jamaica; soon after arrival, some criminal deportees reconstitute their former gangs, join new ones, or create their own. Unemployed local teenagers are easy recruits, eager to learn from their "cultured" cousins.[15] However, despite 2,161 alleged criminals being deported to Jamaica in 2005, concrete evidence regarding the extent to which deportees contribute to criminality in Jamaica remains elusive.[16] What is certain, however, is that convicted criminals – as opposed to those deported for minor infractions or visa violations – often leave with valuable knowledge of sophisticated crimes and crime prevention systems abroad. They also retain connections through which they can receive illegal arms in exchange for narcotics from Jamaica.[17] Deportees without criminal connections may still present a burden to social service institutions and can be a source of tension within communities and families.

Major riots are frequent in Jamaica. In 2001, surprise police raids against former Prime Minister and JLP leader Edward Seaga's "garrison community," Tivoli Gardens, led simmering gang hostilities to erupt into wholesale violence against security forces and rival gangs. The Jamaican Defence Forces (JDF) deployed onto the streets of Kingston to restore order.[18] In response to such persistent problems with drugs and gang-related violence, the JDF combined forces with the Jamaican Constabulary Force (JCF) and law-enforcement agencies from the United States and England for Operation Kingfish, taking aim at organized drug syndicates. Opinions on its effectiveness vary, but it can plausibly be argued that such operations do not address the underlying root causes of violence.[19]

CASE STUDY: HAITI

Background

Haiti is a troubled country, beset by a range of economic and social problems and plagued by recurrent political and social clashes. Unlike the more specific problems faced by Jamaica and most other SIDS, Haiti's problems span the full spectrum of public life.[20] Encouragingly, the country has enjoyed a period of relative peace in the wake of the 2006 presidential and legislative elections, which were widely viewed as successful. The effects of the elections should not be overstated, however. While they represent a significant window of opportunity for the government and international community to initiate a renewed and reinvigorated program of political and economic reform, Haiti's position remains precarious. Core government institutions lack sufficient resources and are tainted by corruption, while armed groups remain active throughout the country. Improvement in the short to medium term will require a degree of mutual tolerance among Haiti's fractious political factions, as well as significant, prolonged, and closely coordinated international engagement in the country.

Proximate Causes of Conflict and Crime

POLITICAL FACTORS. There have been thirty-five changes of government since Haiti won independence from France in 1804; most of these changes have been violent.[21] The most recent cycle of violence began in 2000, following controversial elections that returned Jean-Bertrand Aristide to office for a second term. Only recently have levels of tension lessened somewhat. The recent transition from the interim government headed by President Boniface Alexandre and Prime Minister Gérard Latortue to the newly elected government of President René Préval took place in a relatively peaceful manner. International observers and, more importantly, major factions within Haiti have accepted the result (IMMHE 2006). The country experienced a decline in the level of violence in the wake of the presidential and legislative elections, with most factions appearing to have adopted a wait-and-see approach to how the new government performed (International Crisis Group, 1). Violence has surged again more recently however, with a growing number of kidnappings reported throughout the latter half of 2006.[22]

SOCIOECONOMIC FACTORS. Apart from its turbulent political circumstances, Haiti features a wide range of other potentially destabilizing factors. Chief among these is its moribund economy. According to the World Bank, Haiti's per capita GDP shrank by an annual average of more than 5 percent over the 1985–95 period (World Bank 2006b). By 2003, Haiti's per capita income was just US$441 (in constant 2000 US dollars), more than one third less than it had been in 1990 (World Bank 2006b). This decline clearly has had a devastating effect on the population. Poverty is widespread in the country, with 55 percent of Haitians surviving on less than US$1 per day and 76 percent of the population living on less than US$2 (UNDP 2004). Half the Haitian population is considered undernourished according to the United Nations Development Program (UNDP), and life expectancy has fallen steadily throughout the previous two decades, to 51.8 years in 2003.[23] Finally, HIV infection levels in Haiti continue to be the highest in the world outside sub-Saharan Africa.[24]

Other factors underlying Haiti's current instability stem from the country's demography and geography. Haiti's population density stood at 295 people/km² in 2001, higher even than the

176 people/km^2 in the Dominican Republic and 239 people/km^2 in Jamaica.[25] Haiti's youth bulge is also a cause for concern, with youths comprising 39.4 percent of the Haitian population in 2002.[26] With respect to environmental degradation, only 880km^2 of forest remained in Haiti in 2002, covering just 3.2 percent of the total land area. Thus, the effects of any given tropical storm are magnified in Haiti when compared with other countries in the region, potentially destabilizing affected areas of the country.[27]

CRIME AND CONFLICT IN HAITI. Low intensity conflict continues today, with the Haitian National Police (PNH) and the UN Stabilisation Mission in Haiti (MINUSTAH) struggling to re-establish a government presence beyond the capital of Port-au-Prince. Particular areas of concern include specific neighbourhoods of Port-au-Prince still dominated by armed Aristide loyalists. The militias responsible for Aristide's departure – many with ties to Haiti's now disbanded armed forces (FAd'H) – have also thus far refused to demobilise or disarm. In many parts of the country, the militias have occupied abandoned police stations and now constitute the sole source of order and authority in the region.

Haiti's civil service is an area of serious concern. The PNH, Haiti's law-enforcement body, has not achieved satisfactory levels of professionalism, effectiveness, and impartiality (Vigil). It has been undermined by numerous factors, including: a lack of sufficient and sustained international funding; minimal support from the relatively poorly trained judicial branch and correctional services; increasing dependence on, and subservience to, the country's executive; and the growth of a pervasive culture of corruption engendered by the illicit drug industry. The Haitian judiciary presents another potentially destabilizing institution. Its work has long been considered suspect by many international observers, with a culture of legal impunity extending back to the Duvalier era. The recent release of several key members of Aristide's cabinet suggests that Préval and his cabinet are both actively working to separate themselves from this legacy; however, while important, such symbolic gestures represent only a first step.[28]

More generally, as in Jamaica, corruption continues to be a destabilizing force in both the public and private arena; Transparency International ranked the country 155th out of 158 in their *2005 Corruption Perceptions Index* (Transparency International). The results of a survey performed by La Fondation Heritage Haitian (LFHH) at the end of 2003 indicate the perceived causes of this corruption are numerous and varied, with the most commonly cited being the toxic combination of economic pressure, flawed institutions, the lure of "easy money," and a lack of political will to address the problem (LFHH).

Given the paucity of legitimate economic activity within the country, it is reasonable to expect that unemployed Haitians – particularly young males – may increasingly turn to other sources of income, including illicit activities such as corruption, kidnapping, and drug trafficking.[29] Indeed, figures quoted by US officials suggest some 7–10 percent of the cocaine reaching the US market flows through Haiti, and other reports indicate that kidnapping and other forms of violence continue to play a role in Haitian society.[30] Such high levels of cocaine traffic have numerous adverse effects on the country. Internally, the amounts of money involved dwarf virtually every other economic activity in Haiti. Accusations of drug-related corruption continue to follow Haitians on all sides of the political spectrum, all levels of government, and everyone from police and rebel leaders to judicial officers and the business elite.[31] Some accusations end in conviction; many do not. Even when left unsubstantiated or proven untrue however, such accusations destabilize the country and enhance local and international perception of the entire government system as being unworthy of trust.

THE CANADA SECURITY LINKAGE

From a security perspective, both Haiti and Jamaica are important to Canada, and the two cases provide contrasting linkages. A connection exists between deportees from Canada and crime in both Canada and Jamaica. The evidence is not yet overwhelming, but there is good reason to believe the Canadian experience will mirror that of the US, though perhaps on a smaller scale. Jamaican deportees may commit crime to get back into the country from which they were deported, or live under the radar on the spoils of illegal activity abroad.

Gang activity in foreign cities with large Jamaican diaspora communities – such as in Toronto – is often connected with gang activity in Jamaica, and vice versa. Jamaicans deported from the United States, the United Kingdom, and Canada may re-assimilate into

Jamaican gangs; soon after arrival, some criminal deportees reconstitute former gangs, join other gangs, or form new ones. Recruiting from the large supply of unemployed local teenagers eager to
learn from their "cultured" cousins is not difficult.[32] That said, despite 2,161 alleged criminals being deported to Jamaica in 2005,
the extent to which they contribute to criminality in Jamaica remains contested with contrasting findings from multiple reports.[33]
Those non-criminal deportees may still burden social service institutions in Jamaica and can therefore be a source of community and
family tension. The Associated Press recently reported that ten
thousand deported criminals are living in Kingston alone – the
equivalent of ten thousand criminals "dumped" into Indianapolis
(or Ottawa).[34] That being said, the deportee story is incomplete if
told using only statistics, something the JCF is well aware of.[35]

Those returning to Jamaica with these sophisticated skills are
generally unknown to police, first because only a frail system exists
to monitor deportees (virtually nonexistent), and second because
they know how to avoid detection. The story of two deportees murdered in Jamaica supports this. One had been deported from the
US five times and had served twenty-five months for drug trafficking. Immediately upon repatriation, he and his brother – also deported, but from the Bahamas while attempting to enter the US
illegally – constructed a mansion in a poor Jamaican district (Mont-
ego Bay's Felicity Crescent AKA "Blood Lane" for its high murder
rate). When the men were later murdered – apparently over the
unreturned fee paid for the younger brother's failed attempt to enter the US through the Bahamas – police found immigration documents, a fake driver's licenses, jewellery, money, and other
valuables, despite neither of the brothers being employed.[36] The
author of the MONA study points out that current US immigration
policy deports not only criminals but also instantly deports those
who have in any way violated their visas, whether university students
working to pay university tuition or otherwise.[37]

By contrast, in some ways the Canada/Haiti linkage is more
clearly defined with respect to Haiti's effects on Canadian domestic
security. Canada has repeatedly taken a lead role in international efforts to intervene in the country, providing financial, military, and
humanitarian support to the island on numerous occasions. Within
Canada itself, Montreal's thriving Haitian-Canadian community

forms the nexus of the inter-state relationship. Unfortunately, however, the last twenty years have seen the growth of several Haitian-Canadian-dominated street gangs (HSG) in the Montreal area. Two in particular – the Bo-Gars and the Crack Down Posse – have emerged as formidable and ruthless competitors in Montreal's criminal marketplace. These street gangs were a made-in-Canada phenomenon, emerging out of the nascent criminal activities of a number of Haitian-Canadian secondary school students. The groups found common identity in their ethnicity, and members believed that the gangs provided them with a sense of security and power over their difficult surroundings.

Though not immediately clear from Citizen and Immigration Canada (CIC) documents, it is likely that immigrants arriving from Haiti speaking French are not from the poorest segments of Haitian society, who generally speak Creole. They likely represent more highly educated and urban segments of the Haitian population, a part of the continuing "brain drain" that afflicts the country. Many who have the resources to escape the violence do so. Despite their more educated background, however, Haitians may still be marginalized once in Canada. Regardless of education or background, first generation immigrants typically find themselves disadvantaged relative to the broader Canadian population.[38] As a result, arriving immigrants often tend to congregate in specific neighbourhoods or ghettoes and there form a strong sense of community vis-à-vis broader Canadian society.

Nearly 90 percent of the Haitian immigrants who arrived in Canada after 1981 settled in the Montreal area; moreover, the ten thousand Haitians who immigrated between 1991 and 1996 represented the fastest growing immigrant community in the Montreal region.[39] The reasons for this Haitian-Montreal nexus are clear. As the largest Francophone metropolis in the Americas, Montreal is a natural destination for the largely French and Creole-speaking Haitians. Further, recent immigrants tend to settle in regions close to established ethnic communities, and Canada's immigration system itself ensures that those immigrating in the "family" class are settled in the same region as their sponsoring relatives.[40] Thus, regions that already have a sizeable community of a given ethnicity will tend to receive steadily increasing immigrants from that same ethnic community. These factors combined to ensure that Montreal's Haitian community continued to grow throughout the 1980s and 90s.

Aside from Montreal, other notable destinations for Haitian immigrants to Canada include Toronto and, to a lesser extent, Quebec City.[41] Neither city displays significant evidence of HSG activity, however. Conversely, there have been reports of violent crime involving alleged HSG members in Ottawa-Gatineau, an area with a relatively small Haitian-Canadian community.[42] Though they may have been isolated incidents, one must nonetheless expect that as HSGs continue to grow and enhance their organisational structure and revenue base, they will increasingly look for opportunities to expand their influence beyond the borders of the Greater Montreal Area.

THE DIASPORA'S POTENTIAL CONTRIBUTIONS TO CONFLICT PREVENTION

Having outlined problems fuelling persistent low-intensity civil violence and crime in Jamaica and Haiti and the Canada-security linkage, it is now possible to consider ways in which the sizeable diaspora communities in question might contribute to reducing persistent violence and crime and to preventing large-scale civil conflict in their countries of origin (OECD).

Human Capital and Skills

As with many nations witnessing significant proportions of their population migrating to the developed world each year, there are concerns in both Haiti and Jamaica over losing their best and brightest to developed countries, a process otherwise known as *brain drain*. An estimated 76 percent of Jamaicans with a college education are estimated to live in the United States alone, while 84 percent of Haiti's population with some level of tertiary education eventually emigrates (Lapointe, 5; Docquier and Marfouk). While this flow is generally viewed in a negative light, it also creates significant opportunities; members of the diaspora may use their skills acquired abroad to work on projects in their home country and train local practitioners (Lapointe); they may also play a crucial role in transmitting new ideas and novel ways of doing business back to their home country (Zhang). China and India provide two examples of this alternative phenomenon of "brain circulation," for both countries have benefited tremendously from diaspora

members returning or investing back home; according to some observers, nineteen out of the top twenty Indian software businesses
were founded or are managed by professionals in the Indian diaspora (Zhang).

Clearly, a country's ability to capitalize on such opportunities depends to a great extent on the existence of sound government policy to enable and encourage diaspora investment. A brief survey
indicates developing states have adopted a wide variety of approaches to harness the human and financial resources of its diaspora community (Newland and Patrick). As observed at a recent
conference on Caribbean diaspora communities, a key obstacle to
temporary or permanent return is the widespread perception that
home governments are not overly welcoming. Several participants
at the conference described "a general resentment in home country societies against those who have left," noting that, "such an attitude can discourage diaspora members from playing a more active
role in their countries of origin"; a 2003 SIDS report indicated
much more might be done to encourage repatriation of Jamaican
nationals, or to utilize them as a natural bridge into developed
countries' markets (Jamaica Ministry of Land and Environment).

The Jamaican Government has already taken some notice of this
capacity; in a recent publication for the United Nations Commission on Science and Technology for Development (UNCSTD), it
was explained that working with the diaspora community was crucial to fill the knowledge and technology gap facing Jamaica (Ventura). A decision to work closely with diaspora professionals to
transfer knowledge and encourage investment has apparently been
made (Ventura). Furthermore, the Jamaican Diaspora Advisory
Board (JDAB) was created in June 2004 to advise the Minister of
Foreign Affairs and Foreign Trade on matters relating to the diaspora,[43] while the same ministry now operates the Jamaica Diaspora Foundation, which remains actively seized of the issue.[44]

Capital Flows

In both Haiti and Jamaica, diaspora communities provide significant levels of direct financial support in the form of remittances. In
a recent Canadian survey, Simmons, Plaza, and Piché found that
87.9 percent of Haitian households and 87.8 percent of Jamaican
households had remitted funds at least once in the previous five

years; within the last year, the figures were 84.4 percent and 62.3 percent, respectively. Including households who did not remit funds, Haitian households remitted an average of $401 in 2005, while Jamaican households sent $314.

The effects of these financial flows are substantial. In 2004, these private financial transfers accounted for 17.4 percent of Jamaica's GDP, and 24.8 percent of Haiti's (World Bank 2006b, 90). In a recent study on remittance recipients commissioned by FOCAL, over half of all recipients in Jamaica have been receiving money from their relatives abroad for more than five years, and most receive transfers at least once month.[45] Furthermore, Jamaica's national debt as a percentage of its export revenue falls from 167 percent to 121 percent when remittances are included in the calculation (World Bank 2006a, 90), and the UN Population Fund indicates that Jamaica's remittances to aid (Official Development Assistance) ratio stands at 15:1.[46] In dollar terms this amounted to US$1,425 billion in remittances in 2003, designating Jamaica as the country with the highest volume of remittances per capita in Latin America and the Caribbean that year (IADB).

Though spent primarily on consumption, remittances are also channelled into health care, education, and community development (Simmons et al.). Three broad categories can therefore describe the general ways in which remittances can and are being used by recipient families and communities: consumption, investment, and the provision of public goods. Remittances sent primarily to finance immediate consumption – expenditures on basic needs such as food and housing – are the most common form of such financial transfers. Consumption fuelled by remittances – including not only consumer goods but also expenditures on health care and education – can have a significant multiplier effect on the local economy.[47] Remittances in-kind, however, such as the "barrels" sent home by most overseas Jamaicans, are likely less capable of stimulating a multiplier effect of this sort.

The second category, remittances sent to one's home country specifically to invest in local enterprises, tend to be limited to the most prosperous immigrants with the disposable income to do so and depend heavily on the investment climate back home. Nevertheless, such diaspora-fuelled foreign direct investment (FDI) can still be a crucial addition to recipient countries short on foreign capital. The third broad category, public goods, includes remittances sent home to pay for goods accessible to all members of the community, including infrastructure such as schools and potable water facilities. These types of remittances are often channelled through diaspora organizations known as hometown associations (HTAs), which pool the resources of members of the diaspora and often work in tandem with home country governments in order to maximize the reach of their funding back home. Mexico's "Padrino programme" is an oft-cited example of this type of engagement, while the work of Jamaican diaspora church groups in North America provides further examples of such partnerships (Simmons et al., 11). If managed creatively and effectively by all actors involved in the process (Newland and Patrick, 13), such initiatives have the potential to facilitate substantial long-term development and growth in recipient communities.

While it falls outside the commonly accepted definition of remittances, a final type of capital flow motivated by members of the diaspora, particularly in the United States, is fuelled by the "nostalgic trade" industry. This market, which revolves around travel, communications, and the growing demand for "ethnic" or "nostalgic" exports from home, is composed primarily of small- and medium-sized enterprises (SMEs) in countries of origin (Lapointe). It is also an industry that has significant potential to bolster economic development in Latin America and the Caribbean, given that SMEs account for approximately 50 percent of manufacturing employment in the region (Lapointe).

Conflict Resolution

Diaspora groups have the potential to influence the political realm in their home country in a variety of ways, potentially improving or impairing political processes. They may "lobby host countries to shape policies in favour of a homeland or ... challenge a homeland government; influence homelands through their support or opposition of governments; [and] give financial and other support to political parties, social movements, and civil society organizations" (Vertovec). However, as noted by Elizabeth Riddell-Dixon,[48] the political establishment's tendency to replace itself with the next generation of elite society has made it difficult for foreign-born Canadians to improve their representation in political spheres. Nevertheless, we argue that parliamentary representation is by no means the only way for diaspora groups to influence national policy agendas.

In the case of Jamaica, given the perceived inefficiency and corruption hampering the domestic political climate, diaspora pressure to reform and improve governance may be seen as beneficial. More generally, the diaspora community occupies a unique niche allowing them to lobby both home and "host" governments: they can exert pressure on the home government from abroad, free from the political intimidation and fear of retribution perhaps hampering such efforts at home. They can also lobby "host" countries to pressure home governments to enact policy favourable to their interests, ranging from calls for better anti-corruption measures and governance reform to favourable international trade policies. For example, JAMPACT – though based in the United States and therefore operating in a policymaking environment considerably different from our own – has a mission "to use ... collective energies, intelligence, and resources to make positive contributions toward the improvement of social and economic conditions in Jamaica," and therefore provides a good example of a diaspora group lobbying for change from within.[49]

In contrast, the net impact of diaspora groups on the political process in Haiti is considerably more ambiguous. While apolitical support for homeland conflict resolution efforts are generally positive, overly partisan political engagement by diaspora groups in the homeland may in some cases encourage more intransigent behaviour by homeland politicians, particularly in countries such as Haiti with a history of deep social divisions or open conflict.

Crime

Immigrant groups have the potential to bring with them criminal patterns from their country of origin; examples of such activity extend from the arrival of the Cosa Nostra in North America in the mid-nineteenth century to the proliferation of Russian-based criminal groups worldwide in the wake of the collapse of the Soviet Union. Despite debate over the contribution of criminal deportees to Haitian and Jamaican crime, it seems likely there is at least some connection. As a consequence, we must be careful about encouraging other countries to look to Canada for advice on how to repatriate criminals.[50] Arbitrarily deporting criminals back to Jamaica could be termed a trade in human criminal capital, harmful for both countries when criminals use their newly acquired skills and bypass immigration systems to enter countries illegally (Barrera et al.). The JCF, having recognized both this overseas crime connection and that diaspora groups are often close-knit and cognizant of most of what goes on within their community, has called on the Jamaican diaspora to work with the JCF to fight crime. In February 2006, a senior JCF panel urged the diaspora to be forthcoming in terms of support and intelligence and to relay information that might help police.[51]

As the proportion of immigrants to native-born Canadians grows in this country, lobbying governments from within destination countries such as Canada is likely to become increasingly pronounced. Even though this has not yet occurred on a widespread basis in Canada, ethnic groups or diaspora communities allied with political parties could soon become acceptable practice.[52] At this stage, however, efforts such as those being made by the Jamaica-Canada Diaspora Foundation to lobby for change in what is perceived as unfair deportation practices – noting that Jamaicans account for a full 40 percent of all deportees from Canada[53] – will only continue to grow, if only on a piecemeal basis. In the future, block voting by particular diaspora communities could make or break politicians at election time.

CONCLUSION

This chapter has explored the numerous ways in which Haitian and Jamaican diaspora communities abroad are related to the "drivers" of conflict, tension, or low-intensity violence that dominate the political and economic landscapes of their home countries. Though both are SIDS, the nature and extent of these linkages are defined as much by the unique social, political, and economic histories of each nation as they are by the countries' common small-island geography. Though some of these relationships may appear more straightforward than others, further rigorous analysis is nonetheless needed in order to better understand the full extent of the complex causal relationships that may exist between each country's economic and political stability and their diaspora communities around the world.

In the meantime, however, it is worth revisiting some of the central themes enunciated in the introduction to this volume: how responsive is Canadian foreign policy to demographic changes in

Canada, and in what ways do diaspora communities influence Canadian security in the long term? In answering these two questions, we must first recognize that lobby groups, including those representing diaspora communities as disparate and diverse as Jamaica and Haiti's, are limited in their ability to influence the formal policymaking process in Canada due to the nature of our Parliamentary system of government. The relatively limited power of individual members of Parliament to push forward or veto legislation, particularly when compared to their congressional counterparts in the United States, inhibits the ability of even well-organized groups to achieve their objectives by lobbying elected officials directly (Howlett and Ramesh). That said, however, even if diaspora communities – or politically active groups within them – do not represent a critical mass capable of influencing electoral outcomes in federal elections, diaspora organizations can nevertheless achieve results by channelling their efforts toward raising public awareness of key issues and by providing valuable information and insight to decision-makers both inside and outside of government. A well-informed foreign policy supported by input from members of concerned diaspora communities is likely to always be in high demand by the Canadian public, particularly when such policy has potential repercussions on public security.

Due to the strategic location of both Haiti and Jamaica in the heart of the Caribbean, their proximity to both Central America and Florida, their poorly defended maritime regions, and, in the case of Haiti, their lack of credible law-enforcement capabilities, it appears as though Haiti's political instability and both countries' roles as drug transhipment points will persist as security issues for Canada in the near future.[54] Consequently, the possibility of an emerging criminal nexus between both countries and Canada warrants considerable further study. To the extent that such a nexus exists, it necessitates greater engagement between members of the Haitian and Jamaican diasporas on the one hand and the Canadian foreign policy, defence, and intelligence communities on the other. The former clearly have a role to play in stabilizing political and economic conditions in their respective countries of origin; such stability in turn is a necessary prerequisite of reduced drug trafficking in both small island nations.

When thinking about the responsiveness of Canadian foreign policy to the country's changing demographics, it is useful to examine the positions of the current and previous governments regarding which countries have received priority status in Canadian aid and foreign policy programming. Has the "special relationship" spoken of earlier between Jamaica, Haiti, and Canada translated into priority status for these small island states in the eyes of Canadian politicians and foreign-policy and development planners?

In 2005, neither Haiti nor Jamaica was included amongst the four countries from the Americas that received priority status in the International Policy Statement (IPS) released by former Prime Minister Paul Martin's government. Instead, Bolivia, Guyana, Honduras, and Nicaragua were listed as Canada's "development partners" in the region, while fourteen others were found in Africa, six in Asia, and one in Europe.[55] More recently, Prime Minister Stephen Harper's Conservative Government shelved the IPS after taking control of Canada's minority government in January 2006. Since then, Africa has fallen from the spotlight, while greater collaboration with the United States, the G8, and emerging economies such as Brazil, Russia, India, and China have surfaced as Canada's foreign-policy priorities (CCIC). Nevertheless, according to CIDA, "fragile states such as Haiti, Afghanistan, and Sudan's Darfur region [still] warrant special attention because of the security, stability, and poverty reduction challenges they present to Canada, to their own citizens, and to development cooperation in general" (CIDA 2006).

While the economic and political imperatives emerging from Canada's relationship with the United States and the "BRICS" countries are likely both motivating factors driving such a shift in foreign policy priorities, one can also argue that Canada's evolving demographic structure is another. Undoubtedly, there are considerable economic benefits attached to closer ties to the emerging giants, namely India and China. Between 1990 and 2002, exports to China increased by 136 percent and imports by 1,046 percent, while Canadian FDI in China grew by 11,017 percent and Chinese FDI in Canada increased by 315 percent over the same period.[56] However, the size of these nations' diasporas might also be considered a strong motivating factor, as 58 percent of Canadian immigrants arriving between 1991 and 2001 came from Asia, including the Middle East (Statistics Canada). Given such numbers, it would therefore be presumptuous to conclude that economic and political factors alone drive Canadian foreign policy. Similarly, in the case of

Canada's continued presence in Haiti, the "special relationship" factor cannot be ruled out, either. Since economic imperatives were surely not its primary driver, the presence of a significant Haitian diaspora might provide an alternative explanation for the Canadian Government's decision to continue to "ante up" in Haiti; without the visibility and focus that community has brought to Haitian issues in Canada, the government might have committed its military and political resources elsewhere.

Beyond such priority setting exercises, there is also limited evidence that the diaspora community has had some influence over the way in which Canadian foreign policy is implemented in Haiti. For example, CIDA has recognized both the challenges that Canada may face as a result of Haitian instability and the role that the Haitian diaspora may play in meeting those challenges. In 2004, the agency stated that "Haitian expatriates must play a greater role in society [and that] they represent a change driver and have a lot to offer in rebuilding Haiti" (CIDA 2004). Admittedly, the extent to which such well-intentioned statements have since been acted upon remains unclear, but it would seem that sectors of the Canadian Government are cognizant that segments of Canadian society may be able to play a more active role in the implementation of foreign policy. For example, there has been some exchange of dialogue between members of certain diaspora groups and the Government of Canada. Of particular relevance to Haiti and Jamaica were three conferences organized by the Canadian Foundation for the Americas (FOCAL) in 2005, in conjunction with DFAIT, CIDA and the Inter-American Development Bank (IADB), which gathered together members of the Latin American and Caribbean diaspora in a preliminary attempt to forge productive linkages between these groups and the Canadian Government and better understand the impact of these diaspora communities on economic and social development in their home countries.[57]

A final element shaping the way in which Canada's changing demographic structure influences foreign-policymaking processes is the geographic distribution of diaspora communities. The extent to which various diaspora communities are concentrated in specific cities and neighbourhoods – and are therefore able to influence the outcome of specific electoral contests – might affect their capacity to exert political pressure on the Canadian Government. Both Jamaica and Haiti's diaspora communities are not only concentrated in Toronto and Montreal, respectively, but in particular neighbour-hoods in these cities as well (Simmons et al.).

While such concentrated populations might limit the extent to which the concerns of each diaspora community become nation-wide in scope, they may also create the impression for local politi-cians that these communities make up a larger proportion of the foreign-born population in Canada than they do in reality. For in-stance, elected officials representing Jane and Finch in Toronto or Rivière-des-Prairies in Montreal might be surprised to learn that only 9 percent of immigrants arriving in Canada in 2005 came from South America, Central America, and the Caribbean in 2005.[58] Densely populated diaspora communities in specific cities thus have the capacity to build networks that would not have been constructed or sustained as easily if the diaspora were scattered throughout the country. Moreover, through public demonstrations, media appear-ances, and other methods of public communication, members of such networks may create the impression their respective communi-ties are much larger and more influential than their total popula-tion nationwide might have otherwise predicted. To cite just one example, there are 183 Guyanese diaspora organizations operating in North America as of 2002, most of which are clustered primarily in New York and Toronto. That concentration and presence is no doubt a product of these cities being home to the largest propor-tions of the Guyanese diaspora in each country (Orozco).

Certainly, "Little Jamaica" and "Little Haiti" in, respectively, To-ronto and Montreal should facilitate the growth of strong and vocal coalitions on issues that affect both Canada and the Caribbean; how-ever, it is unclear whether these opportunities have yet been fully uti-lized. It is possible that the influence of such coalitions may increase if the federal government were to give the provinces greater latitude to operate independently in the realm of foreign policy. Given that many diaspora groups are concentrated in one city or in one prov-ince, it is possible that they would be able to exert greater influence on provincial or civic leaders, where their numbers form a greater proportion of the overall population. It will be interesting to see whether diaspora-based coalitions begin to focus more of their ener-gies on influencing provincial or municipal politicians as the federal government begins to devolve certain international responsibilities to other levels of government, as it has already done in the case of Quebec and its membership in UNESCO. It may be that Jamaican and

Haitian diaspora-based coalitions may perceive an increased incentive to focus their lobbying efforts on Queen's Park or Quebec's National Assembly – or for that matter, on Montreal's Hotel de Ville and Toronto's City Hall – rather than exclusively on Parliament Hill, in order to increase their visibility and influence. Having said that, while the presence of a particular diaspora community in Canada might be enough to force the federal government's hand on specific issues, as argued above in the case of state failure in Haiti, it must be recognized that this does not mean members of that community will share the same concerns or agree on what action should be taken by the Canadian Government on the majority of issues. Despite the concentration of various diasporas in particular Canadian cities, such communities are too heterogeneous to make such unanimity possible.[59]

Such speculation aside however, it remains primarily up to the federal government and diaspora communities to seek out opportunities for engagement in the creation of relevant, practical, and representative foreign policy. As Canada's demographic structure continues to change and an increasingly diverse group of foreign-born Canadians come to represent larger portions of the country's population, political, and policy networks between diaspora communities and Canadian decision-makers will become not only more complex but also more influential. Canadian foreign policy is increasingly becoming synonymous with domestic policy, and it is doing so out of necessity. Similarly, politicians and foreign-policymakers should realize that they cannot ignore the implications of their decisions upon diaspora communities in Canada. Events of recent years – from the tsunami that overwhelmed parts of South and Southeast Asia in December 2004 to the conflict between Hezbollah and Israel in summer 2006 – have repeatedly demonstrated that such communities are not only growing in numbers but also becoming increasingly organized and vocal; these voices will doubtless be heard during the next international crisis, and the next federal election.

NOTES

The authors would like to acknowledge the funding support of the Centre for Security and Defence Studies of the Norman Paterson School of International Affairs, Carleton University, for assistance in the formulation of this chapter.

1 Jamaica: Country Reports on Human Rights Practices – 2000 Bureau of Democracy, Human Rights, and Labor, US State Department (23 February 2001); www.state.gov/g/drl/rls/hrrpt/2000/wha/805.htm (accessed 15 May 2006).

2 Transparency International, "TI Report on Jamaica calls for party finance reform and tighter clampdown on corruption in public procurement," www.transparency.org/news_room/latest_news/press_releases/2004/ 2004_08_10_nis_jamaica (accessed 13 May 2006); Amnesty International, "Jamaica," www.amnesty.org (accessed 20 January 2006); "Jamaica's Ruling Party to Elect New Leader on 25 February," Caribbean Media Corporation News Agency (accessed 22 January 2006).

3 Transparency International, "Corruption Perceptions Index," 2004, 2005 www.transparency.org/surveys/index.html (accessed 26 June 2006).

4 Transparency International, "TI Report on Jamaica calls for party finance reform and tighter clampdown on corruption in public procurement," www.transparency.org/news_room/latest_news/press_releases/2004/ 2004_08_10_nis_jamaica (accessed 13 May 2006).

5 Jamaica Gleaner "The Utility of Political Jam Sessions." 23 November 2006. Editorial. Jamaica Gleaner News Online. 11 December 2006, www.jamaica-gleaner.com/gleaner/20061123/cleisure/cleisure1.html.

6 Jamaica's sensitivity to volatile international commodity prices was most recently exemplified by the European Union's recent decision to cut the price paid for Jamaican sugar by 36 percent over the next four years, a policy shift likely to hurt exporters not only in Jamaica but throughout the Caribbean. For more, see Barrera et al.

7 It is worthwhile to note here that the countercyclical nature of remittance flows tends to soften the impact of economic shocks and natural disasters on recipient countries.

8 The Ministry of Finance and Planning, Jamaica, "Total Public Debt and Indicator, 1990/91-2004/05," www.mof.gov.jm/dmu/download/2005/ pubdebt/pd0506fy.pdf (accessed 14 May 2006).

9 The Statistical Institute of Jamaica, "Main Labour Force Indicators 2002– 2005," www.statinja.com/stats.html#3, (accessed 14 May 2006).

10 Jamaica Ministry of Finance and Planning, Debt Management Unit, "Objectives."

11 Jamaica: Country Reports on Human Rights Practices – 2000 Bureau of Democracy, Human Rights, and Labor (23 February 2001); www.state.gov/g/ drl/rls/hrrpt/2000/wha/805.htm (accessed 15 May 2006).

12 Phillips calls in PSOJ – Private sector to bridge gap between parties, police. Jamaica Gleaner (27 March 2002). www.pnpjamaica.com/ innewsmarch27a.htm (accessed 16 May 2006).

13 Mark Oliver, "Violence in Jamaica: Gun Battles Between Law Enforcers and Gangs in Kingston Have Left at Least 22 People Dead in the Past Three Days," The Guardian UK (Wednesday, 11 July 2001); www.guardian.co.uk/print/0,3858,4219933–103701,00.html (accessed 15 May 2006), and see also: Erikson and Minson, 159–71, muse.jhu.edu/ journals/journal_of_democracy/vo16/16.4erikson.pdf (accessed 15 May 2006).

14 Beverley Anderson-Manley, "Facing the Monster," Jamaica Gleaner (Monday, 9 January 2006), www.jamaica-gleaner.com/gleaner/20060109/ cleisure/cleisure4.html (accessed 15 May 2006), "Spanish Town New 'Murder Capital,'" BBC News (Thursday, 9 September 2004), news.bbc.co.uk/2/hi/americas/3635426.stm (accessed 15 May 2006).

15 Joe Mozingo, "Jamaicans Are Living in Fear as Homicide Rate Skyrockets," The Miami Herald (Thursday, 7 July 2005), www.miami.com/mld/ miamiherald/12072505.htm (accessed 29 January 2006); "'Blood Lane' – Guns, Drugs, Deportees and a Cry for Help," Jamaica Gleaner (Sunday, 12 February 2006), www.jamaica-gleaner.com/gleaner/20060212/news/ news2.html (accessed 2 March 2006).

16 At least three reports have been commissioned on the topic, two found contradictory results, while the third, currently being undertaken by the JCF, has yet to release any findings. "Booted from the Lands of Opportunity ... – Deportees a Criminal Link," Jamaica Gleaner (Sunday, 12 February 2006); www.jamaica-gleaner.com/gleaner/20060212/news/ news3.html (accessed 2 March 2006).

17 Ross Sheil, "Guns Found at Kingston's Port," Jamaica Gleaner (Saturday, 6 May 2006), www.jamaica-gleaner.com/gleaner/20060506/lead/ lead4.html (accessed 18 May 2006); Glenroy Sinclair, "Haiti Drug Link – Cops Say Fake Fishermen Smuggling Arms, Aliens," The Jamaica Gleaner (Tuesday, 9 September 2003), archived on Hartford Web Publishing, www.hartford-hwp.com/archives/43a/452.html (accessed 30 January 2006); Philip Mascoll, "The Guns of Jamaica," The Toronto Star (Tuesday, 24 July 2001) archived in Media Awareness Project, www.mapinc.org/ drugnews/vo1/n1335/a05.html (accessed 30 January 2006); Joe Mozingo, "Jamaicans Are Living in Fear as Homicide Rate Skyrockets"; Julian Borger, "Army Ordered to Wage War on Kingston's Gangs," The Guardian UK (Wednesday, 14 July 1999), www.guardian.co.uk/Archive/Article/ 0,4273,3883091,00.html (accessed 30 January 2006); "Gunrunning to Haiti through Jamaica," Caribbean Media Corp. (3 August 2005), archived in Haiti Democracy Project, Haitipolicy.org/content/ 3162.htm?PHPSESSID=c4d02e6e91fb32eba811dc39b135feod (accessed 30 January 2006).

18 Mark Oliver, "Violence in Jamaica."

19 See for statistics and further information: Jamaican Constabulary Force.
    "'Operation Kingfish': About Operation Kingfish," www.jamaicapolice.
    org.jm/kingfish/home.htm (accessed 15 May 2006).

20 Carment et al.

21 Daniel Lak, "Problem of Haiti's Gun Culture," BBC News, 11 March 2004,
    news.bbc.co.uk/1/hi/world/americas/3500290.stm (accessed 16 Octo-
    ber 2004).

22 Joseph Guyler Delva, "Kidnappings, Violent Crime Surge in Haiti," Reuters,
    27 November 2006, today.reuters.com/News/CrisesArticle.aspx?storyId
    =N27175023&WTmodLoc=IntNewsHome_C4_Crises-4 (accessed 1 Decem-
    ber 2006).

23 Steve Schifferes, "Haïti: An economic basket-case," BBC News Online,
    1 Mar 2004, http://news.bbc.co.uk/1/hi/business/3522155.stm (ac-
    cessed 16 October 2004); World Bank 2006a.

24 World Bank 2006a.

25 World Development Indicators, World Bank, quoted in CIFP, *Country Indi-
    cators Database.*

26 World Development Indicators, World Bank, quoted in CIFP, *Country Indi-
    cators Database.*

27 Sonia Verma, "Aid in Haiti a 'Logistical Nightmare,'" Toronto Star,
    25 September 2004.

28 Radio Jamaica, "Haitian Interior Minister Freed of Murder Charges,"
    www.radiojamaica.com/news/story.php?category=6&story=25600; for a
    thorough treatment of the challenges facing Haiti's legal system, see Inter-
    American Commission on Human Rights, "Haiti: Failed Justice or Rule of
    Law? Challenges Facing Haiti and the International Community," Organi-
    zation of American States, 26 October 2005.

29 Though the circumstances are not completely analogous, the argument to
    some extent parallels that of Hudson and den Boer's "surplus males" the-
    ory regarding South Asia. In both cases, young underengaged males be-
    come vectors for social violence. In South Asia, the problem is the result of
    a high male-to-female ratio; in Haiti, the problem stems from a lack of
    gainful employment. Valerie Hudson and Andrea den Boer, *Bare Branches:
    The Security Implications of Asia's Surplus Male Population* (Cambridge, MA:
    MIT Press, 2004).

30 Vigil, "DEA Congressional Testimony;" Gutierrez, "State Dept. Policy State-
    ment: Haiti"; DEA, "Drug Intelligence Brief: The Drug Trade in the Carib-
    bean, A Threat Assessment." Groups such as Amnesty International and
    International Crisis Group report that kidnapping and violence continue

to be prevalent features of Haitian society. See for instance: International Crisis Group (ICG), "Haiti: Security and the Reintegration of the State," www.crisisgroup.org/home/index.cfm?id=4475&l=1, 30 October 2006 (accessed 21 November 2006); and Irene Khan, "Haiti: Open Letter to the President of the Republic of Haiti," web.amnesty.org/library/Index/ENGAMR360112006?open&of=ENG-382, 2 October 2006 (accessed 21 November 2006).

31 Associated Haitian Press (AHP), "Haiti: Electoral Council Member's Past Connection to Drug Trafficking Alleged," trans. FBIS, 27 July 2004; United Press International (UIP) "Drug Trafficker Gets 11 Years in Haiti," 20 July 2004; Signal FM Radio, "Haitian Ex-Soldiers Arrest Two Policemen Carrying Drugs," BBC Monitoring Service, 1 September 2004; NPR, "Haiti's Role in Drug Trafficking," 11 March 2004; BBC Monitoring, "Highlights of Signal FM Radio News," 20 July 2004; AP, "Ex-Haitian Police Director Added to Drug Indictment of Former High-Ranking Officials," 29 August 2004; Voice of America (VOA), "American Airlines Official in Haiti Indicted on Drug Smuggling Charges," 16 October 2004.

32 Joe Mozingo, "Jamaicans Are Living in Fear as Homicide Rate Skyrockets"; "'Blood Lane' – Guns, Drugs, Deportees and a Cry for Help," Jamaica Gleaner.

33 See endnote 16.

34 "US Study Finds Strong Deportee-Crime Links," Jamaica Gleaner (Sunday, 3 October 2004), www.jamaica-gleaner.com/gleaner/20041003/lead/lead3.html (accessed, 2 March 2006).

35 "US Study Finds Strong Deportee-Crime Links," Jamaica Gleaner.

36 "'Blood Lane' – Guns, Drugs, Deportees and a Cry for Help." Jamaica Gleaner.

37 Bernard Headley. "Looking at Deportees (Part I) – 'They Were No Angels,'" Jamaica Gleaner (Sunday, 26 February 2006), www.jamaica-gleaner.com/gleaner/20060226/focus/focus5.html (accessed 2 March 2006).

38 See Metropolis, "Labour Market Outcomes for Immigrants," Conversation Series, December 2003, www.canada.metropolis.net/research-policy/conversation/conversation_report_15.pdf.

39 Citizenship and Immigration Canada (CIC), "Recent Immigrants in the Montréal Metropolitan Area: A Comparative Portrait Based on the 1996 Census," May 2000, 8.

40 For a detailed account of Canadian immigration regulations, see CIC, "Immigrate to Canada," 2003, www.cic.gc.ca/english/immigrate/index.html (accessed 10 November 2004).

41 CIC, "Recent Immigrants in the Québec Metropolitan Area: A Comparative Portrait Based on the 1996 Census," May 2000, 8; CIC "Facts and Figures 2002."

42 Fabrice de Pierrebourg and Jérôme Dussault, "Les Gangs de rue à Laval," *Journal de Montréal,* 2 October 2003, www2.canoe.com/infos/societe/archives/2003/10/20031002-075310.html (accessed 25 November 2004).

43 It should be pointed out that while this organization seems to have good potential, a cursory glance at a forum on its website shows considerable confusion over its precise mandate, doubt, and skepticism as to its effectiveness. Some news articles and editorials express similar concerns. See generally: Jamaica Diaspora Online Forum, jamaicandiaspora.org/forum/index.php?board=1;action=display;threadid=46;start=0 (accessed 16 May 2006); Delano Seiveright, "Jamaican Diaspora Must Open Their Eyes to Jamaica's Realities" (Thursday, 30 June 2005), www.jamaicans.com/articles/primecomments/jamaicanrealities.shtml (accessed 18 May 2006).

44 See their website: The Jamaican Diaspora Foundation, www.diaspora.org.jm/content/home/default1.asp (accessed 14 November 2006)

45 Dade, Carlo, 2006, "Survey of Remittance Recipients in Four Parishes in Jamaica: Analysis of Data," Canadian Foundation for the Americas, www.focal.ca/projects/ privatesector/diasporas/publications_e.asp.

46 Compared to a 34:1 ratio in Mexico, 24:1 in Costa Rica, 8:1 in the Philippines, and 4:1 in Lesotho.

47 Inter-American Foundation (IAF), "Approaches to Increasing the Productive Value of Remittances," Papers presented at a conference held at the World Bank, 19 March 2001, Washington, DC.

48 See her chapter in this volume.

49 The recent murder of two of Jamaica's most well-known gay activists aptly demonstrates the potential dangers of activism within the country, while possible connections between politicians and gangs poses further dangers. See Jamaica Impact Inc. "JAMPACT," www.jampact.org (accessed 19 May 2006).

50 As Jack Granatstein has done in this volume in the case of Europe.

51 Jamaican Diaspora encouraged to work with Police to fight crime. Caymen Net News (Wednesday, 9 February 2006), www.caymannetnews.com/2006/02/1025/jamaican/dis.shtml (accessed 18 May 2006).

52 As Elizabeth Riddell-Dixon argues in her chapter of this volume.

53 Leonardo Blair, "Jamaican Diaspora Disturbed: Vexed and Vocal," Enterprise Reporter, (Sunday, 26 June 2005). www.jamaica-gleaner.com/gleaner/20050626/lead/lead1.html.

54 Nick Caistor, "Haiti's Drug Money Scourge," BBC News, 19 March 2004, news.bbc.co.uk/1/hi/world/americas/3524444.stm (accessed 20 October 2004). Haiti currently possesses no Navy or Air Force. While the country does have a Coast Guard, its training, equipment, and operational range are all extremely limited. See CIA, *The World Factbook: Haiti*, and J. Milford, "DEA Congressional Testimony before the House International Relations Committee Regarding Haiti," Drug Enforcement Agency, 9 December 1997.

55 CIDA, "CIDA Announces New Development Partners: Developing Countries Where Canada Can Make a Difference," news release, 19 April 2005, www.acdi-cida.gc.ca/CIDAWEB/acdicida.nsf/En/JER-324115437-MU7 (accessed November 28 2006).

56 See Elizabeth Riddell-Dixon, in this volume; statistics compiled from Industry Canada, "Canadian Imports (Exports) Year Annual Trend 1990–2002" (Ottawa, 2003), strategis.gc.ca. (29 April 2003).

57 FOCAL, "Latin American and Caribbean Diaspora Group Meeting Report," proc. from the Latin American and Caribbean Diaspora Group Meeting, 26 October 2005. Ottawa: Canadian Foundation for the Americas (FOCAL), www.focal.org; Dade, Carlo, Luz Rodriguez-Novoa, and Jennifer Domise, "Canada – Caribbean Diasporas and Development Conference Series Report," proc. of Canada – Caribbean Diasporas and Development Conference, 30 and 31 May 2005. Toronto and Montreal: FOCAL, www.focal.ca.

58 Citizenship and Immigration Canada. "Facts and Figures: Immigration Overview 2005." Ottawa: CIC, 30.

59 See the section on diaspora heterogeneity in the final report on the University for Peace's Expert Forum on Capacity Building for Peace and Development: Roles of Diaspora, Toronto, 19–20 October 2006, www.toronto.upeace.org/diaspora/index.html.

4

Multiculturalism and Canadian Foreign Policy

J.L. GRANATSTEIN

INTRODUCTION

Let me begin this chapter with two quotations that suggest the problematic relationship of multiculturalism and Canadian foreign policy. The first is by the Toronto journalist, Zuhair Kashmeri, who published *The Gulf Within: Canadian Arabs, Racism and the Gulf War* in 1991. Kashmeri argued that Canada had failed to consider "the views of its large Arab and Muslim communities before it decided to join the us-sponsored coalition in the Gulf." Such action was simply unacceptable to him, and he then quoted the views of a Reverend Tad Mitsui of the United Church of Canada, who saw "race involved in judging who is an enemy and who is a friend. For example, Canadians will never think of America as an enemy, and neither can they think of British or the French as enemies ... But it is so easy to think of Arabs as the enemy. I think this is not fair." Mitsui goes on: "Why can't Pakistan be our friend no matter what? Why can't Iraq ...? And if you expand that logic, if Canada should exist as a multicultural, multiracial country, you cannot take sides with anybody." Kashmeri picks this up to argue that "Since multiculturalism advocates celebrating the differences, allowing the traditions and cultures to co-exist, the extension of that policy in foreign policy is a stance of neutrality."[1]

The second quotation comes almost fifteen years later from the political columnist John Ibbitson of the *Globe and Mail*, who wrote in

August 2005 about Canada's new governor general, Mme Michaëlle Jean. At her press conference the day she was named, the governor general designate spoke about the situation in Haiti, where she was born. Ibbitson wrote that her words were important: "reflecting a subtle but profound shift in recent Canadian foreign policy priorities, the tsunami of last year, the chaos in Haiti, the exploding troubles in Sudan are not foreign-*aid* issues for Canada, they are foreign-*policy* priorities. They reflect our demographic transformation, from predominantly European to truly multinational. Problems in India and China and Haiti are *our* problems because India and China and Haiti are *our* motherlands"[2] [emphasis in original].

Both these quotes, fifteen years apart, in my view reflect a fundamental misunderstanding of the roots and sources of a nation's foreign policy. Both are advocating policies of the heart, not policies of the head. They are values-oriented, not founded on national interests. Foreign policy is not about loving everyone or even helping everyone. It is not about saying a nation cannot do anything or cannot go to war, for example, for fear of offending some group within the country. It cannot be about doing something only to satisfy one or another group's ties to its mother country. Foreign policy instead must spring from the fundamental bases of a state – its geographical location, its history, its form of government, its economic imperatives, its alliances, and yes, of course, its people. In other words, national interests are and must be key.

No nation like Canada can do what its citizens of Sri Lankan or Pakistani or Somalian or Jewish or Muslim or Ukrainian origin want – all the time. No nation like Canada can do what its provinces, or founding peoples, or some of them may want – all the time. A nation must do what its national interests determine it must. And that requires that a nation like Canada know what its national interests are.

Canadian national interests, while difficult to prioritize and harder still to put into effect, are not very difficult to state:

1 Canada must protect its territory and the security of its people;
2 Canada must strive to maintain its unity;
3 Canada must protect and enhance its independence;
4 Canada must promote the economic growth of the nation to support the prosperity and welfare of its people;

5 Canada should work with like-minded states for the protection
  and enhancement of democracy and freedom.

These are very easy to list, but they can and do fluctuate in importance from time to time. In wartime, national interest 1 might be
supreme, but at the time of the Quebec referendums in 1980 and
1995, 2 might have been at the top of the list. The key point, however, is that the five national interests are all important all the time,
though with varying weight.

The first four interests are unquestionably our domestic goals and
are what any nation must do. The foremost goal, the basic task as acknowledged by the government, is to secure and protect the Canadian people and their territory. Unity is a key interest but is difficult
to achieve, as Canadian history amply confirms. Nothing we do
should tear us apart, but at the same time we must be careful lest *not*
doing something strains the polity. Maintaining unity is the test for
any and every government, and we judge our prime ministers by
their success in this area. Sir Robert Borden, for example, has frequently been judged a failure for his inability to hold the country together during the Great War, while Mackenzie King has earned
kudos from historians for his successes in the Second World War.[3]

The third national interest, protecting Canada's independence,
demands that the nation strive to resist the pull of the United
States, the only nation that threatens our independence – in a benign way, thus far in the twentieth and twenty-first centuries –
through the attractiveness of its culture and institutions and the
power of its corporations. This is very hard to do, primarily because
the next interest, the fourth, is most easily met if we work with the
United States. The US takes more than 85 percent of our trade today and sustains 52 percent of our gross domestic product. The
United States, moreover, is where we draw our foreign investment
from and where most Canadian foreign investment goes. There is
simply no other market on which we can depend and none – neither China nor India nor Europe nor Latin America – to which we
can look with any confidence as a replacement for the foreseeable
future. Thus we must balance the need to be independent with the
need to be able to live and prosper.

Finally, the last national interest is based on our history and institutions. We have always fought for freedom and democracy, for our

friends and allies, when we chose to do so. *When we chose to do so.* We did our part in the war against Nazi Germany and during the Cold War because Canadians believed it – correctly – in our national interest to do so. Stopping oligarchies and advancing freedom and democracy remain goals for Canada, and the government recognizes that Canada is not a great power, that it cannot save the world by itself. We need alliances of the like-minded, and Canadians have sought for this. The last of our national interests reflects this necessity.

CANADIAN VALUES

Sometimes, the Canadian people's desire to press their values overrides their good sense to the point that we seem to believe Canada to be the moral superpower of the world. We want equality at home and abroad. We want freedom of religion for all. We believe in human rights, the rule of law, good governance, and a long list of additional virtuous values. These are important, but we have not gone to war for such things. Canada is unlikely to wage a war for gender equality, however important it is. Moreover, our values can and do change, and some of the values Canadians trumpet today are fairly new – gender equality, multiculturalism, and respect for diversity. But our national interests are long-lived. Canada might go to war, Canada has fought wars, to protect its national interests.

But we have gone to war for ethnicity, too. Let us be honest enough to admit that in 1914, the Canadian war effort was shaped by the British connection, not by national interests, at least not initially. Yes, Canada was a colony and thus bound by the British declaration of war. But the size of the Canadian war effort was shaped by the government's and the English-speaking Canadian public's desire to be British, to be part of the Empire, and to accept the burdens and glory of a British war. In World War II, Canada was no longer a colony; after the Statute of Westminster (1931), Canada was independent in its foreign policy, but we used this power only to wait one week after Britain went to war on 3 September 1939, before we too plunged in. Were Canada's national interests threatened in 1939? The United States next door certainly did not think its interests were, nor did any other independent state in the Western Hemisphere. Was Canadian unity not endangered by the war? Of course, it was. Canadians went to war in 1939 because Britain did, because English-speaking Canadians wanted to support the Mother Country. Few cared what Quebec thought or wanted.

Certainly Prime Minister King handled the strains far better than Borden had a quarter-century before, and King's government constructed a vast war effort that did its full share in defeating the monstrous Nazi regime. No one should doubt that Canadian national interests were ultimately threatened in the 1939–45 war. On the other hand, every Canadian historian knows that French Canada's version of the events of 1939–45 is far different and that World War II goes into the long list of issues on which English Canada forced its will on Quebec against the desires of its people. Opinion polls during the war made clear that Quebec took a different view of the war than did English-speaking Canadians, and not just on the subject of military conscription. But conscription is an important measure – the 1942 plebiscite, for example, showed huge support in English Canada for freeing the government's hands to deploy conscripts abroad, while Quebec showed equally high numbers against. Indeed francophones all across the country voted "no" in very large numbers. Almost always forgotten is that other ethnic groups such as the German- and Ukrainian-Canadians also voted heavily "no."[4] The Second World War, like the Great War, was in Canadian terms a British ethnic war in which everyone else was dragged along.

But Canada grew up as a nation and began to recognize its own national interests. In August 1940, after Dunkirk and the fall of France, Canada struck its first defense arrangement with the United States because Canadians recognized that Britain could no longer be counted on to defend them. They continued their defense relations with the United States after 1945 because of the threat posed by the Soviet Union. Canada went into the North Atlantic Treaty in 1949, into Korea in 1950, and into the North American Air Defense Command in 1957–58 for the same reason. Canada's national interests were to the fore. Ethnicity seemed to be very secondary. But it wasn't, or at least not for very long. And certainly not among Canada's ethnic groups.

There are many examples in the recent past. Sikhs based in British Columbia blew up an airliner in the late 1980s to express their support for an independent Khalistan in the Indian subcontinent.

This mass murder was plotted by Canadians on Canadian soil. It stands as a cautionary tale about the importation of a homeland conflict to Canada and of the utter inability of the Canadian Government to respond before terror struck or to resolve the matter in the courts after the fact. Similarly, Canadian Sri Lankans continue to raise money for the Tamil Tigers, a terrorist group – and succeeded a few years ago in getting the then-finance minister of Canada to attend a fundraising dinner in Toronto.

Then during the collapse of former Yugoslavia into warring ethnicities, Serb- and Croat-Canadians got into scuffles on the streets of Toronto, raised funds for the Old Country, and many returned to Serbia or Croatia to lend their political and military muscle to the struggle. One Serb-Canadian was sentenced to three years in jail in September 2005 for taking United Nations personnel – including Canadians – hostage in Serbia in May 1995. Clearly Canada had failed to integrate these people into its nationality.

Carol Off, in her book *The Ghosts of Medak Pocket*,[5] wrote of the quarter-million Croats who arrived in Canada from the 1960s on. "Their continuing identity as Croats was powerful – and much encouraged by the Canadian government," she said. "In 1971 Canada declared itself officially multicultural; and Ottawa began to offer millions of dollars to ethnic communities in Canada to preserve their immigrant identities, a well-meaning policy that unfortunately exacerbated the problem of the angry émigrés who weren't even trying to fit into the society of their adopted country." That was, of course, true for more than Croats. The government, Off goes on, funded language schools and folklore centres and also, as it turned out, publications disseminating radical right-wing messages. What Ottawa did not do was try to make Canadians out of them.

Off continues by noting the pro-Nazi Ustase connections among Canadian Croats, and the fact that the very idea of a Croatian state, including part of Bosnia, was born at the Norval Community Centre, set up by Croatian-Canadians not far from Toronto. This Centre became the heart of Gojko Susak territory.

An Ottawa restaurant owner and house painter when Franjo Tudjman took over the Government of Croatia in 1990, Susak heeded his leader's call for the Croatian diaspora to come home. He quickly became an extremist and provocateur, literally firing what Off calls "the first shot" in the Croatian war for independence. Soon, he was

Croatia's defense minister. He used his connections in Canada to raise money for Croatia, up to $200 million, Off suggests, for weapons and aid.[6] Susak eventually presided over the "ethnic cleansing" of Serbs in the Medak Pocket – where Canadian soldiers, trying to prevent the slaughter of Serbs, killed Croats in a large pitched battle. It is fair to say that Susak was a war criminal, and if he had not died before the International Criminal Court was set up he would almost certainly have been tried.

The point of the Croatian events in this context is that Canada failed to turn Susak into a Canadian. He had arrived here in 1969 and lived in Canada for more than two decades, but his allegiance was to Croatia first, last, and always. Was he any different than the Sikh terrorists? The Tamils? Or the other ethnic Canadians who send money for political purposes, or for guns, to their homelands? Why has Canada failed? Why does the link of "blood and soil" remain so strong? Why don't the people who live here give their first allegiance to Canada's national interests?

In early 1939, a young civil servant, Norman A. Robertson of the Department of External Affairs, was given the task of working out what was to be done about German pro-Nazi Bundists and Italian Fascisti groups in Canada in the event of war. Robertson proposed that the government make full use of the law to block the import of seditious, disloyal, or scurrilous propaganda. He urged the government refrain from any administrative encouragement by stopping advertising, for example, in suspect newspapers. He called for tax audits of suspected Nazis and Fascists and Royal Canadian Mounted Police investigations of applicants for naturalization. In other words, Robertson wanted to use the resources of the state to control propaganda.[7]

Robertson could be tough, but he knew that toughness was not enough. He wanted to integrate immigrants and to make them into Canadians. He recommended English classes for newcomers, the assistance of social workers, legal aid, access to medical care, the use of the CBC and NFB, taking immigrants into political parties, and the enlistment of churches and other groups into making all who came here Canadians. His goal, he said, was "a positive affirmation of the concept of Canadian Citizenship based on loyalty & domicile and a repudiation of 'blood & soil.'"[8] Robertson was right, but unfortunately he was largely ignored.

MULTICULTURALISM

Sixty-five years later we have still not done as Robertson suggested, or not done it very well. The result, for example, is that a Canadian becomes defense minister in Croatia. The result is that Canadian Jews pressed Prime Minister Joe Clark to promise to move the Canadian Embassy in Israel from Tel Aviv to Jerusalem, no matter whether it made sense there or not. The result is that Canadian Jews in 2004 urged Prime Minister Paul Martin's government to "tilt" toward Israel. Canadian Muslims, naturally enough, argue the reverse.[9] Canadian Ukrainians encouraged Brian Mulroney's government to take the lead in supporting an independent Ukraine, just as those from the Baltic states did for their former homelands.

These things may be right or wrong in and of themselves; some of them unquestionably are right. They ought only to be Canadian policy, however, if they meet the test of Canada's national interests. They are not good foreign policy if they are done only to win support from the "padrones" of the ethnic groups who are supposed to be able to deliver votes during Canadian elections.

Even those who do not usually agree with Naomi Klein will recognize that she was surely right when she wrote in summer 2005 after the terrorist attacks in London "that the brand of multiculturalism practiced in Britain (and France, Germany, Canada ...) has little to do with genuine equality. It is instead a Faustian bargain, struck between vote-seeking politicians and self-appointed community leaders, one that keeps ethnic minorities tucked away in state-funded peripheral ghettoes while the centres of public life remain largely unaffected by seismic shifts in the national ethnic makeup."[10] Mme Jean, if we can trust quotes from her life before Rideau Hall, shares this view of multicultural ghettoization.

Canada needs and want immigrants, and most of us believe that the influx of people from all over the world is good for the country. But we must make Canadians of those who come here. Experiences in Holland and Britain and elsewhere suggest that it is not enough to leave immigrants alone and let them become adapted or not as they choose. We need to make clear to those we choose to admit to Canada that we are a nation with national interests, that we are a formed society with values, and if they wish to join us, they must understand this. That is what Canadians want: a Strategic Counsel poll

in August 2005 showed 69 percent wanting immigrants to integrate
into Canada and only 20 percent saying that immigrants should
maintain their own identity and culture.[11] Canadians want immigrants to understand that Canada is part of Western Civilization
with all its values; that we are not a community of ethnic, linguistic,
regional, and religious groups, but a nation. Women must have
equal rights, and religion does not and cannot rule. Canada is a
secular, pluralist, democratic nation.

Yes, Canadians want to be multicultural and to let all flourish
here, but at the same time the government and people absolutely
must stress that it is a requirement that immigrants come to accept
the values of our society, the values of Western Civilization, the values of Canada, which surely are broad enough to accommodate a
wide range of behaviours. Canadians somehow do not even realize
that to not do this causes a problem, and we tell ourselves that Canadian multiculturalism is far more successful than British or
Dutch multiculturalism. We couldn't have filmmakers assassinated
on the street for making the films they choose; we couldn't have
subway bombings, or so we say. But there is no evidence whatsoever
to suggest that Canada's multiculturalism is any better at integrating immigrant groups than the British or Dutch models.[12]

To paraphrase David Rieff (the word "Europe" and its derivatives have been replaced here by "Canada" and its derivatives): the
multicultural fantasy in Canada was that, in due course, assuming
that the proper resources were committed and benevolence deployed, Islamic and other immigrants would eventually become
liberals. As it's said, they would come to "accept" the values of their
new countries. It was never clear how this vision was supposed to
coexist with multiculturalism's other main assumption, which was
that group identity should be maintained. But by now that question is largely academic: the Canadian vision of multiculturalism,
in all its simultaneous good will and self-congratulation, is no
longer sustainable. And most Canadians know it. What they don't
know is what to do next.[13]

Most Canadians recognize that, if we can make multiculturalism
work, if our citizens from every origin can accept Canada's values
and add their own traditions to them – over time – and become integrated into the polity, then Canada can gain a huge advantage in
trade, foreign policy, and even defense. But to make this work Canada needs its leaders to lead, to speak the truth, and to help integrate

those who come to join our society. Among other things, that means not pandering for votes by twisting Canadian foreign policy.

QUEBEC AND FOREIGN POLICY

Now let me turn to another aspect of Canadian ethnicity. If British-Canadians shaped foreign policy questions in World Wars I and II, French-speaking Canadians have largely shaped our defense and foreign policies since Pierre Trudeau became prime minister 1968. There is no doubt – according to opinion polls – that Quebec attitudes to the military and defense spending and to war are very different than those of English-speaking Canadians; moreover, francophone attitudes to imperialism (historically British, and now American) are much cooler. A recent paper by Jean-Sebastian Rioux for the Canadian Defence and Foreign Affairs Institute makes this clear.[14] Canada has had a string of long-lived prime ministers of Quebec origin – Trudeau, Mulroney, and Chrétien – all of whom were exquisitely cognizant of these attitudes and, of course, all too aware of the *independantiste* attitudes in Quebec, ebbing and rising with events and the years. If it is bad policy to let Canadian Jews or Muslims have undue influence on policy to Israel, it is similarly bad policy to let Quebec, or any one province, determine Canadian defense and foreign policy.

Is it too strong to say that Quebec has determined policy? Quebec opinion, if we believe the present leaders of the Bloc Québécois and the Parti Québécois, is pacifist. If we accept the argument made by Stéphane Roussel and Charles-Alexandre Théoret, it is motivated by Pearsonian internationalism in that it supports the United Nations, peace, development, and international law.[15] My instinct is to believe the politicians, not least because Pearsonian-style internationalism, while it believed in all the good things noted above, also took Canada into NATO and the Korean War, not only into UN peacekeeping operations. Pearson had been a soldier in the Great War, a diplomat in the Second World War, and a Cold War protagonist. He was no pacifist, his Nobel Peace Prize notwithstanding.

To me, the decision to stay out of the Iraq War in 2003 was almost certainly shaped by Quebec's anti-military and anti-imperalist (or anti-American) views. These were reflected in the overwhelmingly negative attitudes toward the war in opinion polls in Quebec and by the coincidence of the provincial election (where all three leaders wore anti-war ribbons during the leaders' debate on television). Prime Minister Chrétien saw this – and he heard anti-war attitudes expressed in his own Quebec caucus, from the Bloc Québécois, and also the very anglo-Canadian NDP. The decision by Paul Martin's government to refuse to join the United States in Ballistic Missile Defense early in 2005 again was shaped by overwhelmingly hostile Quebec opinion poll numbers, the same forces in the House of Commons, and by the Liberals' minority government situation. The prospect of winning seats in Quebec, ultimately frustrated for Martin in the January 2006 election, largely drove the issue.

There were good arguments for supporting the United States in Iraq and joining in BMD. The best reasons were based on Canadian national interests. Canada's economy depends on trade with the US, and that is unlikely to change. If Washington being unhappy with us impedes trade, for example, if border crossings are slowed for even a few minutes more for each truck, or if passports are required to cross the border, that will have huge impact on us. In my opinion, the economy, one of Canada's key national interests, ought to have determined those issues for us.

But what of national unity, another of Canada's interests? This is difficult, and there is no doubt that initially on both Iraq and BMD Quebec was of a very different mind than the rest of Canada. Professor David Haglund in fact called Quebec opinion on BMD "unanimity, with near total agreement that missile defence must be bad."[16] The key point, however, is that in neither the Iraq nor the BMD case was there any leadership from Ottawa to try to persuade Quebecers that the economy, their jobs, and their pocketbooks might actually matter more than whether or not Canada supported the US in Iraq or joined it in missile defense. The latter case is strikingly clear – Prime Minister Martin had indicated early on that he supported BMD, but once he saw the opinion poll numbers, once the NDP (a strong anti-war voice in English Canada) and some in his Liberal caucus began a vigorous opposition, he backed away. The BMD issue was decided by a lack of leadership.

It is bad for Canadian unity to have Quebec driving the agenda on Iraq or BMD.[17] On both issues, the poll numbers were initially supportive in English-speaking Canada; on Iraq, there was at one point more than a thirty point difference between Alberta and Quebec on support for the war. Trying to give Quebec, or any other single province, what it wants can hurt the country; trying to follow clear national interests might help keep it together – if we have prime ministers who are willing to educate, explain, and lead – in Alberta and in Quebec.

Leadership actually can be exercised by politicians on sensitive foreign policy issues. Take the example of Louis St Laurent, prime minister from 1948 to 1957. St Laurent took Canada into NATO, into the Korean War, and he raised defense expenditures to more than 7 percent of gross domestic product in the mid-1950s. He spoke of these things in Quebec, and he did so while memories of the wartime conscription crisis were still very fresh. He toured the service clubs and business groups, and he made the case that Canada was threatened by the Soviet Union and needed to re-arm and to work with its allies. Opinion polls showed that Quebec remained opposed to sending troops to Korea or to NATO, that Quebec opposed any idea of peacetime conscription, and that the province was not especially happy with high defense spending. There were even great difficulties in recruiting enough francophones to man the battalions of the Royal 22e Régiment fighting in Korea. Nevertheless, Quebecers still voted for St Laurent: in the three elections he fought (1949, 1953, and 1957) he swept Quebec every time.[18] Why? Because he led. Because he didn't try to shape policy by opinion polls. Because he explained why he was acting, told people what was necessary, and won their acquiescence, if not their wholehearted support. This was leadership. It was also a recognition of the country's national interests and a willingness to make sure people understood them and why they were important. A prime minister needs to talk national interests to Quebec – and to all Canada – and tell the same story from Montreal to Vancouver.

Understanding what our national interests are is the way to make foreign policy, a better way than pandering to opinion polls and ethnic polls, a better way than – *pace* Ibbitson – looking for new motherlands. We have only one motherland now: Canada. Our foreign policy must be based on what is important to Canadians as a whole, not to Canadians wearing only their Old Country/ethnicity/religious hat. Anything else is a recipe for fragmentation, division, and discord.

It may be entirely appropriate that Canada, as Zuhair Kashmeri would prefer, be neutral in all or almost all wars. But not on the grounds he suggested: that a multicultural nation cannot go to war. Neutrality is an option – but only if it serves our national interests.

Advancing democracy and freedom and cooperation with our friends – that should be the test, along with the impact of neutrality on the remainder of our interests.

CONCLUSIONS

Canadians should care for and about the world and be idealistic They want to help in tsunami and hurricane relief and to help clean up Port-au-Prince. But such things are not national interests, however; they are issues that test our values. They are important, but they are not, for Canada as a nation-state, life-or-death issues. These are the national interests: security, unity, economics, democracy, and freedom. It will help greatly if Canadians and their leaders can make the distinction.

This chapter began with two foolish quotes from journalists. It is therefore appropriate to end with the ordinarily sensible James Travers of the *Toronto Star*, writing in mid-July 2005: "Paul Martin's government ... must send a zero-tolerance message to those who bring a new country the troubles that make it so attractive to leave an old one. This isn't racism or cultural insensitivity. It is a categorical rejection of bombs, guns and hatreds as legitimate expressions of political will."[19]

It will also help greatly if our leaders can focus on the aspects of foreign policy that are important to the nation as a whole and stop playing to the ethnicities that make up our population. Prime ministers must lead nationally. Look after the nation's interests first and its values second. Think for more than the present moment. Lead.

NOTES

1 Zuhair Kashmeri, *The Gulf Within: Canadian Arabs, Racism and the Gulf War* (Toronto, 1991), 126ff.
2 "She Is the New Canada," *Globe and Mail*, 5 August 2005.
3 See the accounts in J.L. Granatstein and Norman Hillmer, *Prime Ministers: Ranking Canada's Leaders* (Toronto, 1999).
4 See J.L. Granatstein and J.M. Hitsman, *Broken Promises: A History of Conscription in Canada* (Toronto, 1977).
5 J.L. Granatstein, *Who Killed the Canadian Military?* (Toronto, 2004), chapter 1.

6 Ibid., 48ff.

7 I suspect that in the 1980s and 1990s governments and political parties advertised in the Canadian Croatian (and Serbian, Bosnian, Slove-
nian, and Montenegrin) newspapers that called for slaughtering their
overseas neighbours.

8 J.L. Granatstein, *A Man of Influence: Norman A. Robertson and Canadian
Statecraft, 1929–68* (Ottawa, 1981), 82ff.

9 E.g., John Ivison, "'Pro-Israel' Federal Advisor Must Go, Elmasry Says,"
National Post, 17 August 2005.

10 "Terror's Greatest Recruiting Tool," *The Nation*, 29 August 2005.

11 "Canadian Attitudes Harden on Immigration," *Globe and Mail*, 12 August 2005. Similar results can be found in a Dominion Institute/CDFAI/
Innovative Research Group poll. See *Ottawa Citizen*, 31 October 2005.

12 I will say, however, that the young – those who have gone through our
public school systems – seem remarkably colour-blind and tolerant of
diversity. Whether that applies to those educated in madrassas, Hebrew
schools, and Christian fundamentalist schools, I do not know.

13 *New York Times Magazine*, 14 August 2005 "An Islamic Alienation."

14 "Two Solitudes: Quebecers' Attitudes Regarding Canadian Security
and Defence Policy," Calgary: CDFAI, 2005.

15 See chapter 9 of this volume; but perhaps Roussel and Théoret need a
different descriptor for Quebec.

16 David Haglund, "Does Quebec Have an 'Obsession Anti-Américaine'?"
unpublished paper, 2005.

17 It is also bad for sovereignists to have Quebec so anti-American that it
is bound to make the US even more concerned than it might otherwise
be should Quebec ever succeed in separating from Canada. Somehow
this fact does not appear to enter the debate in Quebec.

18 See J.L. Granatstein, *Who Killed the Canadian Military?* (Toronto, 2004),
109–11.

19 "Underscoring a Message of Zero Tolerance," *Toronto Star*, 14 July 2005.

The Parizeau-Chrétien Version: Ethnicity and Canadian Grand Strategy

DAVID G. HAGLUND

INTRODUCTION

They may not have agreed upon much else, but Jacques Parizeau and Jean Chrétien seemed to take seriously the impact that demographic change could have on domestic and foreign policy. And while it may seem odd, even jarring, to link together in one title these two political adversaries from Quebec, each is remembered (one more than the other) for a trenchant observation made in respect of the role that diasporas could have in shaping national and international policy agendas.

Parizeau's observation, of course, came in the immediate aftermath of the Parti Québécois's narrow loss in the 1995 referendum on sovereignty – a loss that the premier attributed (and hardly in a neutral manner!) to the role of economic and ethnic interests, with his clear intent being to signal the injustice of it all to the "real" Québécois. Chrétien's comment carried less of a politically incorrect sting, though from the point of view of this country's defense and foreign policies, has to be regarded as being as disturbing as was Parizeau's bitter post-referendum obiter dictum.

The prime minister really did get people's attention by some candid remarks made at a NATO summit in the summer of 1997 – remarks that testified to his rather cynical assessment of the reasons why the Western alliance was in the process of enlarging from its then-membership of sixteen states. Alliance leaders had gathered in Madrid that July to bring into the family three former adversaries of the defunct Warsaw pact: Poland, the Czech Republic, and Hungary. Unlike his foreign and defense policy advisors, Chrétien saw no broad strategic or diplomatic issues at stake in NATO enlargement. Instead, he regarded the process as being totally driven by ethnic diasporas in the United States. In an unguarded moment while NATO leaders were waiting for a group photo to be taken, the prime minister remarked candidly (but not, as it would turn out, confidentially) to his Belgian and Luxembourgeois counterparts that the lead item on the Madrid agenda owed everything to President Bill Clinton's "short-term political reasons." Unaware that his words were being picked up by a nearby live Radio Canada microphone, Chrétien said enlargement had "nothing to do with world security – it's because in Chicago, Mayor Richard Daley controls lots of votes for the Democratic nomination" (Harris, A10).

Although the remarks of the respective leaders drew sharp rebuttals, with Parizeau's eliciting particularly strong denunciations, in reality what the two men were saying, had they only been political scientists instead of political leaders, would have passed without notice – and not just because few people accord much attention to political scientists! In the scholarly realm, what the "Parizeau-Chrétien version" represents is a long-standing approach to policy analysis that pays heed to the influence of demographics and diasporas in the shaping of the public agenda, especially on matters relating to foreign policy. And though there may be no agreement (how could there be?) among the scholars as to whether such considerations of domestic politics (*Innenpolitik*) do or should trump external considerations (*Aussenpolitik*) when it comes to foreign-policymaking, few would dismiss as misguided or mean-spirited the attempt to analytically link foreign policy outputs in liberal-pluralist polities to the workings and power of lobbies, including ethnic ones (Smith; Lacorne; De Conde).

This is not to say that those lobbies everywhere and at all times have the means to steer foreign policy in a narrowly parochial direction, for they clearly do not; it is simply to maintain that, on some issues and at certain times, ethnic lobbies can play a role in shaping foreign policy agendas, a claim that has been recently (and controversially) restated by two eminent US political scientists regarding the influence exercised over their country's Middle East policies by what they term the "Israel lobby" (Mearsheimer and Walt). Nor is there anything particularly sinister about this dimension of "pressure politics," even though some will tell you ethnic as well as other forms of lobbying constitute an unwholesome derogation from the "national interest." And though, as the editors of this volume note in their introduction, immigrant communities tend to come "late" to political activism in the Canadian context, they eventually do get there. So long as the pressure is applied in a legal manner, it is hard to object to ethnic groups using whatever means at their disposal to guide policy in directions thought to be congenial to their collective interest.

With this in mind, my purpose in this chapter is to draw attention to the role played by ethnicity in the shaping of Canada's grand strategy. There are two principal foci of my analysis: recent immigration flows, and the question of Quebec. In respect of the former, I ask two questions: 1) is there a danger of illegal activities conducted by certain ethnic groups contributing to a deterioration of the security environment within North America?; and 2) is there a risk that legal activities of such groups might contribute to the growth of anti-American sentiment in Canada, thereby making the successful management of Canada's most important international relationship more difficult in years to come? In respect of the latter, I also ask two questions: 1) does Quebec have a disproportionate role in the shaping of Canadian foreign policy?; and 2) does opinion in Quebec differ from that elsewhere in Canada on defense and security questions, and if so what implications flow from this difference?

ETHNICITY AND STRATEGY: A "CULTURAL" PERSPECTIVE

In recent years, it has become fashionable for a certain kind of scholar of international relations to cloak the object of his or her inquiry in the garb of "identity," and to ask how this latter shapes the assessment of a given country's national interest, including the articulation of its grand strategy. When applied for the purposes of explicating matters strategic, this approach can bear the label "strategic culture." As with most such labels in political science and international relations, this one's meaning is nothing if not contested

(Haglund). At the risk of overgeneralizing, let us say that there are two principal ways to approach strategic culture. One focuses upon social psychology and is interested in cognition as a means by which culture is said to have a bearing on strategy. The other focuses upon societal context.

The cognitive camp emphasizes symbolism, held to be important in two ways. First, it solves the "level-of-analysis" problem, meaning that it helps us generate usable knowledge about the cognitive patterns of collectivities. Individuals, after all, have personalities, but only collectivities could be said to possess cultures, and the trick is to find a way to go from the individual to the collective level of analysis if culture is to mean anything. Symbolism provides the answer, enabling theorists to explore the *social* ideas of individuals (Elkins and Simeon; Lane).

Symbolism can do this because of its second major contribution, which is to draw us to the cognitive devices that social groupings rely upon, as Lowell Dittmer phrased it, to "transmit meanings from person to person despite vast distances of space and time." Dittmer invited us to think of those devices, which include but are not limited to imagery and metaphor, as being identical to what the poet T.S. Eliot called "objective correlatives," namely mechanisms for the efficient expression of feelings. In this regard, symbols become a "depository of widespread interest and feeling" (Dittmer). Analysts whose interest in strategic culture is situated primarily in the cognitive category might, for instance, be drawn to efforts at explicating strategic choice through the study of such nonliteral forms of communication as myth and metaphor, to take just the two most obvious examples.

Those, on the other hand, who want to tap into strategic culture as a means of grappling with the impact of ethnicity upon foreign and security policy will mainly take their concept in the contextual sense; they will want to determine how states might be thought by their own and other peoples as being likely to act based on the "way they are" and will prefer to delve into "national character" as the source of whatever is deemed to be cultural in foreign policy. But they usually do not identify their object of their intellectual curiosity by that name, which is held to be an obsolete and perhaps even nefarious term. So what do they call it? In a word: identity, a category that is held by many to endow meaning to interest – including and especially the national interest.

It can come as no surprise that even those social scientists who continue to employ the concept, national character, by its name disagree over its definition. Indeed, some will willingly concede that it resists defining – but is nevertheless too important to discard! One such scholar is Arthur Schlesinger, Jr, for whom national character raises important questions about the ability of the USA's creedal (constitutional) identity to withstand the challenge of a contemporary ethnic politics subsumed under the name "multiculturalism" (Schlesinger, 169). Although Schlesinger's pessimism on this score may not be justified, he is certainly correct in noting the important part played by ethnicity in discussions about national character in the United States. Nor is it just in the US that such issues arise.

What this implies for analysts who interpret strategic culture as context is, or should be, apparent: the impact of ethnicity as a conditioning element in foreign-policymaking is a worthy object for their scholarly attentions – in Canada, no less than in the United States. They might not think of themselves in this connection, but analysts who attempt to come to grips with the impact of ethnicity and diasporas in Canada and other liberal-pluralist societies can be said to be working in the field of strategic culture.

It should be noted that there also exists an older and broader assessment of demography's role in foreign policy and grand strategy, associated not with strategic culture but rather with old-fashioned "realist" theory in international relations. Here the emphasis is placed more on the quantitative than on the *qualitative* nature of a country's demography, in a bid to try to establish a link between a population's size and the power potential of the state wherein it resides. One scholar, Ray S. Cline, even developed an ambitious formula for measuring demography's contribution to a state's overall power standing: $Pp = (C+E+M) \times (S+W)$. Pp stood for a state's perceived power, held by Cline to be a function of the sum of its territory and population (its "critical mass," or C), its economic strength (E), and its military capability (M), all multiplied by the sum of its strategy (S) and ability to put that strategy into action (its "will," or W).

Whatever else might be said about such a formulaic construct of "power," at least it avoids problems associated with the circular logic of an alternative means of assessing power, namely to consider it a synonym for "influence." But, with apologies to Cline, what I

am interested in here is to take a qualitative not quantitative measure of demography's impact upon foreign and defense policy – in
our case, of Canada's. So let us start by asking whether there is anything related to recent immigration patterns that might be likely to
have an impact upon Canada's strategic situation.

A NEW FENIANISM?

It is generally considered that the Canada-US "security community"
has to rank as one of the world's oldest such groupings – if not its oldest. By security community is meant an entity about which we can say
that war or even the threat of war simply makes no sense as a means of
conflict resolution *within* the group. For a variety of reasons, security
communities are "zones of peace," within which everyone can have
reasonable expectations that disputes, when they occur, will be re-
solved peacefully. If few doubt that Canada and the US form such a
zone of peace, there is more debate as to the timing of the zone's onset, with some dating it from the last quarter of the nineteenth century (which choice, if accepted, would make the North American
security community the world's oldest), while others, including this
author, believe the security community only took shape in the interwar period after the respective countries finally gave up the unsettling
practice of drafting war plans against each other.

Emblematic of the North American zone of peace is the reciprocal pledge the countries have made to regard each other's legitimate physical security interests as being virtually tantamount to
their own. This pledge constitutes the strategic norm that under-
pins the entire apparatus of Canada-US security cooperation.
Though some writers see this norm as dating back to the beginning
of the twentieth century (Sutherland), it really only took shape during the crisis atmosphere of the late 1930s, when a war in Europe
was looming, and when it seemed that US security might be imperil-
led should Canadian involvement in the European war make un-
tenable the Monroe Doctrine.

We can call this norm the "Kingston dispensation," as it first was
made explicit in an address delivered by Franklin D. Roosevelt at
Queen's University, in Kingston, Ontario, during the August 1938
Sudetenland crisis. The president told his audience that the USA
would "not stand idly by" were the physical security of Canada threatened by a European adversary, as a consequence of the country's

participation in a European war. For his part, Prime Minister Mackenzie King, speaking a few days later (though not in Kingston), pledged that Canada would ensure that nothing it did would jeopardize the physical security of the United States. Taken together, the two leaders' remarks constitute the core of the Canada-US security relationship: each country understood that it had a "neighbourly" obligation to the other to demonstrate nearly as much solicitude for the other's physical security needs as for its own (Fortmann and Haglund).

The Kingston dispensation was not quite an alliance, but it would only take two more years before a bilateral alliance did get forged in North America – an alliance that remains the USA's longest-running bilateral security pact. Is there any reason to believe that this normative core could be subjected to severe challenge – so severe, in fact, as to put paid to the North American zone of peace? Yes. The primary, perhaps only conceivable, challenge to the security community resides in what Canada's former minister of transport, Jean Lapierre, concedes to be his "worst nightmare," that of a devastating terrorist attack mounted against US soil from Canada (Allison, 717).

We might label this threat the "New Fenianism," as a way to provide historical context via analogical reasoning. To be sure, analogies can never be anything other than imperfect, and this one looks, at first blush, to be more imperfect than most; for, to Canadian readers with historical knowledge, the New Fenianism conjures up an earlier threat to physical security that really was a Canadian nightmare – the prospect of the country's being invaded by hordes of Irish nationalists based in the United States and possessed of an abiding grudge, not so much against Canada as against Canada's then colonial ruler, Great Britain. For the Fenians of old, whose ranks in the USA had been filled by the massive migration triggered by the Great Starvation of 1847, the most tempting target in the campaign for Irish independence was Canada; their jihad envisioned seizing Canada, and though this central pillar of their strategic campaign may have failed to secure Irish independence, it certainly played a considerable role in uniting the British North American colonies in the tense period following the US Civil War (Jenkins).

Conceptually, what Fenianism in the nineteenth century represented was a diaspora's bid to achieve world-order aims by attacking targets on North American soil. The Old Fenians cared about Canada, but chiefly as a means to get Britain out of Ireland. The

"New Fenians" also have world-order objectives, the servicing of which involves strikes on North American soil as a means of forcing the pace of developments elsewhere. In the case of the New Fenians, the aim is to dislodge the USA not from North America (a patent impossibility) but rather from the Greater Middle East.

But if the comparison might be an apt one in terms of objectives, does not the difference in scale – tens of thousands of Irish-American jihadists versus a necessarily unknown but definitely tiny number of contemporary Canada-based jihadists – render nugatory the analogy?[1] Ordinarily, one would hesitate simply because of these scale differences to suggest the analogy, except that in the case of modern terrorism, as the events of 11 September 2001 showed, it does not require vast numbers to make a major impact on international security. Given the legitimate worry about terrorists acquiring weapons of mass destruction, small numbers can more than equal, in death and destruction, what in an earlier era would have required veritable armies to accomplish. As Robert Cooper notes, ideological groups can today make do with only a fraction of the warriors who used to be required: "Henceforth, comparatively small groups will be able to do the sort of damage which before only state armies or major revolutionary movements could achieve ... A serious terrorist attack could be launched by perhaps sixty people ... 0.000001 per cent of the [world's] population is enough" (ix).

To date, most of the Canadian jihadists involved in combat against the USA (and, when you think about it, Canada as well given the mission in Afghanistan) have done so outside of North American territory; one recalls in this regard the astounding saga of the Khadr family, made even more astounding by an early intervention of a Canadian prime minister, Jean Chrétien, to get freed from custody in Pakistan the now-deceased patriarch of the family, Ahmed Said Khadr, the al-Qaeda operative who enrolled his four sons in the jihad that would eventually take his own life. As Colin Freeze has written apropos the Chrétien involvement in this case, "[t]he widespread chill and embarrassment caused by the prime minister's intervention for Mr. Khadr a decade earlier still ripples through the Canadian government and its counterterrorism cases today" (7).

But there is the even greater embarrassment of the most publicized jihadist who did attempt to strike a US target – the Los Angeles international airport – from a base in Canada, Ahmed Ressam.

Although the so-called "millennium bomber" failed in his plan, his arrest in December 1999 by US border authorities in Washington state occasioned a great deal of concern in the US, and did so well before the heightened state of anxiety as a result of the attacks of 11 September (Collacott). Needless to say, Jean Lapierre's "nightmare" remains one for the entire Canadian security apparatus, and should a major terrorist strike against the US ever materialize from Canadian soil, it would be difficult if not impossible to overstate the severity of its impact not just on Canada-US relations but also on the North American zone of peace.

But, if the patently illegal aspects of the New Fenianism must remain a constant source of concern for security experts in Canada and in the US, there is a legal side of the phenomenon that itself carries with it profound implications for the quality of the Canada-US relationship. Again, the analogy is instructive, for while most of the Irish diaspora did not, in the end, take part in the jihad against Canadian targets, that large diaspora did contribute to keeping UK-US relations from developing into a strategic partnership until it was almost too late. The Irish-Americans were hardly the only diaspora group in the US to delight in urging politicians to tweak the tail of the British lion (the even larger German-American community also encouraged the pastime), but their presence, especially in major urban centres of the northeast, was a constant reminder to political leaders of the danger in working too closely with the USA's fellow democracy across the seas, Great Britain.

So it bears investigating the way in which current immigration sources and patterns in Canada might have an effect on the evolution of Canadian-US relations, given that considerable numbers of new arrivals are hailing from parts of the world that are hardly sympathetic to the USA or its purposes. To be sure, anti-Americanism in Canada hardly needs off-shore diasporas to stoke it; an electoral campaign and a well-publicized trade wrangle seemed to be all that was required to turn Paul Martin into Hugo Chávez during the most recent federal election campaign. But there is a difference between the variety of anti-Americanism as it is articulated in parts of the world where the USA is seen as a cultural and political enemy – parts of the world from which growing numbers of immigrants keep arriving in Canada – and the anti-Americanism bubbling up in parts of the world where the USA is considered still to be an ally and a partner, albeit an occasional annoyance.

If Canada's traditional so-called anti-Americanism is of the "lite" (Naím) and opportunistic variety (call it "Martinism"), it remains to be seen what will be the longer-term impact of immigration flows betraying a rather less salubrious form of anti-Americanism. If the US experience during the first half of the twentieth century in developing a stable partnership with Britain is any indication, one might expect the imported anti-Americanism of new immigrants to render more challenging the fashioning of a mature and rational "America policy" in Ottawa, all things being equal.

THE OTHER DIMENSION OF ETHNICITY: QUEBEC

The issue of anti-Americanism, lite or otherwise, leads directly into the second substantive focus of this inquiry into the connection between ethnicity and strategy: Quebec. Here there are two questions to pursue. The first concerns whether the province exercises too much influence over Canada's foreign and defense policies. The second asks whether opinion in Quebec, both on the US and on matters strategic in general, differs from that in the rest of the country and, if so, what this might portend.

As to the first of these interrogations, we can say that there is broad division among the analysts. One polar view, let us term this the "wag the dog" thesis, maintains that Quebec does possess more – much more – influence over the country's foreign and defense policies than its share of the overall population (about 23 percent and declining) would warrant. Evidence for this thesis is found both in the frequency with which prime ministers have been chosen from Quebec as opposed to the rest of Canada (the ROC) over the past four decades – i.e., for nearly all the time since the onset of the Trudeau era in 1968 – and in the assumption not only that the "Quebec question" dominates the domestic agenda but that solicitude for the province's public opinion has been allowed to alter strategic policy in ways deemed detrimental to the national interest. Examples of such influence would include, but not be limited to, the decision not to participate in missile defense and the unwillingness of the Liberal Government to support traditional allies in the mooted "Anglosphere" over regime change in Iraq in spring 2003 (Granatstein).

Opposed to this view is the opposite polar position, which we might label the "no smoking gun" thesis. Here the argument is advanced that not a shred of evidence exists to support the claim that on decisions such as missile defense and the onset of the Iraq war, public opinion in Quebec was instrumental to the policies eventually adopted (even if, in both cases, the policies were those of prime ministers from Quebec!). Instead, say adherents to this thesis, what is afoot is simply a new version of an old game – the blame game (Martin).

Somewhere in the middle is another view, perhaps the most persuasive of the three: this we could label the "Pettigrew perspective," reflecting as it does the opportunistic (though perhaps misguided) calculations of a seasoned federal politician from Quebec, to the effect that Ottawa does indeed carefully measure the political payoff that might be had in trying to dress certain policies up in a rhetoric thought congenial to the province's opinion. Illustratively, the then-foreign minister identified (possibly mistakenly) tough-talking to the Americans as an electoral asset, one supposed to bolster the federal Liberals' weak standing in the province during the most recent national election campaign, in late 2005 and early 2006. "In Quebec, it is the sort of thing that will help us a great deal in the next election," Pettigrew confided to a journalist in October 2005, basing his point more on hope than on evidence, given the relative unpopularity of his party with Québécois, and especially in light of the continued collapse of Liberal support ever since the Martin Government began in late autumn 2005 to adopt a language of populist nationalism more often heard in Latin America than in North America (den Tandt).

Nevertheless, that the Martin Government might have believed the message to be the medium when it comes to what Rex Murphy calls the "sweet spot" of Canadian politics (the felt need to placate Quebec), does testify to a perception that a major attitudinal gap separates Québécois from the rest of Canadians when it comes to issues related to the grand strategy. And this takes us to our second question, concerning the implications that might flow from such a gap (should it, in fact, exist).

Historically, it is not hard (in fact, it is easy) to make the argument that an ethnic divide existed in Canada on matters strategic, especially when prospects of overseas intervention loomed. From the Boer war through the two world wars of the twentieth century, Quebec appeared to be on a decidedly different page from the rest of Canada when it came to foreign and security policies that would have military implications, with the greatest divisiveness being encountered, not surprisingly, at those moments when Ottawa was confronting the need to contribute to the collective defense of Imperial/ Commonwealth interests. It was thought that with the end of the era in which Britain served as the principal organizer of Canadian overseas military activities – i.e., with the rise of the USA and its panoply of security organizations to international prominence – the old ethnic divide in grand strategy would become a thing of the past.

Recently, there have been signs of its re-emerging, and these have been associated with an apparent change of attitude in Quebec toward the United States. It is probably wrong to argue that Quebecers are "essentially" anti-American; most likely, the differences gleaned from survey data as between their opinion of Americans and the opinion of other Canadians can be interpreted as representing nothing so much as a secular trend, one that has seen Quebec oscillate from being Canada's most to its least "America-friendly" region. A glance at history would suggest that we are simply at the low point in a cycle concerning Quebecers' attitudes toward the US – a cycle that demonstrates nothing so much as their fundamental ambivalence, over time, toward their southern neighbours (Lamonde).

So the issue of the moment is not so much *whether* Quebecers interpret the USA differently from other Canadians; in this respect we can take it for granted that, as Jean-Sébastien Rioux says, compared with their counterparts in English Canada, Quebecers are "more likely nowadays to oppose the United States [and] to feel that they 'cannot trust the United States', that 'the US is behaving like a rogue nation' or that 'the US is a force for evil in the world'" (Rioux, 23).[2] Instead, the issue is what this ethnic divide over strategy might imply, either in the short term or the long.

Let us split the potential implications into three categories. The first concerns Canada-US relations. One should not disregard the prospect that "culture" can play a large role in the shaping of a country's "strategic culture"; if it did not, of what use would the latter concept be? Nevertheless, it is possible to make too much of the Canadian ethnic divide as an element conducing to the worsening of bilateral relations, notwithstanding the above-mentioned willingness of the Martin Government to pander to what it takes to be Quebecers' sensibilities (an electoral tropism that is, as of this writing, being evidenced by one of the candidates for the leadership of the federal Liberal Party, Michael Ignatieff) (Simpson).

If it is true that the Bush administration has not been an easy one for Quebecers to warm to, it is no less true that the ROC is hardly head-over-heels in love with the current US administration. Pollster Michael Adams asserts that not since the days of James Madison has a president been so thoroughly disliked by Canadians as is George W. Bush – and Madison, be it recalled, was president at the time of the last war between Canada/Britain and the US, the War of 1812!

Moreover, one must be careful in overstating the tension in the current bilateral relationship. We are still, thankfully, a long way from the toppling of the democratic North American alliance as a result of *those* issues that have so roiled the bilateral waters; still, as I argued earlier, it *is* possible to imagine scenarios that really could damage the bilateral relationship in such a way as to make all of us wonder about the solidity of the North American security community. That, of course, gets us back to the New Fenianism of the previous section: can we say that this phenomenon is more pronounced in Quebec than elsewhere in the country?

The Ressam affair to the contrary notwithstanding, there is no reason to believe Quebec is disproportionately host to whatever New Fenian menace might be lodged in Canada. There are two reasons for this. One has to do with the relative weakening of Islamist terrorism in Algéria; Ressam's old group, the GIA, is no longer in existence under that name, and most analysts would conclude that, compared with a decade ago, the government in Algiers has been able to contain and turn back what had been a severe challenge to national security. And since the Montreal cells were largely Algerian in origin, it is fair to argue that there has been progress on the counter-terrorism front in Quebec *pari passu* with developments in North Africa – or, more accurately, because of those developments.

And what of the rest of Canada? Judging from the province of choice of this country's leading jihadists, we might be tempted to conclude that, if any province looms as a problem for the North American security community, it is likely to be Ontario not Quebec, as witnessed by the foiled Islamist plot to bomb targets in Toronto and Ottawa during late spring 2006 (Appleby and Freeze). To repeat, for obvious reasons it is difficult if not impossible to do other than speculate on the likelihood of a New Fenianism troubling the North American peace. But there *is* documented evidence concerning some Canadian jihadists, and by far the most celebrated such cases involve a few immigrants (and their children) who came from

English- not French-using source countries, and who settled in Ontario not Quebec. Such is the case not only of the Khadrs and the springtime 2006 plotters but also of would-be martyr Mohammed Mansour Jabarah, a Kuwaiti-Canadian who grew up in St Catherines and joined the jihad, travelling from Afghanistan to Karachi, Manila, Singapore, and Oman, where he was arrested (Bell).

This gets us to our second dimension: might there be national-unity implications of the changed Quebec mood, from the province's erstwhile pro-Americanism of the 1980s and 1990s? Can we say, today, that we are witnessing a reappearance of that earlier cultural cleavage, whereby English Canada shows itself more willing, and Quebec less willing, to defer to or otherwise trust US leadership? Is there a risk that at a moment when some argue an "Anglosphere" is emerging in international politics, the pull of "geo-ethnicity" might cause English Canada to interpret global strategic reality in a manner so profoundly different from Quebecers as to add one more log to the fire of national disunity?

Notwithstanding the short-lived English-French differences over the wisdom of the Iraq war, it is hard to imagine the divergence of views across the cultural-linguistic divide in Canada ever having the consequences for national unity that they possessed in the first half of the twentieth century, and this applies even in the case of Alberta, where a foreign-policy outlook different from Quebec's is the most pronounced, and where – unlike in other parts of the ROC – one might imagine the rise of a sovereignty movement.

With the exception of the aforementioned "nightmare scenario" of a terrorist strike on the US that involves Canadian operatives based in one province and results in the closing of the Canada-US border and the crippling of Canadian economic activity, domestic cultural divisions over foreign policy are unlikely to play themselves out as gravely as they once did. This is due to two conditions. First, while it is true that recent survey data indicate English Canadian opinion to be more favourable to the USA than is opinion in Quebec, whatever "collective identity" might be said to be shared between the ROC and the USA can never approach in strength and emotional significance the attachment that English Canada had to England during the great global upheavals of the twentieth century that so tested Canadian national unity.

Secondly, and directly related to the first condition, there had in the latter half of 2005 been a reduction in the "US-affinity gap" as

between Quebec and the ROC, resulting from the growing frustration in large parts of the latter with a Bush administration that was
seen to be dragging its feet on the softwood lumber dispute,
thereby aggravating a sense of frustration that the USA was cheating
on the rules and norms of "free trade." Whether the narrowing of
the affinity gap continues in the wake of the (partial) settlement of
softwood dispute remains to be seen.

But even if it turns out that the differing attitudes toward the US
as between Quebec and the rest of Canada possess major implications neither for bilateral Canada-US relations nor for Canadian national unity, does it follow that the divergences are of absolutely no
consequence? Hardly, for the third dimension, to which we now
turn our attention, concerns the "place" of the United States in respect of any pending third round of referenda on Quebec sovereignty. By "place" I mean to suggest the real but indirect effect that
a continuation of the current Quebec mood might be expected to
have on the referendum strategy of any future PQ Government.

As Stéphane Roussel and Charles-Alexandre Théorêt have pointed
out, sovereignists altered radically their views on defense and security
policy the closer they came to power provincially, and the closer they
came to winning a referendum. There was more than a touch of
irony in the evolution of Quebec sovereignists' thinking about matters strategic; for if it made sense for a "distinct society" to carve out
a new political and territorial dispensation in North America, then
surely this self-same distinctiveness might have been expected to
have found an echo in a newly independent Quebec's grand strategy. Yet instead of developing a "distinct strategy" to complement
the distinct society, the best PQ defense intellectuals and policy advocates could do, on the eve of the last referendum, was to sing the
praises of *Canada's* grand strategy, to such an extent that the defense policy of an independent Quebec could be safely advertised
as simply more of the same. "Interestingly enough," write Roussel
and Théorêt, "with the exception of some small peace groups, the
alignment with Canadian policy did not occasion any adverse reactions on the part of those desirous of breaking with Canada. Not
only did the majority of Quebec voters seem to like those internationalist ideas; they also saw adherence to them as representing an
insurance policy" (574).

The primary reason that PQ defense intellectuals and policy advisors advertised, back in 1995, a sovereign Quebec's willingness to

mimic Canadian grand strategy and to pledge an ongoing role both in NATO and NORAD was to send reassuring signals both to the Quebec electorate and to its neighbours in the ROC and the US; joining these two collective- defense entities was sought, and this at a time when Quebecers' opinions of the USA were relatively charitable, primarily for reasons having little if anything to do with a desire to contribute to collective defense. Instead, joining would send out a comforting message to those who might be skittish about the possibility sovereignty could negatively affect the North American security community.

Given the alteration in Quebec opinion toward the US, does anyone today believe that a successful referendum strategy could feature the same sort of appeal? Possibly, but it would entail some quick and deep thinking on the part of PQ defense intellectuals. Failing this, Quebec sovereignists will find themselves unable to rely upon one "insurance policy" (to use the words of Roussel and Théorêt) that was thought essential last time a referendum was attempted.

CONCLUSION

Barring the one thing that *could* put paid to the North American security community, namely a devastating terrorist strike on US territory that could be traced back to groups operating out of Canada, the North American zone of peace is remarkably durable. This does not, however, mean that ethnicity has no impact upon the future evolution of the security community. I argue that it does, for two reasons.

First, if anti-Americanism can be a corrosive element even in liberal-democratic security communities – if it can lead, in the minatory words of the US ambassador to Canada, David Wilkins, to a "slippery slope"[3] whose end point no one can glimpse (LeBlanc and Galloway) – then it does appear that one implication of current trends in Canadian immigration is an increased likelihood of Canadian society's becoming more anti-American in disposition than it currently is.

Second, and countering the first implication, is the prospect that should Canadian national-unity be increasingly called into question for *domestic* reasons, we can expect a reversal of the recent state-level practice of opportunistic anti-Americanism of the "lite" variety that I termed "Martinism." This will be so, irrespective of whether Liberals or Conservatives form the government in Ottawa at the time of any future referendum on Quebec sovereignty, for the adage still applies that "a friend in need is a friend indeed." Each time a crisis in national unity looms in this country, federal figures hasten to "make nice" to the Americans. Pierre Trudeau did this in the 1970s after the arrival in power of the PQ, and so did Jean Chrétien in the mid 1990s as the menace of a second referendum loomed. There is no reason to expect the pattern to alter.

Indeed, to the extent that a separatist Quebec Government might also be expected to try to cozy up to the US, it is not out of the question that we will see another shift in the Quebec societal mood regarding what the USA represents. So the picture left by a consideration of ethnicity and diasporas on Canadian foreign and defense policy remains a fuzzy one: on the one hand, an upswing in *societal* sources of anti-Americanism, balanced on the other by a likelihood that *state-level* anti-Americanism will abate as Ottawa once more turns to Washington to support the merits of Canadian federalism.

Whether Washington will respond in future as it has in the past remains in question (Dunsky). Perhaps this is the "slippery slope" to which David Wilkins made allusion?

NOTES

1 Consider that about 140,000 Irish-American fought for the Union during the Civil War, and while most of them had no desire actually to wage holy war against the object of their loathing, Britain, several thousand did join the ranks of the Fenian movement and hundreds took part in "Colonel" John O'Neill's raid on Fort Erie, Ontario, in early June 1866.

2 The words in single quotations are taken from a 2004 opinion survey commissioned by CDFAI, "Visions of Canadian Foreign Policy."

3 Said the ambassador, about Martinist critiques of US policies on a range of issues, including the environment (ironically, where even the US record made Canada's look dismal): "It may be smart election-year politics to thump your chest and constantly criticize your friend and your No. 1 trading partner. But it is a slippery slope, and all of us should hope that it doesn't have a long-term impact on the relationship."

Muslim Communities:
The Pitfalls of Decision-Making
in Canadian Foreign Policy

SAMI AOUN

INTRODUCTION

The question of diasporas has only recently occupied centre-stage in the analyses of international scholars and foreign policy experts. There is no doubt that this recent preoccupation was long overdue, given the expanding role of diasporas as actors in an increasingly globalized post-Westphalian international system. Nevertheless, some studies have emphasized the involvement of diasporas and the reinforcement of their role in international politics (Sheffer; Bruno; and in particular Shain and Barth, 449–79). In fact, free from state-centric reasoning, diasporas as transnational ethnic and cultural groups belonging to both their host country and their countries of origin can build political networks across borders and play a key role in the relations between the two. The issues at stake arise in particular, and are further complicated, when countries of origin approach their nationals for the purpose of furthering and defending their interests with respect to host countries that inevitably belong to the Western liberal-democratic space. These nationals are expected to do so however, without playing the role of "fifth column"[1] (Pipes) and without "treason or infidelity" in cases where the interests of the two countries collide. Thus, in this post-Westphalian system, the communities experience both gains and troubles arising from disruptions on the international stage.

Considering this, and the increasingly important role that is expected of diasporas in the Canadian foreign-policy sphere, it is appropriate to point out that Canada's foreign policy is the result of a constant readjustment between the executive, elected officials, and the media. While diasporas can intervene at the electoral level and even with respect to the media with the aim of becoming political actors that the Canadian decision-maker can deal with, the role these communities[2] play at the level of the executive remains limited. The latter responds to a different logic and different criteria, which are, at least in the short and medium term, beyond the reach of any action or influence from Arab and Muslim diasporas.

The Arab and Muslim communities belonging to Canadian space have the same legal and constitutional rights and privileges as native Canadians. The Muslim community is one of the most important communities in Canada: the number of Muslims in Canada[3] has been estimated at approximately 400,000 in 1997 (Coward et al., 174) and is currently estimated at about 580,000 with an increase of 130 percent over the last decade (Sallot). Members of these communities who have been granted citizenship have the right to adhere to mainstream political parties and to form other parties or cultural and social associations, or create media forums, among other things. These rights are guaranteed by laws that set no bounds on participation in political and social life.[4]

Despite the rights and privileges granted to the Muslim community its participation in this free political space remains limited. In fact, even if the membership criteria for political parties are not difficult to fulfill (adherence simply requires properly filling in a form, regardless of race or religion), the Muslim community from the first generation onward has paid little attention to political participation. Adherence to political parties remains limited, the will to form other parties nearly absent, and even participation in elections is not common practice among members of this community.

That being said, it is important to mention that despite this "renunciation" of the right to political participation, the influence of the "Muslim" vote (Arabs included) has increased through the years (Sallot). Candidates from different political parties consistently court the Arab and Muslim electorate, and Canada's foreign policy toward the Muslim world (Palestine, Iraq, etc.) is among the main issues emphasised by the Muslim and Arab diaspora during elections. This diaspora remains attached to its Arab and Muslim homeland and is very conscious of the role that Canada could play in that region of the world.

Nevertheless, this political consciousness is not accompanied by a clear and consensual strategy (with a near-total absence of debate among the diaspora) to influence Canadian foreign-policy decision-making. This raises an important question as to what the obstacles impeding such influence may be. Thus, the following reflections focus on notable attempts by Arab and Muslim social actors to influence Canadian foreign policy decision-making. The aim is to try to identify the factors that impede a participatory role by Arab and Muslim actors in the decision-making process and to understand the elements that limit this role to sporadic consultations rather than more systematic lobbying.

This diaspora constitutes a significant demographic mass concentrated in Ontario, with 61 percent of all Canadian Muslims, approximately 352,500 people, and in Quebec, with 108,000 people according to the census in 2001. The diaspora also has an important presence in British Columbia. The number of Muslims in British Columbia has more than doubled in recent years, reaching slightly more than 56,200 people (Statistics Canada). Islam is the second religion in the country (after Christianity) and Arabic, Canada's seventh language, spoken by 220,500 people (Heritage Canada; Statistics Canada). The political role of this mass is reflected in the electoral vote at the level of at least thirty federal ridings. Furthermore, the Canadian Islamic Congress (CIC) has identified, in its report *Election 2004: Towards Informed and Committed Voting*, 101 Canadian electoral districts in which a "Muslim vote" could influence future elections, fifty-five of which would be in Ontario and twenty-one in Quebec.

THE ARAB AND MUSLIM COMMUNITY AND
THE DECISION-MAKING PROCESS IN CANADIAN
FOREIGN POLICY: DIFFICULTIES AND WEAKNESSES

Despite the demographic advantages that this community has, difficulties and weaknesses arise that can be considered exogenous factors. In fact, Canada's commercial relations with Arab countries are at a lower scale than those with India and China. Furthermore, Canada is not involved in strategic alliances with Muslim countries, with the exception of Turkey in the context of NATO. Non-commercial relations remain confined to the Commonwealth or La Francophonie (for Quebec) and to assistance for the reconstruction of Afghanistan[5] and Iraq,[6] the first and second most significant recipients of Canadian aid in the region in the 2003–05 period (Government of Canada 2004).

CANADIAN STAKES IN THE ARAB AND MUSLIM WORLD

Thus, the stakes of Canadian foreign policy in the Arab-Muslim space and in particular in the Middle East[7] can be summarized by the following issues of concern. First, Canada does not recognize Israel's control of the Arab territories occupied after 1967 (the West Bank, the Gaza Strip, the Syrian Golan Heights, East Jerusalem) and considers the occupation to be contrary to international law and harmful to peace in the Middle East. Furthermore, Canadian foreign policy clearly supports the creation of a Palestinian state, United Nations resolution 242, as well as all declarations that could lead to peace between the protagonists in the region. Given these non-aggressive positions, Canada has credibility in the eyes of Arab leaders, which could eventually facilitate a deeper involvement of Canadian foreign policy in the Middle East. Canada's Arab and Muslim communities seek the consolidation of, and better adherence to, this principled position on Canadian foreign policy.

Second, with respect to the fight against terrorism, Canada continues to join its efforts with those of the international community. Canada has signed and ratified a dozen United Nations conventions and protocols relating to terrorism, such as the Convention on the Suppression of the Financing of Terrorism of 8 December 1999 and the Convention on the Suppression of Terrorist Bombings of 9 December 1999. Without any doubt, Canada acts within the United Nations system of international law but a close relationships with its US neighbour often leaves very little leeway for an independent Canadian foreign policy on issues related to terrorism. One can also say that Canada acts more in concert with the G8 regarding this issue.[8] In sum, the Canadian message to the Muslim world and to the Middle East in particular involves the achievement of peace, the implementation of international resolutions related to security in the Middle East, and the promotion of democracy and human rights[9] in the region. With respect to the issue of Iraq,

Canadian action consists primarily of humanitarian assistance, political and economic reconstruction, and the training of Iraqi police officers in Jordan.

It is important to point out that the Arab and Muslim world is not perceived as a monolithic geopolitical and economic bloc in Canadian foreign policy. Thus, Canada's current relations with the Muslim world are primarily limited to bilateral relations with each country of the region wavering between the requirements of diplomatic protocols on the one hand and commercial needs on the other (trade with these countries remains more or less modest).[10]

Along the same lines, the Muslim and Arab imagination remains filled with the notion of Canadian foreign policy as based on a pacifist ideal (one can think of the respect granted to Nobel Prize winner Lester Pearson, considered to be the father of the modern-day concept of peacekeeping operations). Accordingly, the perception is that Canadian foreign policy is (or should be) fostering real democracy and good governance in the region, being vigilant about failed and fragile states engaging in intra-state conflicts as mediator and helping conflict affected countries implement meaningful reform through election monitoring and development assistance.

THE MUSLIM COMMUNITY: INTERNAL OBSTACLES AND ENDOGENOUS PROBLEMS

It is important to emphasize that several crucial turning points continue to pose significant challenges to Muslim and Arab political mobilization. The inescapable date of 11 September 2001, the second Palestinian Intifada in September 2000,[11] the war in Afghanistan and subsequently in Iraq, and the "Pax Americana" have all generated various anti-American reactions in the region. Faced with these thorny problems, Arab and Muslim communities in Canada have found themselves in an uncomfortable position. There are several reasons for this:

a) A policy of denial. This policy, which is prevalent throughout the Muslim world, is also the most dominant one among Muslim diasporas. In fact, it persists even among elites and continues to characterize their minimally critical and thoroughly emotional worldview. Being based on faulty logic, but easily transmitted

and perpetuated, the policy of denial has had devastating consequences. Thus, errors made are not acknowledged and are ignored, preventing the self-criticism that would improve the
place of this community within Canadian foreign-policymaking.

b) An ideology of conspiracy. An ideology of conspiracy consists of
attributing one's historical errors to the Other (who is primarily
Western and Judeo-Christian). This ideology is broadly reflected
throughout Arab-Muslim culture and is disseminated by the
elites of the diaspora. The contemporary roots of this mentality
date back to the Sykes-Picot agreements between France and
Great Britain in 1916, which were the basis upon which the Middle East was to be divided between the two powers of that period. It is also worth mentioning European colonialism and its
after-effects. The conspiracy mentality is most often reflected in
an absolute refusal to explain rationally, and especially through
self-criticism, the upheaval in the Middle East since 9/11. This
ideology has become an ideology of resentment and bitterness,
because it absolves the Arab community of any responsibility in
the face of history.

c) A victimization mentality. This mentality has strongly persisted
in the Arab and Muslim community in Canada. It is certainly residual but nevertheless still powerful. It is expressed within
households, in newspaper columns, and in expert analyses. Education and ensuing perceptions of the world are largely responsible for this mentality and for the construction of the concept
of an "enemy, who is the cause of all ills." The promotion of the
community's perception as an oppressed people, renders positive action, and attempts at playing a role in Canadian foreign-
policy decision-making process, disjointed and maladjusted.

Thus, it is important to re-emphasize that diaspora elites are often the bearers of the negative memory of a dark colonial past and
are the generators of a discourse of victimization. These diaspora
elites are those who have not yet achieved a proper synthesis of tradition and modernity.

Moreover, the establishment of the Arab and Muslim community
in Canada is a multi-tiered process consisting of the first necessary
stage of immigration, then moving on to education, economic stability, building places of worship, and then opening up to other communities, integrating into society, and defending economic, cultural,

and political achievements. But a major part of the Arab and Muslim diaspora in Canada has not gotten past the first stage (the Maghreb community, for instance, is still economically unstable and linkages with families in their countries of origin remain so strong that they still perceive their host country, Canada, as foreign). This lack of integration creates obvious impediments for the diaspora to enter Canadian policy circles and to constitute a meaningful political force.

Nevertheless, despite these difficulties and being conscious of their role, the elites of this community began, decades ago, to organize through Arab and Muslim associations and organizations (for example: the Canadian Arab Federation, Canadian Islamic Congress, Muslim Canadian Congress), inquiring into their rights as a community and integrating themselves into many fields: cultural, journalistic, and religious (to reconcile the precepts of Islam with Canadian liberal-democratic space, which is fundamentally secular). In recent years, these elites have understood the importance of better integration into Canadian society in the interests of their community and to ensure a decisive role in Canadian policymaking.

It is also important to point out the difficulties that diminish the role of the Arab and Muslim community in the Canadian foreign-policy decision-making process. As noted, some members of the community still cling to problems inherited from their countries of origin, such as the fear of the Other, the strong sense of belonging at the national or regional level to their countries of origin, and a strong reluctance to politically occupy public space. There are also problems caused by cultural differences within these communities and among its various constituents, which are a function of discord among states of origin. Obviously the Arab and Muslim community is not homogenous; it consists of Arabs, who represent a minority within it, and also Pakistanis, Indians, Africans, etc. The countries of origin are themselves often involved in regional conflict and through that absorb the diaspora as protagonists. Among many others, one can mention the rivalries between Iran and Turkey, Iran and Saudi Arabia, Syria and Lebanon, Morocco and Algeria. This complicates the elaboration of a single vision and the defense of specific interests with respect to Canadian foreign policy in order to influence it. Furthermore, the spread of the diaspora over the vast Canadian physical space and its distribution among the provinces make any emerging agendas more provincial than federal, thus thwarting coordination at the federal level.

Furthermore, 9/11 constituted a stumbling block for the Arab and Muslim community in Canada striving to progress culturally and economically and in particular trying to constitute a real lobby group defending its interests and the interests of its countries of origin. The average Canadian has become more reticent and more suspicious of things coming from the Arab and Muslim community. In fact, the community's reaction in opting for confinement and retreat from the public scene has made the problem worse.

While the situation has considerably improved in the last several years, and the scars of 9/11 have become smoother, 9/11 became for the community a shackle that it brandishes to justify its failures or its unease in the face of internal problems and its incapacity to formulate real recommendations for Canadian foreign-policy decision-makers.

That being said, in general, the Arab and Muslim community fears that Canadian foreign policy is becoming excessively influenced by the US, particularly the George W. Bush administration. To be sure, Canadian foreign policy strives to be consistent with international law, and active in the promotion of peace and security in the world, but it cannot be contrary to US policy. Nor can it entirely subside into, and be a replication of, White House foreign policy. This poses a dilemma for the Arab and Muslim community witnessing the US "battlefield" expand to encompass other choices and political agendas that affect them directly. Nevertheless, through various organizations and associations, the Arab and Muslim diaspora aims to be a bridge between Canada and the Muslim world in order to establish the ground for peaceful dialogue, respect for the Other, and tolerance of difference in the promotion and protection of its community interests.

Arab and Muslim elites in Canada face yet another dilemma. The community has a hard time defending the interests of an Arab-Muslim world ruled by despotic, non-democratic, corrupt, and politically disabled regimes, where any attempt at real change is severely repressed. In addition, these Arab and Muslim states ignore their diaspora communities abroad and do not help them become an active force in an open society such as Canada. In fact, the countries belonging to the Arab-Muslim diaspora do not provide any guidance for these communities and seem uninterested in the role that this diaspora could play in their favour with respect to Canadian foreign policy. In parallel, one may say that these states consider immigration to be a solution to their internal crises. For example, sums remitted every year from Canada to host countries represent a significant part of the countries of origin's foreign earnings. Furthermore, the richest of these states do not invest in the host countries of their diasporas whether in the social and cultural sphere or in the economic sphere (one notable exception is the role of Saudi Arabia or Iran in financing construction of Wahhabite or Shiite mosques, but such investments do not provide benefits to the majority of Canadian citizens).

The Arab and Muslim community in Canada finds itself trapped between the indifference of its countries of origin on the one hand and its internal disorganization on the other. Furthermore, it is far from constituting a lobby group – or it does not want to do so, even if it provides a way to influence Canadian foreign policy. To be sure, most people consider that lobbying is a primary role in foreign-policymaking, but it is important to point out that the strength of a lobby by itself is not what matters. What matters are the economic and strategic interests behind that lobby and as these are still weak in the Muslim world, for reasons already stated, the participation of Arab and Muslim communities will remain limited and of little if any influence.

All of these factors work together to bind Canada's Arab and Muslim diaspora leading them to pursue instead a simpler, less nuanced approach to international relations and, more importantly, to an inaccurate decoding of the foreign-policy decision-making process. The net result is the absence of a unified and coherent vision with respect to many foreign-policy issues.

THE PALESTINIAN CAUSE: AN EFFECTIVE RALLYING CALL

The Palestinian cause certainly remains a long-term unifying and rallying factor. But, since the 1990s and in particular after the intensification of the suicide attacks perpetrated by Palestinians, this cause has presented a dilemma to the Arab and Palestinian community in Canada. In fact, support for the Palestinian liberation movement has now become difficult. These movements, which are highly respected, utilize suicide attacks in their struggle for liberation, even against Israeli civilians. But since 2001 the Arab and Muslim community has continued their support for Palestinian disruption without decrypting the impact of 9/11 on North American sensitivities. This misunderstanding has prevented meaningful criticism of the movements and their methods.

Many conflicts have taken place under the umbrella of the Palestinian cause: the Israeli-Arab conflict, conflicts between the Palestinian Authority and some Arab regimes, or those between Palestinian groups and other Arab countries. This complexity makes objectivity within the Arab and Muslim community in Canada difficult. The resulting differences of opinion have prevented a unified pro-Palestinian position that would help further the Palestinian cause with respect to Canadian foreign policy.

THE WAR IN AFGHANISTAN, AFTER 9/11: CANADA GETS INVOLVED

In 1999, Arab and Muslim positions were favourable to military strikes in Kosovo by NATO, backed by the United States, against Yugoslavia even without the approval of the United Nations. However, in the case of the intervention in Afghanistan, Arab and Muslim communities in Canada generally expressed reservations, with the exception of the Afghani diaspora, which sought to liberate its country from the hold of the Taliban. Pride regarding the Canadian role in Afghanistan is also rarely expressed, except among Afghani immigrants.

In the beginning, Canada's role in the reconstruction of Afghanistan was disregarded by the Arab and Muslim communities because of the way the war was conducted by the United States. To be sure, Canada's participation has, until recently, been limited and its contribution to the war effort has not been as significant compared to US and British efforts, but, given the scale of collateral damage, the diaspora has remained reserved with respect to this war.

THE WAR IN IRAQ: CANADA ABSTAINS

The debate among the Arab and Muslim communities in Canada regarding the war against Saddam Hussein involves more or less the same parameters as those of the war against the Taliban. On the one hand, a mainly Shiite and Kurdish Iraqi community has approved of the action against oppression and, on the other hand, an Arab and Muslim community has criticized the intervention by US and allied forces. This situation is exacerbated when elites from the Arab and Muslim global diaspora have supported an armed resistance led by Iraqis against the occupation, despite the preference of a majority of the Shiites and Kurds for pacific resistance and a political presence. As a result, the elites of the diaspora in Canada have been unable to develop a coherent vision to enlighten Canadian decision-makers.

THE CANADIAN-IRANIAN DIPLOMATIC TENSION

The case of the Canadian-Iranian journalist and photographer Zahra Kazemi, who was allegedly raped and tortured to death in an Iranian prison in 2003, also reveals a priority deficit among Arab and Muslim diaspora communities. The Arab and Muslim community has been unable to articulate a clear position on Iran. Some members support the Iranian regime, and others have denounced it for human rights abuses.

This tension is exacerbated by the fact that Iran has mastered the art of pulling on the sensitive strings of Muslim causes. In fact, Iranian leaders (spiritual and political) have a populist discourse and one that is highly critical of the United States and Israel. This discourse remains attuned to the feelings of the greatest part of the Arab and Muslim community, which makes criticism of the Iranian regime more difficult.

SYRIA AND LEBANON: THE ENEMY BROTHERS

The deterioration of the security situation in Lebanon since the assassination of Rafiq Hariri on 14 February 2005 caused a further weakening in the relationships among different religious groups in Lebanon (Christians and Sunni, Druze and Shiite Muslims) and particularly between those Lebanese who were opposed to Syria's presence in Lebanon and those who were not. An accusatory dialogue between the two groups has prevented the elaboration of a clear position regarding the effects of ongoing political assassinations in that region on political stability and, at the same time, more involvement in the Canadian foreign-policy decision-making process for the region. The Lebanese community has ongoing difficulties in speaking with a single voice about many issues, including: Syria's presence in Lebanon, which has historically

divided the Lebanese diaspora; the question of Hezbollah, considered a terrorist movement by the Canadian Government but very
highly regarded and supported by the Lebanese and Arab community for its role in the Lebanese resistance; and the problem posed
by the presence of political refugees formerly belonging to the
South Lebanon Army, allied with Israel in Lebanon. On these and
other points, the Lebanese community remains divided, and this
division has translated into inertia with respect to involvement in
Canadian foreign policy.

THE SITUATION IN DARFUR: SUDAN'S MISFORTUNE

The Darfur crisis represents another confusing case for the Arab
and Muslim diaspora. The community has remained divided between the perspective of the Sudanese Government, accused by international organizations of having directly contributed to the
massacres perpetrated by the Janjaweed militias by facilitating their
raids through its aerial bombardments, and the perspective of the
Sudanese opposition, which has taken a strong position against the
government in this crisis. The hesitations of the Sudanese refugees
themselves are worth noting. These refugees did not send a clear
message to Canadian decision-makers; and Canada's decision to
get further involved in the resolution of the crisis in Darfur has
largely been result of its own initiative and not due to pressures by
the concerned diaspora groups.

IN CONCLUSION

What to do? Faced with a situation (as described here) that is both
critical and self-critical, Canadian decision-makers have no other alternative but to continue to expand consultations with the representatives and elites of the Arab and Muslim diaspora community
and to remain abreast of the different developments within this
community pertaining to crucial and thorny issues. They also have
to make sure, on the one hand, that an open and democratic debate takes place within these communities in order to avoid the en-
trenchment of any religious or secular fundamentalism and, on the
other hand, that these Arab and Muslim diaspora communities are
in touch with the important issues engulfing their countries of

origin. Canada's foreign-policymakers must also emphasize to this diaspora community that Canada's concepts of social contract and civil peace are the key democratic reference points that will help the diaspora become positive and assertive actors in Canadian foreign-policy decision-making.

To this end, the Arab and Muslim community needs to evolve toward critical thought, free of polemics and debates and of emotion. Furthermore, it is important to mention that this community needs to further express its opinions and ideas regarding the democratization and reform of its countries of origin, free itself from any misleading nostalgia, and formulate clear ideas, exempt of any anxiety and concerns regarding questions about the future of their countries of origin, to better enlighten Canadian foreign-policy decision-makers and to influence their decisions. For these reasons, a better Arab and Muslim representation in Canadian forums would be desirable. An internalization of democratic Canadian values would be a necessary step to transcend any cultural cleavages and overcome contradictions between the original values of these diaspora and their newly acquired Canadian values.

NOTES

The author would like to thank Souleima El Achkar and the editors for assistance in translating this chapter and Mohamed Ourya for his substantial contribution to this article.

1 For instance many authors argue that Muslims in the West constitute a fifth column. Daniel Pipes, among others, considers that Muslims in the United States are a fifth column representing the interests of the enemy.
2 It should be noted that it is not our objective to discuss the role of the multicultural communities in Canadian foreign policy, but only that of the Arab-Muslim Diaspora.
3 This statistic is generally estimated at approximately one million Muslims living in Canada, see:www.islammemo.cc/west/one_news.asp?IDnews=20.
4 For more information about the Canadian policy on the integration of ethnic communities, see chapter 5 of this book: David G. Haglund, "The Parizeau-Chrétien Version: Ethnicity and Canadian Grand Strategy."
5 The aid given to Afghanistan by the Canadian International Development Agency (CIDA) was primarily humanitarian assistance: usually 10 million dollars a year to satisfy basic human needs. See the Canadian Government's

official site on Canada-Afghanistan relations: www.canada-afghanistan.gc.ca/
background-en.asp.

6 Aid to Iraq includes partial debt-forgiveness.

7 About this point, see Marc J. O'Reilly, "Canadian Foreign Policy in the
Middle East: Reflexive Multilateralism in an Evolving World," in Patrick
James, Nelson Michaud, and Marc O'Reilly, eds, *Handbook of Canadian
Foreign Policy*, Lanham: Lexington Books, 2006.

8 For example the G8 Member States' 22–23 January 2002 meeting in
Ottawa for the elaboration of legal measures to combat the financing
of terrorism.

9 For further analysis, see Bethany Barratt, "Canadian Foreign Policy and
International Human Rights," in Patrick James, Nelson Michaud,
and Marc O'Reilly, eds, *Handbook of Canadian Foreign Policy*, Lanham:
Lexington Books, 2006.

10 For a presentation on these relations, see www.dfait-maeci.gc.ca/
middle_east/menu-fr.asp.

11 The first Intifada began in 1987.

Just How Liberal and Democratic Is Canadian Foreign Policy?

CHRISTIAN LEUPRECHT AND TODD HATALEY

INTRODUCTION

We wondered why Canadian foreign and defense priorities (outputs) appear to diverge markedly from Canadian public opinion (inputs) on foreign and defense policy. In this chapter we seek to postulate a plausible explanation for this puzzle – the institutional constraints imposed by Canada's relationship with the United States complemented by growing structural constraints due to greater ethnocultural heterogeneity – and work out the broader implications for Canadian democracy. Rather than being aligned with the will of "the Canadian people," this chapter hypothesizes that Canadian foreign policy is actually structurally contingent upon the Canada-US relationship as well as institutionally contingent upon a ruling political party and its elite whose horizon is the next federal election. With the Statute of Westminster of 1931, Canada as a country may have become sovereign in the area of foreign policy, but sovereignty for the Canadian "people" in the area of foreign policy, by contrast, remains a work in progress – one that, due to exogenous and endogenous constraints, may be unattainable. If this chapter's argument turns out to be tenable, it follows with a high degree of probability that the misalignment between Canadian foreign policy and the will of the Canadian people is a permanent phenomenon of democracy in Canada.

Although it is now little more than a historical relic, the Paul Martin Liberal Government's (2004–06) International Policy Statement can

still serve as a benchmark. It encapsulated an attempt – however er-
ratic, chaotic, and rushed – at crafting a cohesive mission statement
on the one hand and at formulating Canadian foreign policy re-
sponsively and democratically on the other. The first section of this
study uses a systems-analytic approach to provide a cursory overview of the IPS, which we then contrast with (1) the process of public consultation that was involved in crafting the document and (2)
public opinion on the subject matter. The second section subjects
to empirical scrutiny two hypotheses – one exogenous, the other
endogenous in explanatory character – that purportedly explain
this divergence. The first proposition is premised on an institution-
alist approach that seeks to develop "more explicit theorizing on
the reciprocal influence of institutional constraints and political
strategies and, more broadly, on the interaction of ideas, interests,
and institutions" (Thelen and Steinmo, 14). This first proposition
postulates that, insofar as foreign and defense policy is concerned,
the Canadian capacity to act in a sovereign manner – and thus its
capacity to govern democratically – is contingent upon Canada-US
relations. As Charles Doran observes: "If the United States tends to
look outward toward the world system, Canada, because of its size
and priorities, tends to look towards the United States" (38).[1]

The second proposition has a statist rational-choice premise. Inherent to party politics in a democracy is the governing political
party's goal to get re-elected. In the Westminster parliamentary system, this constraint is especially pronounced when the party in
power has to govern as a minority. Since few studies have dealt with
political parties as a domestic source of foreign policy (Haas;
Holsti, 192–3; Risse-Kappen; Simmons, 281) and taken into account domestic institutions and collective political actors as foun-
dations of foreign policy (Hudson and Vore, 219; Risse-Kappen,
484–5; Hagan 1993, 26–31; Hagan 1995, 137), this study's contribution to the political circumstances that exacerbate the magnitude and nature of the influence of partisan politics on foreign
policy has ramifications beyond this chapter. The chapter draws on
two case studies to test this point. First, it contrasts the economic-
policy priorities of Canadians with those of business interests and
then looks at how these interests might – or might not – be reflected in voting patterns. Second, it contrasts spending on overseas development assistance (ODA) and recent deployments of the

Canadian Forces' Disaster Assistance Team (DART) with voter concentration and support in some key urban areas across Canada.

The broader implications of this analysis for pluralist democracy in Canada are discussed in the conclusion. Pluralism presumes that all members of society share interests with some other members. Pluralism, as a theory of politics, has as its premise that society as a collection of groups's defined by differing interests (Dahl 1956). Pluralist theory, therefore, holds a healthy liberal-democracy to be one where (1) there is widespread citizen participation in group life, (2) groups can freely form and compete for political influence, (3) there is fair and equal competition among groups in the political arena, (4) no one group possesses a disproportionately large share of resources to influence government decision-making, and (5) public policies accurately reflect the balance of power among groups (Connolly, 3–4). How does the IPS measure up against these criteria? The chapter's analysis confirms the neopluralist caveat that money, organization, and leadership seem to work in favour of business interests and that, as a result, one would expect their interests to be reflected disproportionately in the policymaking process and outcomes (Dahl 1985). Yet, two other constraints emerge that moderate this finding. One is the growing importance of demographic change, its impact on political behaviour, and its consequences. The other is the continentalist constraint imposed by Canada's geostrategic location. The analysis in this chapter suggests that these contingencies present a formidable challenge for pluralist democracy in Canada. Pluralist democracy presumes that individual interests are represented and aggregated by interest groups and, subsequently, by political parties. Such is the constructivist take on foreign policy: international relations theory in general and foreign policy in particular cannot be understood in isolation from domestic politics (Waltz; London; Rosenau 1967, 1997; Hughes; Piper and Terchek; Smith; Keohane and Nye, 267; Milner, 492; Maoz; Delvoie; Ignatieff). The most fundamental transformations of our time cannot be explained by international factors alone (Kratochwil, 63).

However, the analysis in this chapter suggests that the converse may obtain as well: with respect to foreign policy, political parties and elites are subservient not to the way in which values and principles are institutionalized at the domestic level in general (Thérien and Noël 1994, 2000) but to particular domestic interests. Jean-Jacques Rousseau famously distinguished between the "general will" and the "will of all" (book II). The former is a sort of common interest that transcends and stands above the particular interests aggregated in the form of the latter. The IPS may represent a moment in Canadian foreign policy when the ruling political party endeavoured to align the "general will" more closely with the "will of all." If that was indeed one of its purposes though, this chapter posits that momentary realignment to have been thwarted by institutional and structural constraints. Depending on whether those constraints converge or diverge, however, the trajectory of these two constraints is bound to have interesting implications for Canadian foreign policy and the way it balances its relations with the United States relative to those with the rest of the world.

CANADA'S INTERNATIONAL POLICY STATEMENT

In 1993, the Liberal Caucus Committee on External Affairs and National Defence, chaired by future Minister of Foreign Affairs Lloyd Axworthy, committed the Liberal Party of Canada to the "democratization of foreign policy" in its *Liberal Foreign Policy Handbook* and subsequently to a more "open process for foreign policy making" in the so-called Red Book election platform. To expand the ideas, options, and advice available to the minister, policymaking was to become more responsive (Lee, 64). The results, however, were mixed (Ayres, 498–504).

In the run up to the IPS, the then Department of Foreign Affairs and International Trade (DFAIT) started an online dialogue website with weekly updates that attracted sixty thousand hits in the first six months of 2003 (Canada 2003). In addition, representatives of the Department of Foreign Affairs held fifteen town-hall meetings across the country with the minister, a session with the National Forum of Youth, and nineteen expert roundtables and meetings with provincial and territorial governments.[2] Purportedly, Canadian foreign policy as set out subsequently in the IPS thus "reflects the views expressed by Canadians during the 2003 Dialogue on Foreign Policy, the 2002–2003 Defence Update and consultations on aid effectiveness" (Government of Canada).

After reviewing the process Jeffrey Ayres concluded: "It is doubtful that much more consensus exists today between government officials and civil society groups than existed ten years earlier in terms of determining what is meant by the democratization of foreign policy" (506). One might infer, as Kim Nossal cautioned early on, that efforts to democratize foreign policy are simply an "elusive ideal" (1995). The more interesting question, however, is why Foreign Affairs consults in the first place. Is it to clarify to the government what Canadians want? Or does it consult to put it in the clear when asked if Canadians have had any input into the making of foreign policy?

The purpose of this section is to provide – as objectively as possible – a cursory overview of Canadian foreign policy as it is set out in the IPS. In keeping with the structure of the IPS, we shall differentiate between two areas of foreign policy: the Canadian role in the North American community and the Canadian role in the global community. The most recent overhaul of Canadian foreign policy, tabled in Parliament on 19 April 2005 is the latest instalment in an "integrated" Canadian approach to foreign policy. According to former Liberal Prime Minister Martin, rapid and radical global change necessitated the need to recast Canadian foreign policy. The proliferation of new, failed, and failing states, global terrorism, disease, climate change, and non-state actors threatens to diminish the international clout of smaller countries, such as Canada, turning it from a middle power to a little power (Welsh). Martin figured that Canadian interests would be served best by a stable and prosperous global environment. That line of thinking, of course, is nothing new. It actually reflects the traditional "closet" realism that marks Canadian foreign policy. Martin wanted to adjust Canadian foreign policy to this end. That meant actively promoting Canadian interests and values abroad for the purpose of maintaining a position of influence in the global community, while at the same time ensuring the prosperity and security of Canadians.

The fundamentals of Canadian foreign policy thus remain unchanged since Canadian foreign policy's last review in 1995 (Canada 1995). Canadian foreign policy is guided by three basic principles. First, foreign policy shall be premised on the "joint pursuit of democracy, human rights and the rule of law." Second, Canadian foreign policy shall maintain a commitment to free-market principles and a commitment to shared risk and the equality of opportunity. Third, Canada remains committed to the development of multilateral institutions and multilateral governance.

The IPS differentiates the goals that flow from these principles by two geographic areas: goals that apply to Canada and the North American community, and goals that apply to Canada's position in the international community. The continentalist priorities are:

1 collaborate with the United States and Mexico to protect North American territory and citizens from twenty-first-century threats;
2 protect Canada and Canadians by implementing the National Security Policy, and updating the approach that the Canadian Forces take to domestic operations;
3 establish Canada as an attractive business gateway for those establishing a foothold in North America;
4 develop deeper knowledge of, and new channels of influence with, the United States and Mexico;
5 collaborate with our regional partners to build a competitive economic space that facilitates the free movement of goods, services, capital, and people and enhances the quality of life of all North Americans.

The internationalist priorities are:

1 contribute to UN, NATO, and G8 efforts to counteract terrorist organizations and cut off their support networks;
2 establish a Stabilization and Reconstruction Task Force (START) to plan and coordinate rapid and integrated civilian responses to international crises;
3 maintain combat-capable Canadian Forces, focused on the challenge of restoring peace and stability to failed and fragile states;
4 prevent the spread and reduce the existing stocks of WMDs;
5 strengthen international export control regimes on proliferation-sensitive technologies and build the capacity of countries to enforce them;
6 optimize Canada's economic framework;
7 develop new frameworks to promote trade and investments with our mature markets, while reaching out to take advantage of emerging economic giants;
8 create a level playing field in international trade and investment through active participation in the WTO;
9 pursue sustainable development through both domestic and international strategies;

10 refocus Canadian development assistance to target states with the greatest need and greatest potential for successful intervention;

11 focus our contribution to the Millennium Development goals on governance, private sector development, health, basic education, and environmental sustainability;

12 establish Canada Corps as a key mechanism for providing governance assistance to developing countries;

13 contribute ideas, expertise, and resources to reform efforts aimed at improving the effectiveness and legitimacy of existing international institutions;

14 revitalize Canada's core international relationships, while strengthening our ties with key "pathfinder" states and organizations;

15 strengthen Canada's influence in the Western hemisphere;

16 create a new framework for international policymaking that engages multiple departments and levels of government;

17 support the good international work of existing networks of Canadians.[3]

Central to the integrated approach to foreign policy is the Canada-US relationship. At a macro level, economic and security ties to the United States have enabled Canada to advance domestic and international issues. The predicament thus precipitated recognizes, on the one hand, the need for an institutionalized relationship with the United States and, on the other, the potential consequences for Canadian sovereignty. In other words, an internal contradiction marks Canada-US relations in general and the IPS specifically: the Canada-US relationship is key to enhancing Canadian sovereignty – but it has the potential to reduce it as well.

Canada's perilous walk along this tightrope has been highlighted further in the post-9/11 period as Canada has been forced to deal more directly with US security concerns inherent in the shared space of the Canada-US relationship. As a result, the Canadian Government has made it a priority to "engage cooperatively with the US on measures that directly affect Canadian territory and citizens, and to maintain our ability to influence how the North American continent is defended" (FAC 2005). Pursuant to the logic of the IPS, the Advanced Passenger Information/Passenger Name Record (API/PRN), the Container Security Initiative (CSI), the Customs

Trade Partnership Against Terrorism (C-TPAT), the Safe Third Country Agreement, and the Smart Border Declaration all manifest Canada's national interests.

The government acknowledges that it is in the best interests of Canada to strengthen relations with the United States, particularly where trade and economic links are concerned. How then is it that the "national interest" – as concretized by a democratically elected government – does not neatly map on to the desires of the Canadian population?

PEOPLE VERSUS INSTITUTIONS

In a series of four recent polls[4] – taken between April 2004 and October 2005 for the express purpose of gauging Canadian attitudes toward foreign policy – a distinct pattern emerges: although Canadians and Americans always put the opposite country near or at the top of the countries with which they identify most closely (O'Reilly), those surveyed repeatedly expressed their desire to search for alternatives to the dependence Canada now has on its US neighbours. As visualized in figure 1, Pollara's poll from April 2004 found that 48 percent of Canadians felt that Canada should focus more on its relations with other countries of the world, as opposed to 35 percent who believed in its foreign relations Canada should focus primarily on the United States. However, Canada's demographic concentration somewhat falsifies the aggregate results. Whereas Quebecers, Ontarians, and British Columbians tend to have internationalist leanings, the Prairies and Atlantic Canada tend to be more continentalist. Even there, though, continentalist feelings are moderate compared to the fairly strong internationalism elsewhere in the country.

The Innovative Research Group's poll taken in November 2004 posed the question of Canada-US relations slightly differently, asking whether or not Canada should pursue a foreign policy that focuses on Canada's ability to influence the United States. In this instance, 52 percent of respondents opposed the US-centric approach of Canada's foreign policy. Ipsos-Reid's poll, released on 11 October 2005, asked if Canadians favoured an independent foreign policy even at the expense of causing a rift in Canada-US relations; 83 percent of respondents agreed that an independent foreign policy should trump the Canada-US relationship. Finally,

Canada's International Focus by Region, 2004

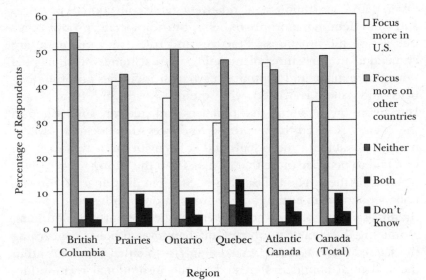

Figure 1: Canada's international focus by region
Source: Pollara, 2004 (see endnote 4).

Innovative Research Group's poll released on 31 October 2005, found that a majority of Canadians questioned the reliability of the United States within the Canada-US relationship. Fully 72 percent of respondents agreed that Canada would be better off deepening relations with other countries. A trend emerges of a discrepancy between the goals of the government vis-à-vis Canada's relationship with the United States and the desires of Canadians in general.

It could be argued that a US-centric foreign policy is simply the logical outcome of Canada's physical, economic, and political location in the world. A model of institutional constraint, however, posits a more parsimonious explanation. Institutional approaches to understanding policy choices are concerned with analyzing the effects of rules and procedures on the preferences expressed by human actors (Immergut). Institutions have two roles: they constrain some behaviours while inducing others. Institutions are mediators that privilege some interpretations (over others), either in the goals that political actors seek to achieve or in the means they use to achieve these goals. Institutions do not determine behaviour. However, they "provide a context for actions that helps us to understand why actors make the choices they do" (Immergut). March and Olsen define institutions as a "relatively stable collection of practices and rules defining appropriate behaviour for specific groups of actors in specific situations." Practices and rules, they maintain, are embedded in "structures of meanings and schemes of interpretations that explain and legitimize particular identities and the practices and rules associated with them." Borrowing from Émile Durkheim, they contend that practices and rules are embedded in the resources – and the way those resources are allocated – which make it possible for individuals and collectivities to act in a certain way, and to penalize those that deviate from the "norm."

Assessing the position of the United States in the Canadian foreign-policy equation, an institutional approach would posit structural constraints as playing perhaps not a deterministic role but, at a minimum, as framing the climate in which Canadian foreign policy concerning the United States is forged. Accordingly, actors that function within the structural boundaries created by the institutional relationship, and who have the resources to influence policy development within the given constraints, hold a hegemonic position.

From the IPS one might deduce a Canadian preoccupation with economic security: "establishing Canada as an attractive gateway for those establishing a foothold in North America" and to "collaborate with our regional partners to build a competitive economic space." The same preoccupation spans Canada's *National Security Policy – Securing a Free and Open Society*: it is in Canada's economic interests to ensure that Canada is neither a base of operations nor a gateway to the United States for terror groups (Canada 2004). Ergo, stronger cross-border law enforcement, counterterrorism programs, and infrastructure development and improvement all serve to secure Canada's economic ties to the United States. In this light, the economic elite should be the best positioned to influence the development of Canada's foreign policy vis-à-vis the United States. The role played by elite economic actors in the development of Canadian policy toward the United States should come as no surprise given the dependence of the Canadian economy on the US market.

The role of economic elites in the process of setting the foreign-policy agenda is further evidenced by the degree to which the section of the IPS dealing with the Canada-US relationship concurs with and supports the US homeland security agenda. Birkland's

study on policymaking and agenda-setting after disasters and catastrophic events maintains that policy changes after "focusing
events"5 will reflect the preference of certain segments of society.
Advocates of policy change reap substantial benefits from focusing
on events because they shore up the perception that previous policies were a failure. The status quo (ante) becomes unacceptable. As
a focusing event of unparalleled magnitude, 9/11 was an opportunity to promote the development of mechanisms that would ensure
the viability of Canada's economic linkages to the United States.
The centrepiece of this agenda, the *Smart Border Declaration*, was
heavily endorsed by the Coalition for Secure and Trade-Efficient
Borders. The Coalition is part of the Canadian Manufacturers and
Exporters Association, one of the largest business coalitions ever
formed in Canadian history. Perrin Beatty, former Conservative
Cabinet minister in the Mulroney administration and now President and CEO of the Canadian Manufacturers and Exporters Association spearheaded the development and lobby efforts of the
Coalition for Secure and Trade-Efficient Borders. He told *Canadian
Ports Magazine* that the *Smart Border Declaration* signalled a recognition on the part of the Canadian Government to accept recommendations made by the coalition. Applying Birkland's thesis to this
outcome suggests that the Canadian Manufacturers and Exporters
Association was well-placed to use its resources effectively to influence the development of Canadian policy toward the United States,
specifically the economic agenda.

If Canadian policy toward the United States is a matter of elite ac-
commodation, then the process is captured by the neopluralist
model of policymaking. In this paradigm, economic actors, by virtue of their financial, organizational, leadership, and networking
resources, figure prominently. The case study thus supports the
neopluralist assertion that economic elites have disproportionate
clout over the policymaking process. For neopluralists, that is old
news. What is news, however, is the apparent clout of non-
economic, ethnocultural groups as it emerges below.

CANADIAN FOREIGN POLICY AND OFFICIAL DEVELOPMENT ASSISTANCE

By its own admission, the strategy taken by the Canadian Government in the distribution of official development assistance (ODA) is

intended to advance Canadian interests in the global community. As
stated in the IPS: "Canada will strive to make a greater difference in
fewer places. In so doing, we will further the interests of our development partners, the international community at large and Canada itself" (Canada 2005). This strategy of tying aid to national interest is
part of a growing trend in Canada that regards aid with increasingly
commercial motives (Macdonald and Hoddinott). That approach de-
viates ever so slightly from the more altruistic approach to ODA,
which Cooper has called a pillar of Pearsonian internationalism that
shaped Canadian foreign policy for so many years.

The trend of using ODA to further Canada's interests is incontro-
vertible. But who decides and what constitutes "Canadian interests"? Can "national interests" be homogeneous in a pluralist
society such as Canada? Noël et al. observe differential attitudes toward ODA between two groups they distinguish as liberal and conservative internationalists. This distinction, they argue, is a function of
domestic and partisan differences. Insofar, then, as foreign policy
in general and ODA policy specifically are contingent, one might
posit domestic and partisan politics as a point of departure.

Polling evidence indicates that a majority of Canadians endorse
development spending as a form of financial aid (Noël et al.).
Ipsos-Reid (2005) found that 54 percent of Canadians made "helping reduce hunger and poverty around the world" a top priority for
Canadian foreign policy. A poll by Pollara (2004) eighteen months
earlier, by contrast, found that only 24 percent of Canadians
deemed spending more on foreign aid to be in the interests of Canadians. These results highlight a contrast identified by Noël et al.
in the domestic attitude toward spending on development assistance: whereas most Canadians agreed that foreign aid matters,
that is not necessarily reflected in the government's program. A reduction in spending as a percentage of GDP during the 1980s and
1990s notwithstanding (Smillie), when public satisfaction with
spending on foreign aid is tracked over the long term, Canadians
generally feel the government is spending enough on development
assistance. From these findings one may infer that although Canadians stress spending on aid and development, the issue does not
garner much attention and Canadians are generally satisfied with
the performance of the government in this area. This begs a question: insofar as it is not really a highly politically charged issue, if

the Canadian public is inattentive to spending on foreign aid, what motivates the government's formulation of ODA policy?

It is a truism in Canadian foreign policy to observe that as a trading nation it is in Canada's best interests to work toward maintaining a stable global order that allows for the maintenance and development of external markets for Canadian products. The IPS does not depart from this goal with regards to ODA: "The establishment of good governance in other societies around the globe will make Canadians safer and more prosperous. In a globalized world, where threats are transnational and greater wealth depends upon deeper forms of exchange, the creation of stable and capable states will form a major part of Canada's global agenda" (Canada 2005). The inference that ODA is somehow tied to the development and maintenance of global markets to advance Canada's economic interests gives some indication as to the catalysts that drive ODA spending. Ergo, one would expect ODA distribution to reflect Canadian trade patterns. From this public-choice perspective, one would expect ODA to be concentrated in geographic areas with the greatest potential for increased returns from trade. However, according to the *Statistical Report on Official Development Assistance* for the 2003–04 fiscal year prepared by the Canadian International Development Agency (CIDA), the top three recipients of Canadian development aid in 2003–2004 were: Iraq, Afghanistan and Ethiopia (Canada 2003–04).

These countries are hardly significant trading partners for Canada. To illustrate the point, tables 1, 2, and 3 evidence just how relatively insignificant Canada's trading relationship with Afghanistan used to be. Compare the steep rise in exports to Afghanistan since 2001 with the moderate growth of exports to Iraq and Canada's flatlining trade relationship with Ethiopia.

By 2005 Canada exported about 120 times the amount to Afghanistan it did only four years earlier. Most of this growth is a function of ODA. Contrasting exports with imports for Afghanistan thus belies the claim that the primary purpose of ODA for Canada is to promote economic prosperity.

Figure 2 shows that, a decade ago, neither Afghanistan nor Iraq were a foreign-aid priority for the United States. A decade later, both countries find themselves among the top recipients of USAID development aid. This development is significant in that the figures show that a handful of countries tend to receive the bulk of USAID

Table 1
Afghanistan, Trade Balances

		Canadian Trade Balances, Total for all industries, Latest 5 years, Value in thousands of Canadian dollars.				
		2001	2002	2003	2004	2005
Afghanistan	Total Exports	167,371	1,884,503	9,022,516	9,673,121	19,069,588
	Total Imports	415,608	364,440	618,889	374,099	457,703
	Trade Balance	-248,237	1,520,063	8,403,627	9,299,022	18,611,885
Others	Total Exports	404,084,905,976	396,376,122,913	380,856,973,072	411,792,178,783	435,622,306,884
	Total Imports	343,110,092,319	348,848,818,990	335,961,864,210	355,710,302,137	379,576,151,570
	Trade Balance	60,974,813,657	47,527,303,923	44,895,108,862	56,081,876,646	56,046,155,314
Total (all countries)	Total Exports	404,085,073,347	396,378,007,416	380,865,995,588	411,801,851,904	435,641,376,472
	Total Imports	343,110,507,927	348,849,183,430	335,962,483,099	355,710,676,236	379,576,609,273
	Trade Balance	60,974,565,420	47,528,823,986	44,903,512,489	56,091,175,668	56,064,767,199

Source of data: Statistics Canada

Table 2
Iraq, Trade Balances

		2001	2002	2003	2004	2005
		Canadian Trade Balances, Total for all industries, Latest 5 years, Value in thousands of Canadian dollars				
Iraq	Total Exports	6,669	13,667	5,425	31,620	75,873
	Total Imports	874,059	1,089,670	1,126,295	1,101,571	1,206,427
	Trade Balance	-867,389	-1,076,004	-1,120,870	-1,069,951	-1,130,555
Other countries	Total Exports	404,078,404	396,364,341	380,860,571	411,770,232	435,565,504
	Total Imports	342,236,449	347,759,513	334,836,188	354,609,105	378,370,182
	Trade Balance	61,841,955	48,604,828	46,024,383	57,161,126	57,195,322
Total (all countries)	Total Exports	404,085,073	396,378,007	380,865,996	411,801,852	435,641,376
	Total Imports	343,110,508	348,849,183	335,962,483	355,710,676	379,576,609
	Trade Balance	60,974,565	47,528,824	44,903,512	56,091,176	56,064,767

Source of data: Statistics Canada

Table 3
Ethiopia, Trade Balances

Canadian Trade Balances, Total for all industries, Latest 5 years, Value in thousands of Canadian dollars

		2001	2002	2003	2004	2005
Ethiopia	Total Exports	7,075	6,034	23,873	15,140	26,936
	Total Imports	6,072	6,111	6,060	6,421	8,633
	Trade Balance	1,003	-77	17,812	8,719	18,303
Others	Total Exports	404,077,998	396,371,973	380,842,123	411,786,712	435,614,440
	Total Imports	343,104,436	348,843,073	335,956,423	355,704,255	379,567,976
	Trade Balance	60,973,563	47,528,901	44,885,700	56,082,457	56,046,464
Total (all countries)	Total Exports	404,085,073	396,378,007	380,865,996	411,801,852	435,641,376
	Total Imports	343,110,508	348,849,183	335,962,483	355,710,676	379,576,609
	Trade Balance	60,974,565	47,528,824	44,903,512	56,091,176	56,064,767

Source: Statistics Canada

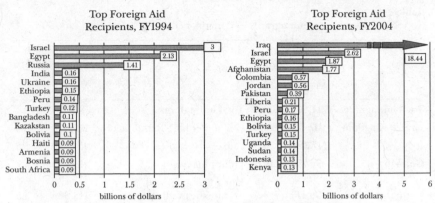

Figure 2: Top foreign countries receiving USAID funds, 1994 and 2004
Source: Tarnoff and Nowels, 2004, based on USAID and the Department of State.

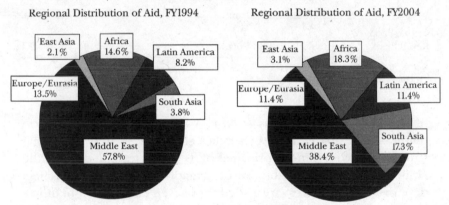

Figure 3: Regional distribution of USAID funds, 1994 and 2004
Source: Cited in Tarnoff and Nowels, 2004, based on USAID and the Department of State.

spoils. And it is all the more remarkable in light of figure 3, which shows a precipitous decline in the proportion of USAID spending devoted to the Middle East over the same period (with much of the balance being diverted to South Asia).

Insofar as the pattern of the distribution of aid is concerned, then, Canadian and US interests appear to overlap. One may speculate that this overlap is explicable in terms of shared geostrategic interests. However, in view of the divergent approaches to foreign policy illustrated by the Martin and Bush administrations, this line

Table 4
Top source countries of immigrants to Canada, before 1961 and 1991–2001[1]

	Immigrated before 1961			Immigrated 1991–2001	
	Number	%		Number	%
Total immigrants	894,465	100.0	Total immigrants	1,830,68	100.0
United Kingdom	217,175	24.3	China, People's Republic of	197,360	10.8
Italy	147,320	16.5	India	156,120	8.5
Germany	96,770	10.8	Philippines	122,010	6.7
Netherlands	79,170	8.9	Hong Kong, Special Administrative Region	118,385	6.5
Poland	44,340	5.0	Sri Lanka	62,590	3.4
United States	34,810	3.9	Pakistan	57,990	3.2
Hungary	27,425	3.1	Taiwan	53,755	2.9
Ukraine	21,240	2.4	United States	51,440	2.8
Greece	20,755	2.3	Iran	47,080	2.6
China, People's Republic of	15,850	1.8	Poland	43,370	2.4

Source: Statistics Canada.
[1] Includes data up to 15 May 2001.

of reasoning seems tenuous at best. A more plausible explanation might be that ODA enhances Canada's economic security by playing strongly to the foreign-aid priorities of its largest trading partner, the United States. The distribution of Canadian ODA does not reflect democratic preferences – provided those even exist. As a tool of foreign policy, however, ODA is used to further the goals of the Canadian economic elite as part of the larger strategy of maintaining strong economic ties with the United States. Realism, in other words, does not trump economics. Instead, the evidence confirms Joel Sokolsky's assertion that the two are linked: economics is impossible without security, and security is impossible without economics.

The case of Canadian bilateral ODA is also telling. Although in the overall scheme of things Haiti ranked twelfth in terms of total bilateral assistance dispersed by Canada in 2004, Haiti and Nigeria are the two countries in the world where Canada ranks among the top three donor countries (Canada 2003–04, table T). Mali and Pakistan are the only countries where Canada ranks in the top four. In many cases, Canada averages sixth. In other words, for Canada to rank among the top three or four donors to a particular country is

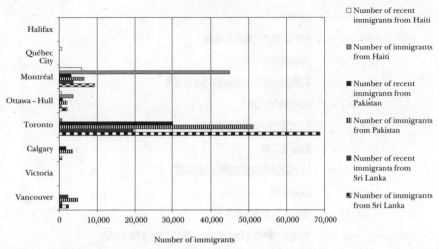

Figure 4: Immigration from Haiti, Pakistan, and Sri Lanka to major Canadian urban centres
Source: Statistics Canada. 2001 Census of Population (46 Large Urban Centres, Census Tracts (Neighbourhoods). E-Stat. Online

unusual. Clearly, a decision was made to single out certain countries. Like Canada, Haiti and Mali belong to La Francophonie.[6] As table 4 shows, Pakistan ranks among the top source countries for immigration to Canada.

Ahead of Pakistan in terms of immigrants to Canada ranks Sri Lanka. As may reasonably be inferred from figure 4, a relationship is plausible between where in Canada these immigrants settle and that – after many years of sitting mostly idle – in rapid succession these two countries also happened to be the sites of two recent deployments of the CF's DART.

Figure 4 shows that immigrants from Haiti, Pakistan, and Sri Lanka settle in specific metropolitan clusters: Haitians overwhelmingly tend to settle in Montreal, Pakistanis and Sri Lankans tend to settle predominantly in Toronto. If the network theory of migration holds, we would expect each community to concentrate in specific parts of the city. Indeed, figures 5, 6, and 7, in turn, confirm a disproportionate concentration in a small number of key ridings.

Under the Paul Martin Liberal Government (2004–06) all the ridings with strong Pakistani and Sri Lankan representation in Toronto and strong Haitian representation in Montreal were held by members of Parliament running for the Liberal Party of Canada. In

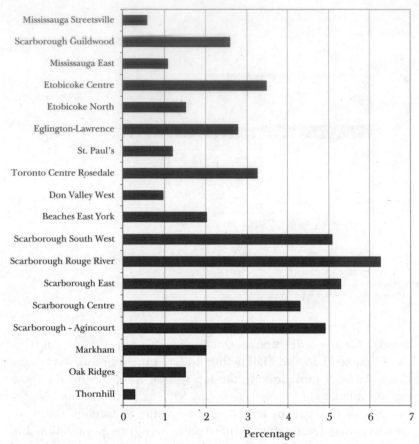

Figure 5: Immigrants from Sri Lanka in Toronto ridings as a percentage of select federal riding populations in Toronto, 2001
Source: Statistics Canada.

Toronto, the Liberals were able to hang on to almost all those ridings in the January 2006 election. While they did not generally fare as well in Montreal in ridings with strong Haitian representation, they were able to retain the Montreal riding with the greatest Haitian population.

Based on these observations one may postulate that there appears to exist a relationship between the way ODA is dispersed, the way the DART is deployed, and the way ethnic-minority disporas congregate in Canada's electoral ridings. No causal relationship per se follows necessarily from these findings. However, there appears to be a pattern. The pattern is further reinforced that Liberals show considerable resilience in those ridings.

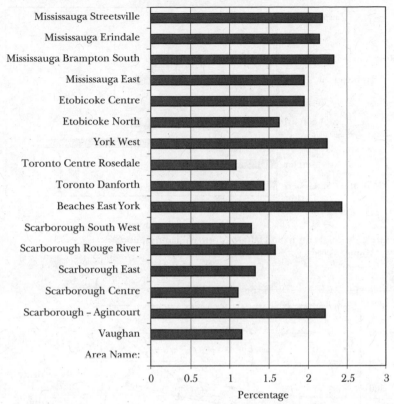

Figure 6: Immigrants from Pakistan to Toronto ridings as a percentage of select federal riding populations in Toronto, 2001
Source: Statistics Canada.

The observation that members of recent ethnic immigrant communities exhibit a propensity for voting Liberal is not new. What is novel in this analysis, however, is the link between ethnic minority diaspora communities, electoral behaviour, and foreign policy. It is difficult to speculate about the direction of causality at work here. Do ethnic minority diasporas vote Liberal because they feel they have more clout over the Liberals' foreign-policy agenda (as opposed to another party's foreign-policy program)? Did the Liberals orchestrate foreign policy to shore up their vote among specific ethnic minority communities? Whatever the case may be, there seems to be a trend.

The trend is not as strong in the larger scheme of things. Figure 8 depicts the way the regional distribution of ODA has evolved in recent years.

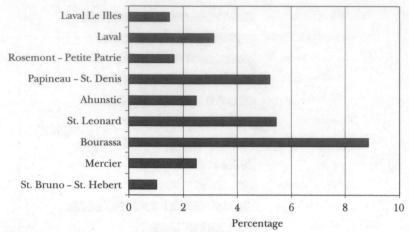

Figure 7: Immigrants from Haiti to Montreal ridings, 2001
Source: Statistics Canada.

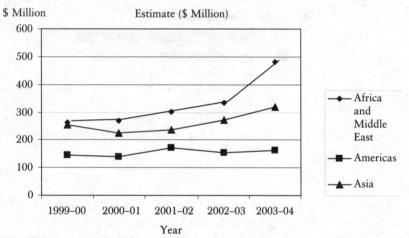

Figure 8: Overseas Development Assistance by Region
Source: Canadian International Development Agency, 2003, 2004, 2005.

While Canada's commitment to the Americas has remained constant and its pledge to Asia has grown moderately, the amount of aid to Africa and the Middle East almost doubled between fiscal years 1999–2000 and 2003–04. Contrast that with immigration trends in figure 9. At first glance, there is no obvious relationship.

On closer examination, however, as immigration from Asia has increased, so has the Canadian Government's ODA commitment in that region. Similarly, while ODA spending on Africa seems to have

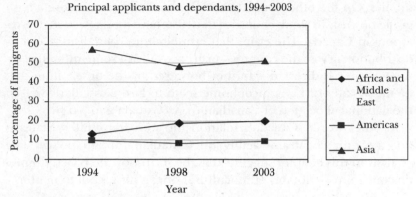

Figure 9: Immigration to Canada from different regions of the world
Source: Statistics Canada, 2001; Citizenship and Immigration Canada, 2005.

Table 5
Selected ethnic origins, for canada, 20% sample data, 2001 census

Ethnic origins	Total responses	Total population (%)
Total population	29,639,035	100
Afghan	25,230	0.085
Iraqi	19,245	0.065
Ethiopian	15,725	0.053
Haitian	82,405	0.278
Pakistani	74,015	0.250

Source: Statistics Canada.

increased markedly, as immigration from the Americas has held fairly constant, so has ODA spending in that region.

For neopluralists, this observation is interesting because it suggests that socioeconomic factors are not the only ones skewing policy. Ethnocultural demographic factors among diaspora communities in Canada also seem to impose a policy constraint. Table 5 shows that the same contention does not hold for Canada's aforementioned ODA investment in Afghanistan, Iraq, and Ethiopia, for their diasporas are far smaller a proportion of Canada's population than the Haitian and Pakistani diasporas.

Two different dynamics seem to be at work with regard to Canadian ODA priorities. On the one hand, disproportionate amounts of ODA seems to flow to some countries that also receive a lot of USAID monies. On the other hand, Canada's seems to want to score a high grade on ODA in some countries that also have a relatively strong diaspora in Canada. The claim that ethnocultural pluralism – and its distribution across the country – may have at least some influence on the way ODA is directed is further bolstered by the observation that member states of La Francophonie seem to fare particularly well in the national allocation of Canadian ODA (Canada 2003–04).

In other words, Canada's relationship with the United States is not the only constraint acting on Canadian foreign policy. The analysis in this chapter suggests that, be it ODA or the DART, domestic constraints – notably ethnocultural ones – also seem to matter.

CONCLUSION

We started out by observing a disconnect between Canadian foreign-policy priorities and the apparent preferences of Canadians. We postulated neopluralism as a possible explanation: some groups wield more influence over the policy process than others. If there were an unambiguous national interest on issues such as ODA or peacekeeping, then interest groups may be of less interest in the study of foreign policy. On most global issues, however, there is no clear national interest. In a democracy the national interest is what it is judged to be after debate and discussion (Nye). Those groups with a particular interest in a subject, be it for ethnic or economic reasons, will dominate and shape the debate. The debate, hence the policy, both reflect particular interests. The conventional statist/realist take on Canadian Government decision-making is thus turned on its head[7]: Larger amounts of ODA end up not necessarily with developing states that are of strategic importance to Canada per se but with developing states that are of strategic interest to pivotal electoral constituencies and to the Canada-US relationship.

Neopluralism is particularly concerned about the undue power exerted by particular, notably economic, interests. Indeed, the analysis turned up economic interests as an overriding concern in Canadian foreign policy. That outcome, however, was expected, especially in light of the geostrategic continentalist constraints with which Canada has to contend when exercising its sovereignty.

Yet, the analysis also turned up another set of constraints: it suggests that changing demographic trends may also have some bearing on the government's foreign-policy agenda. Canada's geostrategic location in the world is unlikely to change; Canada's demographic footprint, by contrast, is changing. The symbiotic relationship between growing ethnocultural diversity and Canadian foreign-policy priorities is an emerging structural story, one worth watching. The institutional constraints within which Canadian foreign policy has traditionally operated thus seem to be increasingly mediated by evolving structural constraints.

In short, the rapid sociodemographic changes to which the Canadian population is subject are likely to become an ever more salient intervening variable impinging on the Canada-US. relationship. How likely depends on the electoral expediency – in the guise of "democratic responsiveness" – of Canada's federal political parties and elites. If growing ethnocultural differentiation, diversity, and fragmentation among the Canadian population and growing electoral posturing for "ethnic votes" are any indication, domestic structural considerations in Canadian foreign policy are probably on the rise. How well the cross-border relationship will fare is thus at least partially a function of the concurrent evolution of structural and institutional constraints. If their trajectories diverge, the Canada-US relationship is likely to fare worse than if they converge. And if convergence were to bolster the same policy constraints that economic globalization imposes on national governments, congruent institutional and structural constraints end up reinforcing one another so as to curtail the Canadian Government's flexibility on foreign policy.

NOTES

The authors are indebted to research assistance by Nicolette O'Connor.

1 Doran goes on to write that the United States looks at the world through the prism of its relations with the world. In the first, the US may loom larger than it really is; in the second, Canada may seem smaller than it really is.
2 This is not to say this process was actually reflective of Canadians' views. The department's travelling road show was largely hijacked by special interests and the selection bias intrinsic to digital democracy is considerable (e.g., Alexander and Pal). Still, in good Milibandian fashion (see Miliband), the process was, supposedly, not entirely elite-driven; at least it had a facade of popular legitimacy.

3 These priorities are taken directly from *Canada's International Policy Statement: A Role of Pride and Influence in the World* (Canada, FAC, 2005).

4 The four polls are: Pollara, *Canadian's Attitudes Toward Foreign Policy*, report prepared for The Canadian Institute of International Affairs, Toronto, April 2004; Innovative Research Group, *Visions of Canadian Foreign Policy*, report prepared for The Dominion Institute of Canada and the Canadian Defence and Foreign Affairs Institute, Toronto, November 2004; Ipsos-Reid, *Canadian Views on Canada's Roll in International Affairs*, report prepared for the University of Ottawa, Vancouver 2005; Innovative Research Group, *The World in Canada: Demographics and Diversity in Canadian Foreign Policy*, report prepared for the Canadian Defence and Foreign Affairs Institute, Toronto, October 2005.

5 Birkland (22) defines a focusing event as "an event that is sudden, relatively rare, can be reasonably defined as harmful or revealing the possibility of potentially greater future harms, inflicts harms or suggests potential harms that are or could be concentrated on a definable geographical area or community or interest, and that is known to policy makers and the public virtually simultaneously."

6 Canada's disbursement of ODA has already been shown to have been influenced by its membership in international organizations such as the Commonwealth and La Francophonie (Rioux; Thérien 1989).

7 For examples of the statist approach to Canadian foreign aid, see Spicer; Triantis; Nossal 1988.

8

Public Perceptions of Canada-US Relations: Regionalism and Diversity

EVAN POTTER[1]

One of the perpetual questions in any examination of the Canadian mindset concerns attitudes toward the United States. This is not surprising given the dominant role played by US culture, politics, and economics in daily Canadian life and, therefore, in Canada's self-image. With the blurring of lines demarcating national policy and international policy, a process that has accelerated in post-9/11 North America, US security concerns – at home and abroad – have had increasing implications for Canada's own security postures and economic prosperity.

Calling for a more "sophisticated relationship," the Liberal Government of Paul Martin issued an International Policy Statement in April 2005 advocating a global foreign policy anchored by a closer partnership in North America. It was understood that by continuing to play an active, global role, Canada would, in fact, be reinforcing its bilateral relationship with the United States.

Public attitudes toward the United States are a source of great interest – some would say obsession – north of the forty-ninth parallel. There are good reasons for this. As shown by the national debate on free trade in the 1980s, the Chrétien Government's refusal to participate in the US-led invasion of Iraq in 2003 and the Martin Government's difficulty in arriving at a position on missile defense in 2005, an understanding of the public mood is essential to making political decisions and calibrating policy positions when Canada-US relations are involved. For this reason, Canadian attitudes toward the United States and, to a lesser extent, US attitudes toward Canada, have been a focus of considerable media attention and subject to detailed examination by Canada's public opinion researchers.

Since the terrorist attacks of 11 September 2001, for example, there has been continuous polling on Canadians' attitudes toward the border, ballistic missile defense, terrorism, and Ottawa's decision not to join the Bush Administration's "coalition of the willing" in Iraq. There has also been an ongoing debate with respect to whether Canadian values are diverging or converging with those of Americans. However, relatively less attention has been paid to whether there are significant regional differences in attitudes toward the United States and whether Canada's growing multicultural society portends a shift in Canadian opinion in the years ahead.

In light of public statements by both prime ministers Paul Martin and Stephen Harper about the need to put Canada-US relations on a new footing, this study's purpose is to raise questions for future research by probing to see whether there are any indications of significant national cleavages with respect to Canadian attitudes toward the United States. This probe will be based primarily on data compiled by Ekos Research Associates' syndicated study, Rethinking North American Integration (2005), an annual research program that started in 2001.[2] The 2005 version explored four themes: images of the United States; security and borders; trade and economics; and attachment to Canada.

To illuminate any changes within the Canadian mindset with regard to relations with the United States, I will report selectively on the Ekos study by summarizing and analyzing some of the findings that compare the attitudes of first-generation Canadians and those who are longer established as well as compare Quebecers' attitudes with those from the rest of Canada.[3] The underlying question is whether the traditional public-opinion cleavages between Canada's regions (and particularly between Francophone Quebecers and the rest of Canadians) on matters of Canada's relations with the United States are being mirrored – given an increasingly diverse Canadian society – by an emerging set of cleavages between foreign and native-born Canadians.[4] If such new cleavages do exist, they may have profound effects for how Canada manages its relations with the United States in the future. However, this chapter's analysis of Ekos's findings will not resonate without first sketching the state of Canada-US relations from 2001 to 2005.

THE CONTEXT

Canadians, since at least Confederation, have expressed who they are by who they are not, namely, Americans. More precisely, Anglophone Canadians have expressed a nationalism based on being different from Americans; Francophone Quebecers are more likely to base their identity on their distinctiveness from the rest of Canada. For most of Canada's short history as a country, Canadians have thus expressed a form of default national identity. However, by the 1990s, as Darrell Bricker, president of Ipsos-Reid, and Edward Greenspon report in their book *Search for Certainty: Inside the New Canadian Mindset*, the trends of accelerating globalization and an increasingly diverse society at home had created a more confident population, less worried about us economic and cultural encroachments and more likely to embrace a less "reflexive and more situational" nationalism.[5] Canadians are ranked third in the world after Americans and Austrians with regard to their level of pride in their country.[6]

The vicissitudes of Canadians' attitudes toward their southern neighbour cannot be understood in isolation from bilateral histories in North America, the tone of bilateral relations (with the perceived degree of warmth of personal relations between the us president and Canadian prime minister acting as a barometer), domestic politics in Canada (and in the United States, as well, given Canadians' access to us mass media), trade relations and the role of the United States in the world (e.g., how it projects its cultural, economic, and military power). The mass media – Canadian and American – through its agenda-setting role, has a significant role in interpreting the state of bilateral relations. This study's examination of Canadians' attitudes toward the United States must therefore be seen as a snapshot of attitudes at a particular period of time that are influenced by a particular set of circumstances. Such a snapshot is not only valuable because it can validate historical continuities in attitudes, but also because it can isolate particular discontinuities that may portend more significant change in Canadian public opinion toward the United States.

The inauguration of George W. Bush in January 2001 crystallized for Ottawa the new face of the United States: the ineluctable shifting of the locus of political and economic political power from the Northeast to the Southwest. A further signal was sent when the new president's first state visit was to Mexico rather than Canada. With a Liberal Government in Ottawa and a new Republican administration in Washington, the Canadian media was alert to what status the new administration would accord its northern neighbour, with some observers assuming that there was every possibility that there would be a continuation of the "benign neglect" that had come to characterize how Canadians view Americans' attitudes toward Canada.[7]

The 9/11 terrorist attacks in many ways reinforced existing public-opinion trends in Canada and the United States and, in other ways, changed the public-opinion equation. There was, for example, a perceptible change in the attitudes toward Canada among US opinion leaders, particularly within Congress. The initial positive image garnered by Canada because of its prompt response in welcoming more than thirty-three thousand stranded US airline passengers was soon overshadowed by the incorrect perception in the United States that Canada was a haven for terrorists. Canadians may have thought that their welcome mat was going to pay some lasting public-opinion dividends south of the border (similar to the long public-opinion afterglow that accompanied Canada's successful efforts to save US embassy staff in Iran in 1979), but this perception was short-lived and soon overshadowed by a consensus among a cross-section of US decision-makers that the "world's longest undefended border" was no longer a source of pride but one of vulnerability. The off-hand reference to the president of the United States as a "moron" by Prime Minister Jean Chrétien's director of communications at an international NATO conference in 2002, silently applauded by a segment of the Canadian population, did not go unnoticed by the Bush White House and represented a further cooling of the tone of bilateral relations. Still more seeds of doubt were sown about Canada's worthiness as "America's best friend" when the Liberal Government refused to join the US Government's "coalition of the willing" to remove Saddam Hussein from power in Iraq in 2003, followed two years later (after ambiguous signals) by the Martin Government's refusal to have Canada involved in the US missile defense program.[8] Canadians were split on Ottawa's decision not to join the US "coalition of the willing," with Quebecers the most adamantly against Canada joining the fight; the largest opposition to Canada's participation in missile defense was in British Columbia and Quebec. Quebec's position should not be surprising. Jean-Sebastien Rioux's review of the historical and sociological literature shows that Francophone Quebecers, who are often described as isolationist, are actually supportive of collective security; however, they are less likely than other Canadians to support Canada's involvement in "concrete military commitments" – in other words, the sending of troops into the field.[9] Roussel and Theoret[10] support Rioux's findings insofar as they see Quebecers – including sovereignists – as being more internationalist (even "Pearsonian") in their outlook and realistic about the benefits of defense cooperation with the United States in such institutions as NORAD. At the same time, softwood lumber, a seemingly intractable trade irritant, and the Bush administration's refusal to ratify the Kyoto Treaty, were demonstrating the growing distance between Ottawa and Washington.

Much to the chagrin of federal officials and Cabinet ministers who had been busy trying to prove Canada's security bona fides to skeptical Americans, British Prime Minister Tony Blair, closer in political persuasion to Chrétien's Liberal Party than he was to Bush's Republican Party, was being hailed as a hero in the United States. It was not long before the UK was perceived in the United States and around the world as the US's "best friend" – a role that Canada had always coveted. While this moniker may have been noticed mostly by the editorial page writers of the National Post and The Globe and Mail, the fact was that, while more than eight in ten Americans had held a favourable view of Canada in 2002, only a year later this approval rating had fallen precipitously to 65 percent.[11] From the Canadian perspective, the US-led invasion and occupation of Iraq would, over the next two years, begin to erode the overwhelming sympathy shown by Canadians toward the United States after the 2001 attacks. Canadians, meanwhile, were surprised to find out that they had become the destination of choice for elderly Americans who needed to purchase lower-cost prescription medication (raising questions about fairness of US society) and that Canada was seen as a "model" nation for a large segment of Americans, primarily in so-called "blue" (or liberal) states. The US media's coverage (including ongoing criticism by pundits on Fox News) of Canada's same-sex marriage legislation was played back to Canadians by Canada's media, further reinforcing a sense among Canadians of fundamental difference between the two nations.

Adding it all up, Canada's stock was falling with its vital trading and security partner, causing the US Ambassador to Canada Paul Celluci, in an unusual breach of diplomatic protocol, to publicly berate Canada about its position on missile defense. These uncertain bilateral relations combined with the sense that Canada was losing its overall influence led some long-time Canadian observers of public opinion in both countries such as Frank Graves of Ekos Research Associates and Michael Adams of Environics Research Group to examine whether some of the bilateral misunderstandings and misperceptions could be attributed to a fundamental divergence of values in the two societies.

A review of Canada-us value changes by the federal government's Policy Research Initiative (PRI) in 2004 concluded that value differences between Canada and the United States are small and that, when observed across a range of indicators, the differences "are often a matter of degrees rather than direction, except for religious and moral issues, where larger gaps are found."[12] To cite just one obvious example of a large values-gap, while nearly three in five Americans (58 percent) say a person has to believe in God to be moral, only three in ten Canadians agree.[13] The PRI's review of research on Canada-us differences and similarities in the categories of economic, political, social and moral domains concluded that there was a "net effect toward divergence between 1981 and 2000," which corroborated the thesis propounded by Michael Adams (2003) in *Fire and Ice: The U.S., Canada, and the Myth of Converging Values*.[14] The data on North American value sets by the Pew Global Attitudes Project also showed that when it came to the values of engaging the world Canadians were more internationalist than Americans, with 28 percent seeing the United Nations as good for their country in 2002, while only 18 percent of Americans agreed.[15] Only 58 percent of Americans believed that the UN contributed a great deal to world peace compared to 80 percent of Canadians who felt this way.[16] These findings were corroborated by surveys commissioned by the Centre for Research and Information (CRIC) on Canada for its "portraits of Canada" series in 2003 (essentially an analysis of the national zeitgeist), which indicated that about two-thirds of Canadians believed that their values were different from those of Americans. A curious paradox was emerging: Canadians acknowledged that their values were different, but it did not stop them from agreeing to closer economic and security relations with the United States by, for example, favouring the expansion of the Canada-us free-trade agreement to cover labour in addition to goods and services or by expanding cooperation (as opposed to harmonization) on border security.[17] As noted, analysts have attributed this apparent paradox to Canadians growing more confident. The

Some uncertainty in relations between Canada & the U.S.

Q: How would you currently describe relations between Canada and the United States?

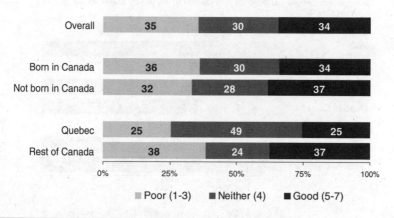

Base: Most recent data points from Jun. 05, Canada n= half sample; U.S. n= half sample

Figure 1

above provides the public environment context within which the following findings on Canadian attitudes toward the United States, as reported by Ekos Research Associates and other major Canadian public research firms, need to be understood.

THE FINDINGS

When Ekos asked Canadians to describe the current state (June 2005) of relations, one-third of Canadians rated relations as good, which was roughly the same proportion that believed they were poor. When the data were broken out for those not born in Canada there was little significant difference. As noted in figure 1, the difference in perception was most pronounced among Quebecers, for whom relations with the United States are not high priority,[18] with a quarter saying relations were poor and a quarter saying they were good but with almost half saying relations were neither good nor bad. As reported in the Innovative Research Group's survey (2005), 81 percent of "established French Canadians" were most likely to agree with the statement that "the United States has proven to be an unpredictable and unilateral trading and security partner and Canada would be better off deepening our relationships with other countries" compared to

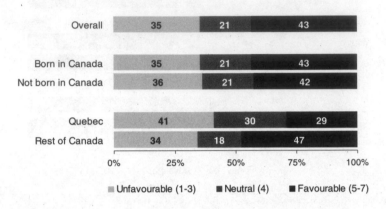

Images of the United States

Q: In general, would you describe your opinion of the United States as favourable or unfavourable?

Base: Jun. 05, Canada n= half sample; U.S. n= half sample (Source: *Rethinking North America*)

Figure 2

72 percent of "established English Canadians" and 68 percent of "newcomers." Only 57 percent of the residents of the Atlantic provinces were likely to agree with this position.[19] To illustrate the significant regional disparities in Canadian attitudes toward the United States it is instructive to look at attitudes in 2003 after the US-led invasion of Iraq. In July of that year, 75 percent of Quebecers blamed the US Government for the deteriorating relationship as compared to 33 percent of Albertans (51 percent of Albertan respondents blamed Ottawa).[20] To be sure, responses to such a question must be put into perspective as this is a snapshot of public opinion at a particular point in Canada-US history and will largely reflect the mass media's coverage of the relationship.

A better way of probing the vicissitudes of Canadian attitudes toward the United States is to track the level of favourable and unfavourable views. According to Michael Adams, in 2005, the US and its government were less popular in Canada than at any time since polls were first conducted in this country in the 1930s. To find similar anti-American sentiment, he writes, one would have had to go back to the federal election of 1911, when Wilfrid Laurier's espousal of trade reciprocity with the United States cost him re-election. Adams goes on to note that in 1981, the year Ronald Reagan was inaugurated, 7 percent of Canadians held an unfavourable opinion of the US, while ten times that proportion (72 percent) reported a favourable impression of the United States (Adams 2005).

When Ekos (2005) asked Canadians about their images of the United States, about 43 percent of Canadians had a favourable opinion of Americans (75 percent of Americans had a favourable opinion of Canada).[21] As shown in figure 2, 41 percent of Quebecers had an unfavourable view, with one in three saying they were neutral (significantly above proportion of other Canadians voicing a neutral position); 18 percent of French-speaking Canadians said that they had a very unfavourable view of the United States. What is even more revealing in available surveys since 2000 is that Quebec's youth had become viscerally anti-American (more than youth in the rest of Canada), which suggests that there may be a wholesale rejection of the idea of the USA among a particular demographic cohort rather than just a rejection of the policies of a particular administration. Not surprisingly, with the US's negative international image (as described in regular surveys undertaken by the Pew Global Attitudes Project) because of the perception that it is involved in a largely discretionary occupation of Iraq, the number of visible minorities who said that they had a very unfavourable view (21 percent) was double the number for those born in Canada.[22]

To put these historically high negative ratings into perspective, it is useful to compare Canadians' views with those of citizens in other countries. According to the Pew Global Attitudes Project (2004), Canadian opinion of the US people – as opposed to views of the United States – did not decline with the Iraq war (though other Canadian data suggests that it did so among French Quebecers). In nine of fourteen countries surveyed by Pew in 2002 and 2003 public attitudes toward Americans worsened, but 77 percent of Canadians maintained a favourable attitude toward Americans, with 34 percent holding a very favourable view, the second highest among those surveyed. When people were asked around the world about their views of the US Government, the responses of Canadians stood out again. Even after the image of the US administration in Canada slipped once the US invaded Iraq – going from a 72 percent favourability rating before the war to 63 percent after the war began, this was, according to Pew, still a "relatively modest" drop

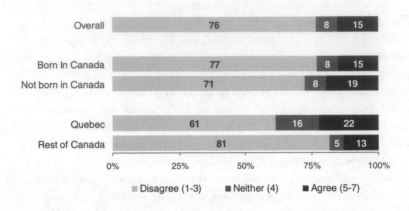

Attitudes towards integration with the U.S.

Base: Jun. 05, Canada and U.S. n= half sample; Oct. 03, Mexico n= 1499 (Source: *Rethinking North America*)

Figure 3

compared to the responses by some of the United States' other allies. While there is certainly no suggestion in these statistics that the United States is being given a free ride by its neighbour to the north, it is nevertheless true that certain regions of Canada – notably Alberta – have greater sympathy for the policies of the Bush White House, which may in turn account for a smaller percentage of Canadians who intensely dislike the US administration.

Bricker and Greenspon (2001) describe a "fascinating snapshot in the annals of Canadian public opinion" when a pair of identical questions were posed in 1964 and 2001 to measure Canadians' support for a union with the United States.[23] They write: "In 1964, a period in which the Walter Gordon Liberals had begun beating the drum about American economic domination ... 29 per cent favoured a union and 62 per cent opposed it. A generation and a half later ... support had fallen in half to 15 per cent and opposition had grown to 81 per cent ... Moreover, those disputing the assertion that such a union was, in any way case, inevitable had grown from 59 per cent to 68 per cent."[24] In contrast to the more lukewarm attitude toward the idea of Canada prevalent among Canadians in the mid-1960's, as figure 3 shows, eight in ten Canadians assert that they would be concerned if Canada joined the United States, suggesting

Rating the response to terrorism

Q: Thinking about Canada's security response to the issue of terrorism, would you say
we've gone too far, not far enough or responded appropriately?

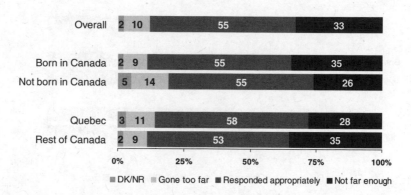

Base: Canada Sep. 05, n= 1031 (from the *Security Monitor*); U.S. Jun. 05, n= 1505 (from *RNA*)
Figure 4

that there is strong desire to maintain an independent identity.
Quebecers continue to be less concerned than other Canadians
about such a prospect, probably because they feel that their distinc-
tive culture, language, and institutions would continue to prevent
Quebec from being assimilated by US culture.

A second dimension of the Ekos (2005) study concerned attitudes toward security and safety, which both Canadians and Americans rate as the dominant consideration in terms of their shared
border. Of the four options – freedom of movement, national sovereignty, economic advantages, and safety – that were tested by
Ekos, safety as a consideration outranked all the other issues by at
least a margin of two to one in Canada and, not surprisingly, three
to one in the United States.

This raises the question of how the predominant concern for
safety at the border could correlate with risk perception regarding
the Canadian Government's response to terrorism. As figure 4
shows, the majority of Canadians believe that Ottawa responded appropriately to the terrorist threat with a third of Canadians, particularly those born in Canada, actually indicating that they could
tolerate Ottawa doing more. The Ekos questionnaire did not probe
what specific civil liberties Canadians were prepared to give up in

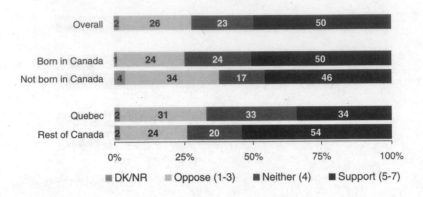

Support for a common security perimeter

Q. Would you support or oppose Canada, the United States and Mexico establishing a common security perimeter?

Base: Jun. 05, Canada n= half sample; U.S. n= 1505 (Source: *Rethinking North America*)

Figure 5

order to increase their safety. The overall Canadian position of relative satisfaction with the government's response may reflect the fact that Canada has not had terrorist attacks on its soil since the days of the FLQ in the 1960s and early 1970s and, consequently, that terrorism is not a first-tier security or foreign-policy concern for Canadians. (The 1985 terrorist bombing of an Air India flight originating from Canada, the largest mass murder of Canadians in Canada's history, occurred off the coast of Ireland.)

Given that borders became very strongly associated with safety after 9/11, it is not surprising that there were initially high levels of public support for strong borders and perimeters. However, with the memory of the attacks receding in the collective memory, Ekos reports that support for a common North American security perimeter dropped significantly in Canada – down 12 percent – between 2003 and 2005. Figure 5 shows that half of Canadians supported such a position. Quebecers were split on the idea of a common security perimeter with a third neither opposing nor supporting.

After more than a generation of divisive debate about the threat of growing continental integration on Canada's identity and independence, there is now broad public acceptance of continental free trade. In Canada, support for free trade plummeted in the early

Gauging support for NAFTA

Q: Do you agree there should be free trade between Canada, the U.S., and Mexico?

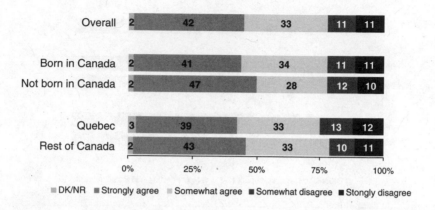

■ DK/NR ■ Strongly agree ■ Somewhat agree ■ Somewhat disagree ■ Stongly disagree

Base: Most recent data points; Jun. 05, Canada n= half sample; U.S. n= half sample (Source: *Rethinking North America*)
Flgure 6

1990s and then rebounded later in the decade. Figure 6 shows that a strong majority of Canadians – including visible minorities and Quebecers – agree with the idea of continental free trade and the national level of support, ranging between 75 percent and 79 percent (depending on which firm has done the survey), has been stable since 2001. As a reflection perhaps of their value orientations, Canadians are more positively disposed to references to "North American relations" than to "Canada-US relations."

However, as figure 7 shows, the real story is not the level of Canadian support for free trade, but the perception of its effects on Canada. North American publics continue to express mixed views as to whether NAFTA has had an overall positive or negative effect on their countries. The plurality of Canadians (38 percent) lean to seeing NAFTA as having a positive impact on Canada (with 27 percent seeing it as having negative impact). There are no significant differences in perception between those born in Canada and those born outside. A third of Quebecers are likely to perceive this free-trade agreement as having no impact, and they are less likely than other Canadians to see NAFTA having a positive impact. Canadians in the prairies are the most likely to think NAFTA has had a negative impact; those living in Atlantic Canada are most positive.

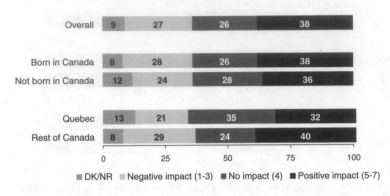

Figure 7

The biggest divergences – despite largely similar levels of support for free trade – are between North American decision-makers and their publics. Four in ten Canadians see NAFTA making a positive impact compared to two in three Canadian decision-makers. Decision-makers in Quebec and Ontario are the most inclined to characterize the impacts of NAFTA as being positive (76 percent and 70 percent respectively). The gap between the Quebec elite's views of NAFTA's benefits and the Quebec public is striking (Ekos 2005).[25]

While a political union is a non-starter for most Canadians, as figure 8 shows, a slight majority of Canadians (58 percent) think that Canada, the us, and Mexico will form an economic union in the next ten years. Again, on this question, Quebecers seem not to have taken any definitive position; those not born in Canada are more likely than Quebecers and native-born Canadians to have made their minds up one way or the other. Ekos (2005, Decision-Maker Survey) reports that there is stronger majority support for the idea of a common-market union like the European Union.[26]

Returning to this study's discussion of the growing values gap between Canada and the United States along certain indicators, a portrait has emerged over the last two decades of two distinct societies. As figure 9 shows, a significant portion of Canadians continue to want Canada to be less like the United States. These proportions are similar

Likelihood of a North American economic union

Q: Over the next 10 years, how likely is it that Canada, the U.S. and Mexico will form a North American Economic Union?

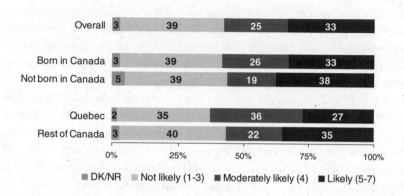

Figure 8

Attachment to Canada

Q: In the future, would you like to see Canada become more like theUnited States, less like the United States, or would you like things to remain as they are?

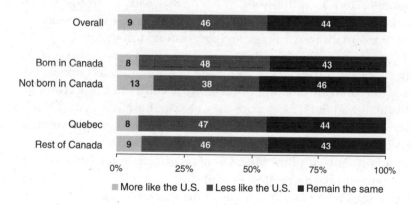

Base: Canada, most recent data point Jun. 05 n= half sample (Source: *Rethinking North America*)

Figure 9

to survey findings in 1998, 2000, and 2002, and they seem to cut across linguistic or ethnic differences, though it appears that Canadians who are not born in Canada may be less likely to think this way.[27]

The implications of these differences in values for understanding Canadian attitudes toward issues in bilateral relations as well as forming opinions on how to resolve global conflict are profound. For example, they explain the wide differences in views on immigration and foreign aid in both countries. With the Canadian public continuing to be split on whether relations with the United States are well-managed or not, there appears to be a practical strain in how Canadians perceive relations with their southern neighbour. Public opinion research by a variety of firms (Ekos, Environics, CRIC) since 2001 has shown that Canadians are prepared to support greater cooperation with the United States on border security, trade, and national defense out of necessity and a sense that there are tangible benefits for Canada. On the other hand, they oppose any rush to harmonize social or fiscal policy (e.g., dollarization of North American currency) or even border policy for fear of relinquishing Canadian sovereignty.

CONCLUSION

Overall, the Ekos study suggests that while Canadians generally support closer integration with the United States across environmental, economic, and security issues, this coexists with a strong, values-based desire to maintain national identity. Canadians, in particular, want to maintain control over immigration and their foreign policy and place less emphasis on the "war on terror." There is steady long-term support for the principle of trade liberalization in Canada, but this is mirrored by ongoing uncertainty about benefits accruing to individuals and families. According to Ekos, there is a shared North American mosaic with strong shared economic and security orientations but a desire for separate national societies. Despite the clear disappointment with how the us is managing its international role, Canadians still have a positive view of the United States.

Based on a select number of questions that were examined for the purposes of this study, the differences in attitudes in Canada toward the United States, when they do occur, appeared to be greater between Canadians living outside of Quebec and those inside Quebec than they were between those Canadians born inside Canada and those born outside. The exception to this pattern seems to be on questions that seek to measure the level of general support for the United States (favourable/unfavourable). As noted, those not born in Canada tend to hold the United States in a more negative light than those born in Canada. It is not clear how this finding can be reconciled with the commonly accepted observation that Canadians are more confident about their national identity and less reflexively anti-American. These findings are broadly consistent with the Innovative Research Group's findings on Canadian attitudes toward the United States, which showed that there was "no major issue with a majority of any major ethno cultural group on one side and majorities in the other two [Established French Canadians and Established English Canadians] opposed." They did, however, find differences in the levels of support for particular policy *direction* between Established French Canadians and Established English Canadians.

As memories of the 9/11 attacks recede further in the public consciousness and as particular segments of an increasingly diverse country[28] grow ever-more confident challenging the primarily secular humanist values of contemporary Canadian society, the cleavages in attitudes between those born inside and those born outside of Canada may begin to rival those that currently exist among regions, creating a much more complex public environment in which to manage Canada-US relations. Indeed, it will become progressively more difficult for Canadian politicians to invoke the "values card" in discussions about Canada's international vocation, or the nuance of engaging in a "common cause" with the United States while appearing to follow Washington's lead.

With the expanding populations of Alberta and British Columbia now virtually equal to Quebec and with Quebec's overall population growth expected to atrophy (in the absence of significant in-flows of new immigrants), we should expect Quebec public opinion to have a decreasing – though by no means inconsequential – influence on Ottawa's calculus in its relations with the United States.[29] As long as a majority federal government in Ottawa depends on a critical number of Quebec seats in the House of Commons, Canada's international security policy will continue to be substantially influenced by how Francophone Quebecers view the United States. For this reason, no matter how active Canada's diaspora populations become in the years ahead, they will never be able to rival the critical influence of Quebec public opinion on Canada's foreign policy.

Finally, we should be concerned about what appears to be the more crystallized, negative attitudes of young Quebecers toward the United States. If these attitudes become more entrenched within the next generation of Quebecers (the children of the baby boomers' children and newcomers to the province), then it may become more difficult to count on a broad domestic consensus for the development of Canada's future foreign policy.

NOTES

1 The views in this chapter are those of this author alone and do not reflect the views of the Government of Canada. The author would like to thank Ekos Research Associates for allowing him to use survey data and graphs from the 2005 Rethinking North American Integration project.
2 Innovative Research Group, *The World in Canada: Demographics and Diversity in Canadian Foreign Policy.*
3 The study examines shifts in attitudes in us, Mexico, and Canada. The first wave of the survey took place in June 2005 with a large sample size in Canada of two thousand; 1,505 in us, and 1500 in Mexico. All the results are statistically accurate to within +/- 2.5, nineteen out of twenty.
4 One in five Canadians is foreign born and by 2017 one in five Canadians will be a visible minority.
5 Darrell Bricker and Edward Greenspon, *Searching for Certainty: Inside the New Canadian Mindset*, 301.
6 This fact was included in a Power Point presentation delivered by GPC Research (Ottawa) to the Department of Foreign Affairs and International Trade on 15 December 2004.
7 See reference to "benign neglect" in Colin Robertson, "Getting Noticed in Washington: The Hard Part of Canada's Job," an essay posted on the Canadian Washington, DC, web site. (This essay was accessed by the author in May 2007 at geo.international.gc.ca/can-am/washington/secretariat/p200502-en.asp.) See also Conference of Defence Associations Institute, *A Nation at Risk: The Decline of the Canadian Forces*, 2002, 43.
8 For a description of us disappointment with Canada's decision, see Paul Cellucci, *Unquiet Diplomacy.*
9 Jean-Sebastien Rioux, "Two Solitudes: Quebecers' Attitudes Regarding Canadian Security and Defence Policy," 22-3. This report, prepared for the Canadian Defence and Foreign Affairs Institute in February 2005,

contains a comprehensive bibliography on literature that examines Quebecers' attitudes toward defense.

10 See chapter 9 of this volume.

11 The Pew Research Center for the People and the Press, "Americans and Canadians: The North American Not-so-Odd Couple."

12 Christian Boucher, "Canada-US Values: Distinct, Inevitably Carbon Copy, or Narcissism of Small Differences?"

13 The Pew Research Center for the People and the Press, "Americans and Canadians: The North American Not-so-Odd Couple."

14 Michael Adams, *Fire and Ice: The United States, Canada, and the Myth of Converging Values.*

15 Ibid.

16 Presentation by Continuum Research, "Diverging Paths – Common Goals."

17 Andrew Parkin, "Pro-Canadian, Anti-American or Anti-War? Canadian Public Opinion on the Eve of War," 6.

18 This finding is from a July 2004 survey by Environics Research survey made available to this author. Only 29 percent of Quebecers rated Canada-US relations as a high priority compared to 44 percent of citizens in the rest of Canada.

19 Innovative Research Group, *The World in Canada: Demographics and Diversity in Canadian Foreign Policy.*

20 These statistics are taken from Environics' *Focus Canada* omnibus survey. This survey was made available to the author.

21 According to Environics' data, the sudden increase in unfavourability ratings started in 2001 and peaked in March 2003 at 40 percent.

22 See pewglobal.org/reports for the complete list of survey reports since 2001.

23 Bricker and Greenspon, 300. The question was asked again in July 2002 with different results. As reported by the Centre for Research and Information on Canada, this time the change was not as striking, with 36 percent of Canadians saying that union with the United States was inevitable and 61 percent saying it was not inevitable. With findings that echo the results of the 1964 question, it is hard to pinpoint the reason for such a significant shift in attitude in a little more than a year except to suggest that perceptions on the issue of a full union have not crystallized and are still volatile. See Centre for Research and Information on Canada, "Canada and the United States: An Evolving Partnership," 23.

24 Ibid.

25 Ekos Research Associates, "Decision-Maker Survey: Canada and the U.S.," 12.

26 Ibid., 16–17.
27 Centre for Research and Information on Canada, "Canada and the United States: An Evolving Partnership," 22.
28 See the chapter in this volume by Elizabeth Riddell-Dixon, on the impact of immigration, and the chapter by Jack Granatstein on multiculturalism.
29 As noted by David Carment and David Bercuson in the introduction to this volume.

Defense Policy Distorted by the Sovereignist Prism? The Bloc Québécois on Security and Defense Questions (1990–2005)

STÉPHANE ROUSSEL AND
CHARLES-ALEXANDRE THÉORÊT

When the Liberal Party of Canada assumed power in autumn 1993, it was faced with an unexpected official opposition: the Bloc Québécois (BQ). This organization, then led by the former Conservative minister Lucien Bouchard, was a sovereignist party that intended to defend Quebec's interests in Ottawa pending the province's accession to the status of independent state. The title of official opposition implied among other things that the sovereignists, who had until then been mainly present on the provincial scene, would in future have to delve into questions falling under federal jurisdiction that they'd almost never had to deal with in the past. Among these questions were the defense-related issues that the Parti Québécois (PQ) had only touched upon in a relatively superficial manner in the development of the broad political directions of a sovereign Quebec.[1] Thus, elected representatives from the Bloc were going have to make decisions regarding delicate questions such as the budget of the Department of National Defence, the deployment of troops abroad, or the purchase of equipment for the Canadian Forces; all of which are issues they had no experience with and probably very little interest in. In doing so, the sovereignists were going have to be specific about their positions and their vision of the world.

In 1993, observers were attempting to assess the consequences of the remarkable entry of the *indépendantistes* into the federal Parliament, particularly in the foreign affairs and defense fields. Given the Bloc's commitment to the sovereignist cause, it was possible to expect its position on these issues to be primarily dictated by this goal or at least by the objective of making "Quebec's interests" prevail (Fortmann and Mace). Fifteen years after this party's formation, it is possible to systematically take stock of these interventions and positions. Have they effectively been distorted by a certain "sovereignist obsession"? This is the question that this paper aims to answer.

This exercise also allows a better definition of the premises and objectives of the sovereignist Québécois movement in a field where it has remained quite discreet. Moreover, this overview provides an opportunity to observe (and maybe explain) the evolution of this discourse over time, with its eventual twists and contradictions, along the flow of national and international events, and through changes in defense and security affairs. In order to better observe the details of the Bloc members' set of arguments, this study focuses on four important files: cooperation with the United States, military interventions abroad, the defense budget, and military assistance to civil authorities.

THE EVOLUTION OF THE BLOC AND OF THE SOVEREIGNIST MOVEMENT FROM 1990 TO 2005

The Bloc Québécois was formed in summer 1990 in the aftermath of the failure of the Meech Lake Accord, which was intended to seal Quebec's inclusion in the 1982 Constitution. A dozen Conservative and Liberal representatives from Quebec, led by Lucien Bouchard, got together to found the new party. The first representative elected under this banner was Gilles Duceppe, who won a by-election the following year. In March 1997, he would become party chief.

The 25 October 1993 elections that brought Jean Chrétien's Liberals to power also saw the election of fifty-four Bloc representatives who, having two elected representatives more than the Reform Party, would form the official opposition. This status conferred significant resources to the Bloc not only in terms of a budget for research and research personnel but also in terms of speaking time in the House and increased visibility. The Bloc also inherited the duty – paradoxical at the very least – of having to speak for Canada, and to do so about all topics featured on the agenda and no longer strictly about the issues that primarily concern Quebec. Thus, elected Bloc representatives would pay more attention to questions of national defense than representatives of the sovereignist movement had ever done.

The caucus chose Jean-Marc Jacob, elected representative for Charlesbourg, as party spokesperson on defense issues, which did not prevent Lucien Bouchard from frequently intervening on the topic. The Bloc also hired researchers who would be in charge of keeping the representatives informed on these files. Other representatives who, over the years, would have foreign-policy or defense responsibilities include René Laurin, Claude Bachand, Daniel Turp, and Francine Lalonde.

The first major contribution of Bloc members to the debate on Canadian defense was made in 1994, when following the *Report of the Special Joint Committee on Canada's Defence Policy,* Jacob and Jean Leroux, his colleague from the Shefford district, handed in a dissenting report on the revision of foreign policy (Parliament of Canada 1994a). Four of their colleagues handed in a similar report at the time of the presentation of a report of the Committee on Foreign Policy but made almost no mention of international security problems (Parliament of Canada 1994a).

The dissenting report on defense is surprising, to say the least. The United Nations is given more importance in it than in the majority report and is considered as the principal reference point for Canada's defense policy. The Bloc members recommended, among other things, prioritizing collective security and peace missions at the expense of territorial defense, for which there is little need given Canada's privileged geostrategic location. It is, however, the North American Aerospace Defense Command (NORAD) that is the subject of the most curious proposals, as will be discussed subsequently.

As for NATO, the Bloc's project proposed maintaining Canada's political participation but with a "reduction of its military and economic contribution" in favour of "new international institutions called upon to play a greater role in conflict resolution."[2] Other sections pertain to the organization of Canadian Forces (which must be based on their contribution to the maintenance of collective security), their budget (which we will revisit), the purchase of material (for which the main acquisition programs were subject to review), and policies on the non-proliferation of nuclear weapons.

The very (if not overly) innovative character of the Bloc's propositions drew some criticism to the party (for example, Coulon 1994), but mainly considerable indifference from English Canada. We will return later to the evaluation that one could conduct on this report. For now, it will suffice to say that the positions expressed in the report remain consistent with the principles of "Pearsonian" internationalism, but pushed to the extreme.

Between 1993 and 2005, Bloc members intervened on nearly all files specifically pertaining to defense. For the record, these include:

- the purchase of new shipborne helicopters (1993, 1998, 2000);
- the peacekeeping missions in Bosnia and Croatia (1994–95), Haiti (1994), Zaire (1996), and East Timor (1999);
- the re-establishment of order by Canadian Forces in aboriginal territories or the territories claimed as such (1993–94);
- US cruise-missile testing in Canada (1994);
- the purchase of new armoured vehicles (1995);
- the successive crises in Iraq (1996, 1998, 2003);
- the purchase of British submarines (1998);
- the training of Canadian Forces and the idea that this could involve an attack on an eventual sovereign Quebec (1999);
- the Kosovo war (1999);
- the US anti-missile defense system (2001–05);
- the war on terrorism, in Canada and abroad (2001);
- the war in Afghanistan (2002);
- the North-American Security Perimeter (2001–02);
- Bill C-42/55/17, the Public Safety Act (2001–02);
- the Israeli-Arab conflict;
- border security.

One of the most intense debates took place during and immediately after the 1995 referendum on the future of Quebec. On 26 October 1995, elected representative Jacob invited Quebecers serving in the Canadian Forces to join the ranks of an eventual Quebec Forces shortly after a victory of the "yes" camp. This invitation, prompted in part by the fact that National Defence employs nineteen thousand people in Quebec (among whom are thirteen thousand military personnel), resulted in charges of sedition against him in March 1996 by an elected representative of the Reform Party

(*Le Soleil* 1996); nevertheless, he was acquitted the following June. In general, however, the Bloc left the Parti Québécois in charge of outlining the policies of the potential future state, including defense (Roussel and Robichaud, 186–9).

During the 1997 elections, the Bloc presented a platform akin to the 1994 dissenting report because it included a reinforcement of the UN role and a reduction in military expenditures (Bloc Québécois 1997). The result of the campaign was a disappointment, however, and the Bloc lost its official opposition status, although this did not come as a surprise. The 2000 elections were even more of a disappointment because the Bloc found itself tied with the federal Liberals in Quebec in terms of seats.

In the first few years of the twenty-first century, the Bloc seemed destined to suffer a long period of stagnation. But the sponsorship scandal, which reached its peak shortly after December 2003, gave it new life. In the 2004 elections, the Bloc won fifty-four districts, equalling its 1993 performance. The following year, while Paul Martin's minority Liberal Government vacillated, the Bloc equipped itself with a new political program describing its vision of a sovereign Quebec. The latter is an important document, because until then, the Bloc would only react to federal files, leaving the description of the broad political directions of an independent Quebec to the Parti Québécois. The positions detailed in the document reflected even more of an internationalist approach than did the 1994 document: importance of the United Nations and other international institutions (including NATO and NORAD), preference for multilateralism and associated values (solidarity, equality of peoples, dialogue, peaceful conflict resolution, rule of law), adoption of niche policies and identification with states often described as "middle powers," such as Switzerland, Denmark, and Sweden (Bloc Québécois 2005, 48–56). Beyond these broad directions, it is appropriate to examine some of the most important files, most importantly defense relations with the United States.

MILITARY COOPERATION WITH THE UNITED STATES: AN AMBIVALENT RELATIONSHIP

In 1994–95, on the eve of the second referendum and at a time when their party constituted the official opposition in Ottawa, elected representatives from the Bloc Québécois did not forgo any opportunity to demonstrate their interest in Canadian-US military cooperation. The objective was certainly to demonstrate to Washington that the Quebec sovereignists were responsible and conscious of US sensitivities regarding defense matters. Anticipating a referendum battle, they wanted to avoid a situation where concerns expressed by the United States could be used as ammunition by the federalists and subsequently complicate the establishment of the new state.

In addition to advocating, as did the leaders of the Parti Québécois, the participation of a sovereign Quebec in NORAD, Lucien Bouchard supported, in January 1994, the continuation of US cruise missiles testing over Canadian territory. With respect to this issue, he argued that "insofar as it benefits from the collective security largely provided by the United States, Canada must be willing to collaborate in the establishment of a strategic deterrence capability."[3]

However, Bloc members appear to be very sensitive about matters pertaining to Canada's political and military sovereignty, especially when they feel that the "internationalist" conception of security, which they uphold, is in danger. Thus, cooperation with the United States would not be achieved at the expense of multilateral institutions and international law. This tension has become particularly evident since the George W. Bush administration assumed power in January 2001. The evolution of the Bloc's attitude toward the United States is particularly discernable in two specific files, which are the debates concerning NORAD's functions (including antimissile defense) and the long show of force between Washington and Baghdad that culminated in the March 2003 invasion of Iraq.

NORAD AND THE ANTIMISSILE DEFENSE SYSTEM

One of the most revealing files of the evolution of the Bloc's attitude towards the United States is that of NORAD, and in particular, of this command's contribution to the functioning of the antimissile defense system set up by the United States. In 1994, the Bloc put forth, in its *Dissenting Report*, rather surprising proposals regarding NORAD's future. This document, which first stresses United Nations reform, proposes that the military alliances of which Canada is a member (NATO and NORAD) "adjust their strategic orientation according to the needs of the UN." Thus, NORAD would have to progressively open up to all countries in the Americas, starting with

Mexico, and would carry out peacekeeping tasks when necessary. The agreement would then become "a military alliance providing new member states with political and economic stability and thus allowing for the expansion of economic and commercial treaties to include new partners, thus consolidating the American economic bloc." This NORAD, profoundly reconsidered and reformed, could also allow a "revaluation of public institutions" by being placed "under the direct responsibility of a permanent conference of the Heads of State."[4] Thus, NORAD would be transformed from an aerospace command into nothing more and nothing less than an institution of collective regional security, comparable to the Organization for Security and Co-operation in Europe (OSCE)!

This document, like many others, reveals a lack of understanding of the nature and role of NORAD and of US interests in terms of defense by both the Bloc and the Parti Québécois. First, the sovereignists have a tendency to limit Canadian-US military cooperation to NORAD. Nevertheless, there are numerous other agreements that are never mentioned – such as the Permanent Joint Board of Defense (PJBD) and in which Quebec's participation does not seem to be considered desirable or essential. Second, the sovereignists have a tendency to reduce North America's air defense to nothing more than NORAD. As the US political analyst Joseph T. Jockel emphasized as far back as 1980, this attitude prevented them from considering alternative options:

> From a tactical perspective, Quebec's membership in NORAD
> and the consequent placement of Quebec's air defense under
> NORAD's operational control would be the best type of air
> defense cooperation between Quebec and the other two North-
> American countries. Nevertheless, effective methods can be
> found to integrate Quebec in the continental air defence system
> without however integrating it in NORAD. These methods had
> constituted the basis for the relations that pertained strictly to air
> defense, which existed between the United States and Canada
> prior to the establishment of NORAD in 1957.[5]

These alternatives will never be brought up by the sovereignists. Finally, in the third place, the sovereignists have a tendency to put the North American Aerospace Defense Command, a purely military structure, on the same footing as organizations that have a

largely political vocation, such as NATO. This is a recurrent problem. For example, in 1978, Jean-Pierre Charbonneau and Gilbert
Paquette explained in a document describing the Sovereignty-
Association project, that "NORAD's situation is exactly the same as
NATO's but on a smaller scale. It constitutes a Canadian-American
mutual defence pact."[6] However, the NORAD agreement is not a
treaty comparable to the North Atlantic Treaty, nor an organization
comparable to NATO, nor even a regional command comparable to
the Allied Command Europe (ACE) or NATO's Allied Command Atlantic (ACLANT). It is an "executive agreement" between the governments of Canada and of the United States. NORAD's command
is entrusted with very restricted powers compared to the authority
of NATO's regional commands. As well, the entire content of the accord aims to reduce the two countries' military – and a fortiori political – involvements to a minimum.

Furthermore, the United States has always been very reluctant
to set up mechanisms that could give another state oversight rights
in the organization of the defense of the US territory or on the
control of their nuclear deterrence system. Therefore, they would
probably not welcome the Bloc's 1994 proposal, which aims to
transform NORAD into a « a military alliance [expanded to include
Latin-American states] providing political and economic stability to
the new member states." Ten years later, Mexico's eventual participation would remain a taboo subject in Washington – and even in
Mexico. A government of an independent Quebec that would
champion such a project, or any other measure aiming to politicize
or multilateralize the continent's defense, would have considerably
reduced Quebec's chances of being integrated in NORAD.[7]

The debate on antimissile defense, which intensified particularly
after the announcement of a first deployment phase in 2002,
points to the fact that this lack of understanding has not completely
disappeared – even if the Bloc's position in this field is certainly
better informed. Furthermore, this debate allows us to measure the
aversion of this rather left-leaning (although very moderately so)
organization toward a very conservative US administration.

The arguments used by the Bloc parallel those of the majority of
the opposition and echo a position consistent with Quebec's public
opinion, which is rather unsympathetic to the project. Thus, Canada should not follow the United States along a course that risks increasing military spending, leading to the militarization of space,

and being harmful to nuclear non-proliferation policies. Furthermore, such a program could be harmful to Canada's international
image and compromise its multilateral relations. Instead of participating in a project of questionable reliability and effectiveness, Ottawa should remain loyal to its internationalist tradition and
address, as priorities, environmental problems and real sources of
international insecurity such as poverty, ignorance and weak democratic institutions (Bachand; Bloc Québécois 2006).

Although reflecting the established consensus within Québécois
society on this question, the Bloc's position creates a contradiction
that is particularly visible in the "Proposition principale" handed
out in October 2005: whereas article 270 states that a "sovereign
Quebec must participate in NORAD," article 271 states that a "sovereign Quebec must not participate in the American antimissile
shield," which implies that the former is possible without the latter
(Bloc Québécois 2005, 54). This is an illusion that the federal government itself has, because, despite its February 2005 "refusal," a
bilateral agreement allows NORAD to transmit to the defense system
command information concerning the trajectory of objects to in-
tercept. In fact, regardless of what then Prime Minister Paul Martin
said, Canada contributes to the "shield." The problem with the
Bloc's position is that it would probably be very difficult for a sovereign Quebec to negotiate its participation in NORAD without at
least reaching a similar agreement, unless it succeeds in convincing
the Pentagon to go without the information that the two commands transmit to each other, which seems at best unlikely.[8]

THE IRAQI QUESTION

The debates on Canada's position throughout the different epi-
sodes of the long conflict between the United States and Saddam
Hussein's Iraq also illustrate the evolution of the Bloc's attitude towards Washington, as well as the party members' discomfort with
the use of force.

In 1990, in the months preceding the launch of Operation
Desert Storm (January 1991) against Iraqi forces occupying Ku-
wait, the Bloc was ambivalent, at times backing the Conservative
Government, at times taking the side of the Liberal and NDP opposition (Coulon 1992, 89–99; Lortie and Paquin, A5). Thus, after
having preferred to maintain economic sanctions, hold a peace

conference for the entire Middle East, and implement a peace plan proposed by France, the Bloc (along with the federal Liberals and also the Parti Québécois) ultimately supported the government's decision to go to war against Iraq. This position incurred significant criticism against the two sovereignist parties by several militants. The two parties justified their position by invoking internationalist principles, such as the necessity of ensuring respect for international law, and emphasizing that the coalition forces' offensive was supported by the UN (Lessard).

In November 1996, the Bloc reluctantly backed the Chrétien Government's decision to support the US response to Iraqi attacks against the Kurdish population, "while calling upon Prime Minister Chrétien not to blindly follow Bill Clinton's administration but to take the necessary measures to ensure that the United States' actions are within reason."9

A similar reluctance appeared during the February 1998 debate on the means to force Iraq to respect United Nations resolutions and to rid itself of any weapons of mass destruction it may eventually possess. The Bloc believed that diplomatic efforts had to be given greater opportunity to succeed but did not oppose military action as long as such action was authorized by the UN (Coulon 1998, A1; Young 1998, 18).

After having committed to support "without reservation" any initiative that Canada would take to help the United States following the 9/11 terrorist attacks (Buzzetti and Cornellier, A4), Gilles Duceppe specified that the response had to be one that would uphold the democratic values that had been targeted by these attacks, and therefore advocated an active participation by the UN to the war on terrorism, as well as the creation of an international criminal tribunal to try suspects (Duceppe 2001). He also wanted Canada to avoid using the principle of solidarity with the United States as a pretext to blindly support all of Washington's initiatives. Although supporting Canada's participation in the offensive against al Qaeda in Afghanistan, Bloc members deplored the fact that this intervention was made outside the UN framework. They were also among the first to be outraged by the treatment of Taliban prisoners. In their opinion, Canada was an accomplice to what they perceived to be an unjustified violation of the Geneva Convention and a setback in terms of upholding the fundamental principles of the lawful state (Buzzetti 2002a, A1).

The Bloc's opposition during the international diplomatic crisis that preceded the onset of the second Gulf War in March 2003 constituted without any doubt, along with the opposition to the antimissile defense project, the most virulent expression of Quebecers' aversion to the Bush administration's security policy. Reflecting the attitude of their political clientele, Bloc representatives were adamantly opposed to Canada's participation in any military intervention, which did not meet the conditions that usually justify resorting to armed conflict; specifically, legitimate defense, a significant threat to international security recognized by the United Nations Security Council, or the perpetration of genocide (Duceppe 2001). Instead, they supported the continuation of negotiations and the intensification of Canadian diplomatic action. For instance, MP Francine Lalonde proposed that Canada serve as an intermediary between the US and Iraqi governments, a role that, according to her, conformed more with Canadian tradition than that of "waging war" (Buzzetti 2002b, A3). Furthermore, elected representatives from the Bloc were systematically opposed to any measure that could give the impression that Canada was indirectly helping the United States. They required among other things the repatriation of Canadian soldiers embedded in US units in the Gulf region; also, they criticized the decision to increase Canadian participation in Afghanistan following the onset of the war in Iraq (Massie and Roussel, 74–5).

There is a striking evolution between Lucien Bouchard's support for cruise missile tests in 1994 and the Bloc's stubborn refusal to encourage the government to take part in the United States' ballistic missile defense project. This evolution can first be attributed to the aversion of this centre-left organization to the conservative policies of the US administration and, in particular, for those that run contrary to the fundamental principles of internationalism, specifically respect for international law, multilateralism, and institutionalism (Roussel). However, this attitude transcends a simple ideological disjuncture. In fact, it probably also involves electoral calculations. This feeling of discomfort with regards to the Republican administration is widespread among the francophone Québécois population.[10] In that sense, not only are the Bloc's positions consistent but they are also on the same page as those of the population it seeks to represent. Finally, in the absence of a referendum date, the need to win Washington's favour also became less pressing.

In 2002, Francine Lalonde summarized quite well the discomfort of Bloc members regarding the United States: "The necessary counterbalance to the dominant United States influence, which can only be achieved by a game of alliances built through multilateral institutions, has become even more intensely felt since the terrible attacks of 11 September 2001 [...] The instinctual defensive reaction that followed, though understandable, has subjected us to strong pressures. While being sensitive to the security needs of our neighbours, we must not lose track of our values and interests. For this reason, certain aspects of the cooperation with the United States in terms of security are a source of concern for us."[11]

Again here, the internationalist instinct prevails in as much as multilateralism has historically been considered by Canadian leaders and diplomats as a means of containing the excesses of US policies (Haglund and Roussel).

THE BLOC AND MILITARY INTERVENTIONS ABROAD: "INTERNATIONALIST" ACTIVISM

Despite their attachment to mediation and peaceful conflict resolution, elected officials from the Bloc accept the use of force for the resolution of certain crises, particularly when it is supported by a consensus at the United Nations and among Canada's Western allies.

When Jean Chrétien raised the possibility of a unilateral retreat of the Canadian Blue Helmets participating in the United Nations Protection Force (UNPROFOR) in Bosnia in January 1994, Lucien Bouchard opposed it. According to him, "Canada cannot break the pact of solidarity that it wisely, generously and courageously knitted through the years with its partners and friends within the Atlantic Council"; a retreat by Canada "would be contrary to our own perception of our humanitarian obligations" and would "signal other departures."[12] In April, the Bloc also supported the government's decision to join the United States and its NATO partners and comply with the United Nations' request for air support in Bosnia. During an emergency debate in Parliament, Bouchard argued that the credibility of the UN and of Western democracies was at stake (Bouchard 1994b).

In December 1994, Canada participated in the multinational Implementation Force (IFOR) under NATO command. The Bloc deplored the fact that by participating in this mission of peace *imposition* Canada got further away from its peace *keeping* tradition but nevertheless supported the initiative (Jacob). As they had done during the Gulf crisis, sovereignist leaders justified their support for the use of force and a Canadian participation in NATO operations by the necessity of protecting human rights and participating in peacekeeping abroad.

In 1999, as a new crisis arose in the Balkans, Bloc members upheld the government's decision to participate in NATO's air strikes against Serb troops operating in Kosovo and were among the first to require sending ground troops. The representative Daniel Turp, then foreign affairs critic, who regretted that Canada was diverging from its traditional role of peacekeeping champion and denounced the absence of a UN mandate, proved to be among the most dedicated supporters of an armed intervention in Kosovo (Bloc Québécois 1999). The sovereignist agenda inevitably influenced the attitude of Bloc members with regards to the Kosovo crisis. Gilles Duceppe, for instance, refused categorically to see the Yugoslav province torn between its different constituent groups, fearing that this could set a precedent that could then be applied to Quebec if it were to obtain independence. However, most of the Bloc's interventions would pertain to the conduct of the war or the Parliament's privileges in such circumstances (Rempel, 80–1), making the Bloc's attitude little different from that of other opposition parties.

In addition to supporting military interventions to resolve successive crises in the Balkans, the Bloc supported, during the 1990s, the principle of UN-sponsored military interventions in Haiti, the Great Lakes region of Africa, and East Timor. It also frequently took the Canadian Government to task for its lack of initiative in terms of seeking diplomatic solutions to international crises.

Thus, in general, the Bloc supports operations aiming to preserve international order as long as these conform to a given number of rules related to collective security. Nevertheless, the case of Kosovo demonstrates that these principles have not been applied in a dogmatic manner and that some of these interventions could be undertaken outside of the legal framework constituted by the United Nations Security Council resolutions when the Security Council itself seems unable to fulfill its functions. The tolerance threshold of the Quebec sovereignists was revealed to be slightly higher than generally expected.

REDUCTION IN MILITARY EXPENDITURES
AND QUEBEC-STYLE *PORK BARRELLING*

Military expenditures constitute another defense-related issue that often poses a dilemma for Bloc Québécois members. On the one hand, the party inherited the pacifist ideas that have characterised the sovereignist movement. On the other hand, it purports to be a "defender of Quebec's interests," including issues such as employment and industrial development. The problem is that the two do not always go hand in hand.

The influence of pacifist groups varied across time (Roussel and Robichaud) but became most visible in the period between the failure of the Meech Lake Accord and the return to power of the Parti Québécois in 1994, which corresponds to the time of the foundation and reinforcement of the Bloc. Military expenditures feature among the favourite targets of the pacifist faction of sovereignist militants for whom these expenditures were at best a waste of resources urgently needed in other sectors and at worse as a cause of wars (see, for example, Tremblay; Confédération des syndicats nationaux).

During the period leading up to the 1995 referendum, the Bloc's positions were clearly influenced by this perception. Thus, during the 1993 electoral campaign, the Bloc proposed among other things to reduce by 25 percent the amounts awarded to the Canadian Forces, cancel the contract for the purchase of EH-101 helicopters, and proceed to the reconversion of military industries (Tramier, A1). In the 1994 dissenting report on defense, the Bloc proposed a "rationalization of spending" on human resources and infrastructure. It also suggested abandoning certain acquisition programs such as those for submarines or armoured vehicles (Parliament of Canada 1994a, 90–5).

This approach is consistent with another idea defended by the Bloc: a focus of the Canadian Forces on specific missions, mainly in peacekeeping. The proposed rationalization should therefore subscribe to this niche logic. It would allow for the reduction of military expenditures through the concentration of resources.

The problem is that the will to reduce the sums allocated to defense hurts some of Quebec's economic interests. During the controversy over the purchase of EH-101 helicopters in 1993, some Quebec commentators accused the Bloc of harming the interests of the aerospace industry in the Montreal area. Since then, Bloc members have shown more prudence and are no longer systematically opposed to military spending. They resign themselves instead to demanding that, when decisions are made regarding such expenditures, Quebec, which according to them bears a deficit in this regard compared to other provinces, receive its "fair share" of the contracts. In doing so, they find themselves in the delicate situation of demanding for themselves what they condemn for others.

Thus, when the government announced the elimination of 16,500 positions at the Department of National Defence, the restructuring of eleven bases, six stations, and thirteen units, and a 12 percent reduction of the defense budget in 1994, the closing down of the Collège Militaire Royal de Saint-Jean became, for the sovereignists, a symbol of this inequity. The same year, when the Liberals proposed to cast aside one quarter of the CF-18 fleet in order to increase the ground forces' amount of equipment and number of troops, the Bloc accused them of threatening the future of the Bagotville base. In 1995, Bloc members denounced the Chrétien Government's decision to grant Ontario a contract of $2 billion over ten years for the construction of 651 armoured vehicles for transporting troops, without having issued a call for proposals. In addition to framing this decision as "shameless waste," they deplored the fact that no guarantee was made to Quebec regarding any fallout from which it could benefit (Gauthier, B1). In the file of the used submarines purchased from the United Kingdom in 1998, the Bloc suggested instead that this money should serve to build ships with multiple vocations intended for peace missions, which would promote the revival of Quebec's maritime industry. Finally, when the government again brought up the purchase of helicopters in 2000, the Bloc lobbied for these to be made in Quebec.

The caution henceforth demonstrated by the Bloc with respect to this file is reflected in the content of the *Dissenting Report* annexed to the *Report of the Standing Committee on National Defence and Veteran Affairs* tabled in May 2002 (Chambre des communes 2002a). Taking stock of the deplorable condition of the Canadian Forces, the Bloc accepted the idea of a substantial increase in the defense budget, as long as such an increase has been subjected to public debate and conditional upon the formulation of a new policy stance.

THE MILITARY ASSISTANCE TO
CANADIAN CIVIL AUTHORITIES

The sovereignists justify the creation of a future Quebec army on the basis of the necessity of ensuring Quebec's participation in UN missions and of assisting the civil authorities in the case of a major crisis.[13] It is therefore not surprising that the Bloc welcomed the intervention of the Canadian Forces to assist civilians during natural disasters such as the flooding of the Saguenay River in 1996, the floods in Manitoba in 1997, and the ice-storm crisis in Quebec and Ontario in 1998. Furthermore, the party is in favour of an increased collaboration between the army and the police in the fight against marijuana grow operations in Quebec and against contraband tobacco.

However, even in this file, the Bloc's position is not without inconsistencies. The participation of armed forces in the maintenance of domestic order is perceived as a double-edged sword. From the repression of the Métis Rebellion in 1885 through the October Crisis in 1970, Quebec Francophones have mainly considered military institutions as an Anglophone bastion and even as an instrument of oppression. Even if the Oka crisis (1990) and the ice-storm crisis have helped to soften this perception, the tendency has nevertheless remained.

Thus, in as far as the sovereignist movement constitutes, in the eyes of its detractors, a threat to Canadian public order, Bloc representatives fear that the Canadian Forces may be used for political ends. Throughout the Oka crisis, the Bloc appeared to be ambivalent about the military intervention. According to Lucien Bouchard, Quebecers felt "uncomfortable" because the Aboriginals were themselves claiming sovereignty. The Bloc leader considered that things would have been different if Quebecers had confronted the events as a sovereign people. In fact, according to Bouchard, a sovereign Quebec would not have had to use force because, although it would not have granted the Aboriginals territorial sovereignty, it would at least recognize their autonomy (Berger, A8).

The fear that the army could be used against Quebec resurfaced in 1999, when the *Ottawa Citizen* revealed the existence of secret military documents describing a training exercise ("the Royal Flush") during which Canadian Forces had to confront the army of an independent Quebec to repel it from Ontario. The Bloc Québécois then suspected that this information leakage was intended to intimidate Quebecers and requested a public inquiry. In 2001, the Bloc's opposition to Bill C-42 – which would have authorized, in case of emergency, the creation of a military security zone to protect all "the goods, places or items that the Canadian Forces had received instructions to protect in order to fulfill their legal obligations" – was also motivated by this fear of abuse. From the Bloc's perspective, this measure, along with the powers conferred by the Anti-Terrorism Act (Bill C-36), would facilitate a military intervention in Quebec following a unilateral declaration of independence. These concerns were partly responsible for the several amendments to this bill, which was renamed C-55 and then C-17 in 2002.

CONCLUSION

Despite its independence option, the Bloc Québécois is not fundamentally different from the other major Canadian political parties in terms of defense and security. Its positions reflect first and foremost an insistence upon the internationalist values and ideas that have dominated foreign policy since the end of the World War II (see Nossal, 154–9). In this regard, the Bloc reinforces rather than questions the consensus uniting Canadian society on this point – at least in terms of the substance of these ideas if not in the modalities of their application.

The main distinction between the Bloc and other federal political organizations – which is the support for the sovereignist project and the will to defend what is perceived as Quebec's interests – results in only marginal changes in the party's position on defense issues. This distinction has played a role in some files including the US cruise-missile tests, the purchase of some equipment or the role of Canadian Forces in the war on terrorism. However, the Bloc's position on most files is determined more by its ideological position (centre-left) or by a desire to echo the concerns of its political clientele.

Regarding this last point, the Bloc is certainly an excellent transmitter of francophone Quebecers' concerns regarding defense and security. When taking internationalist stands, opposing Canada's participation in the war on Iraq and the antimissile system, opposing the increase in military spending, or agreeing to have armed forces play a more important role of support to civil authorities, the Bloc is merely reflecting widely accepted ideas in Quebec society.

The Bloc's contribution to the debates regarding Canadian defense policy is probably difficult to evaluate. If, as claimed by J.L. Granatstein in the *Ottawa Citizen*, Quebecers have too much of an influence on foreign and defense policy (which is a highly debatable claim), it is nevertheless difficult to attribute this to a direct influence by the Bloc. In fact, it is probably more realistic to state that the contribution of *indépendantiste* representatives is in general quite marginal given the little relevance that their rhetoric has for English Canada. It is true that few Bloc representatives are truly interested in these questions, with the notable exceptions of Daniel Turp, Francine Lalonde, and Stéphane Bergeron. However, the Bloc is not significantly different from other political parties, and the problem has more to do with the Canadian parliamentary class in general (Bland and Rempel; Rempel) than with Bloc members in particular.

If the Bloc tends to represent the opinion of most Quebecers in terms of defense, it is difficult, on the other hand, to determine if it has played a role in changing this opinion. On the electoral front, these security questions are rarely (even never) decisive factors in Quebec. The Bloc has certainly gathered all the support it could hope for by opposing Canadian participation in the war in Iraq and the US antimissile defense system. Furthermore, it has little to gain by attempting to change the consensus that seems to have formed within Quebec society.

Nevertheless, this society has changed since the 1960s and 1970s. Having become more educated and considerably more interested in contemporary international affairs, its opinions have become more nuanced and better defined than they used to be. If the sovereignists contributed to this change, they were most likely but one factor among many. On the other hand, the evolution of the *independantiste* movement's positions is certainly a reflection of the changes in Quebec society over the last thirty years or so (Roussel).

In fact, the most original contribution of the Bloc may reside within the sovereignist movement itself. The Parti Québécois has only rarely debated these questions, at least in public. The Bloc, which was forced to take positions on a series of issues that did not directly concern the sovereignists, has therefore had to clearly articulate the movement's positions on such matters. Since 1990, the ideas of sovereignists have become more profound, subtle, and coherent. They have also come to rest upon more solid data and more experienced research. The electoral platform (known as the "proposition principale") submitted by the BQ's executive at the party's October 2005 conference attests to this evolution, since foreign affairs and defense were given critical attention (Bloc Québécois, 2005).

Nevertheless, weaknesses and inconsistencies remain. It is very tempting, especially for the Bloc's political opponents, to attribute these to the pacifist tendencies of part of its political clientele, to the purported "amateurism" of sovereignists in the military domain, to a distortion engendered by the *independantiste* project, or by the difficulty to reconcile the defense of "Quebec's interests" in a Parliament representing Canada as a whole.

The Bloc's line of thinking, even if influenced slightly by the pacifist ideas that persist (although to an increasingly marginal extent) in the sovereignist movement, remains very traditional, from the perspective of Canadian strategic culture. Since the mid-1970s, sovereignists have clearly been more internationalist than pacifist (Roussel and Théorêt 2004). In fact, the explanation for this resides most likely in the centre-left position of the Bloc, which makes it a critic of everything labelled "security" or "defense."[14] Thus, throughout its history, the BQ has encountered the difficulties faced by any political party having to deal with contradictions between the desires of its political clientele and the necessities of diplomacy and military planning.

NOTES

1 The Parti Québécois's evolution in this field is described in Roussel and Robichaud and in Roussel and Théorêt.

2 Translated from French. Parliament of Canada 1994a, 85.

3 Translated from French. Dion, A1.

4 Translated from French. Parliament of Canada 1994a, 88–9.

5 Translated from French. Jockel 1980, 320.

6 Translated from French. Jean-Pierre Charbonneau and Gilbert Paquette, 466.

7 Chances that seem somewhat reduced judging from comments such as those of Joseph Jockel (1995, 9).

8 An observation first made by David G. Haglund. See, as well, Roussel.

9 Translated from French. Young 1996, A5.

10 To the extent that some, like David Haglund, even suspect that Quebec public opinion has spilled over into anti-Americanism.

11 Translated from French. Parliament of Canada 2002b, 351.

12 Translated from French. Bouchard 1994a.

13 According to the text of article 17 of the Future of Quebec Bill presented to the population for approval at the time of the 1995 referendum.

14 The New Democratic Party (NDP), which is generally further to the left than the Bloc, faces similar contradictions and sometimes takes positions that surprise or irritate military officials and defense experts.

10

Interpreting Quebec's International Relations: Whim or Necessity?

NELSON MICHAUD

INTRODUCTION

During the past few years, a forty-year-old debate centred on the nature of Quebec's international presence has surfaced once again. In summer and early autumn 2005, two Quebec ministers, Monique Gagnon-Tremblay in International Relations and Benoît Pelletier in Intergovernmental Affairs, voiced opinions that were dissenting from Ottawa's position that calls for "One country – one voice" in the conduct of international relations. They argued that Quebec should be actively involved in the crafting of Canada's international stance in areas that fall under provincial jurisdiction and that it should speak with its own voice in some forums, such as UNESCO, where matters under Quebec's constitutional responsibility are discussed on a regular basis (Ministère des Relations internationales).

In fact, Premier Jean Charest's government did have reason to expect more from Ottawa on this question. During the 2004 election campaign, Canadian Prime Minister Paul Martin had promised to devise a formula that would enable Quebec to play a more active role in the international arena, specifically in those areas that fall under its domestic authority and constitutional jurisdiction (Martin 2004). Much to Quebec's surprise, the International Policy Statement issued by the Martin Government just one year later adopted the exact opposite position (Government of Canada). Once again, an old wound had been opened, and Paul Martin's

Quebec lieutenant, Jean Lapierre, and Quebec's Benoît Pelletier eventually exchanged harsh words through the media on this issue.

Now that Canadians have given Stephen Harper the mandate to run the country, the question could take a new turn.[1] The newly elected prime minister, in a speech delivered before the Quebec City Chamber of Commerce during the campaign, committed his government to a greater international presence for the provinces (Harper). Some might feel that we are back to the days of Paul Gérin-Lajoie and Paul Martin Sr as the arguments from an activist Quebec are met with the familiar fears and reticence emanating from both the Privy Council Office and the Department of Foreign Affairs. In order to avoid playing the same old record once again, it is important to take a fresh look at the issue. It is time to call upon analysts who can provide some perspective before tackling that most fundamental question as to whether Quebec's involvement in international relations are necessary, as some maintain, or whether it is only a pretentious whim, as others believe. This study will attempt to answer that question.

Since the onus of demonstrating the necessity for such an involvement is more demanding and, as a result, more compelling, I will base my analysis on this hypothesis. I will try to validate this hypothesis from parameters that will bring into the limelight two key dimensions that define the issue: the interests and the constraints. By leaving aside the visceral argument advocating the uniqueness of Quebec, these two variables offer objective grounds on which to test the hypothesis. Hence, I will first define these two dimensions, and I will then briefly review a few cases of some other federated entities in order to map out options that exist and are implemented. This will lead to considering which options Canada, Quebec, and all provinces who wish to play an international role might choose from. But first we must put this study into the proper context by looking at the actual basis of Quebec's claims for an international role.

BACKGROUND

To overcome the complexity of the issue, we must first take an in-depth look into what constitutes the foundation of Quebec's claim for a right to be present on the international stage. In spite of arguments presented here earlier, one must conclude that there is still no real consensus as to the strength of such claims. In addition, this is an area that has not attracted a lot of attention from academics, as the number of specialists in this field is very small. The literature is admittedly quite sparse, but available studies confirm that Quebec's claims are not just a reflection of several generations of opportunistic politicians seeking international visibility for short-term political gain.[2] Rather, there are easily identifiable historical roots for this position, one which has been supported by all political parties in Quebec, as well as by the business community and the general population.

Quebec's presence abroad dates back to the nineteenth century, when commercial agents were sent to London, Dublin, Paris, and later Brussels. By contrast, it is interesting to note that in those days Canada had to operate from the British legations around the world since it was not allowed to conduct its own foreign relations, these being under the Empire's responsibility until the adoption of the Statute of Westminster (1931). Quebec's agents were the precursors of today's *délégués* and *délégués généraux*, who are contemporary Quebec representatives around the world.

These first attempts were followed much later, in 1940, by the opening of a trade office in New York City under the Liberal Government of Adélard Godbout. The rationale for this initiative was largely economic and financial in nature and was one of the tools designed to help pull the province out of the Great Depression. Despite his reluctance to get involved in international affairs, Premier Maurice Duplessis, who succeeded Godbout in 1944 and ruled the province for the next fifteen years, kept the office open. These meagre operations were strengthened substantially after the Duplessis era and became an important part of the overall vision of the Quiet Revolution.

When Quebecers elected Jean Lesage and his Liberal "Thunder Team" in June 1960, the province was ready to take on the many challenges associated with the impending transformation of Quebec society. The people of Quebec had made the choice to form a modern polity and to become credible partners equipped to meet the many needs of the twentieth century. At the heart of the process was a strong will to modernize its tools of governance, in part through the establishment of a professional public service. However, these sweeping changes would not have been possible had Quebec not had the ability to draw upon the experience and expertise of other francophone governments in this area. In order to assist with this gargantuan task, the Quebec Government signed agreements, first with the Government of France. The initiative met strong opposition from Ottawa, a reaction that grew stronger when Quebec received an invitation directly from Gabon to participate in an international summit on education, a matter under the sole jurisdiction of provincial authorities (Martin 1985, Morin).[3]

The rationale for Quebec's presence in the international arena was first set out in April 1965 by Paul Gérin-Lajoie, Quebec's minister of education, during an address before Montreal's Consular Corps. He added to his "Doctrine" a few weeks later in Quebec City at a dinner with a host of European scholars, and it was at the Legislative Assembly in 1967, during the second reading of the bill creating the Ministère des relations intergouvernementales, that he phrased his arguments the way they have been cited and relied upon to this day: Quebec's international relations, he argued, are "the foreign extension of its domestic jurisdiction" (Quebec Legislative Assembly). Almost forty years later, Premier Jean Charest paraphrased this very same position in a speech delivered at the École nationale d'administration publique when he stated that "ce qui est de compétence du Quebec chez nous, est de compétence du Québec partout."[4]

The man most responsible for the Gérin-Lajoie Doctrine was André Patry, a constitutional lawyer and an artisan of the Quiet Revolution (Aird). Patry grounded his policy proposal on a number of important decisions rendered by the Judicial Committee of the Privy Council in the 1930s. These rulings clearly established that provinces have full responsibility over the application and implementation of international treaties and standards in areas that come under their jurisdiction. This interpretation is based in part on the total silence of the Canadian Constitution on questions of international relations and foreign policy. It also draws upon on an important body of jurisprudence relating to section 92 of the British North America Act, which defines legislative responsibilities of the provinces.[5]

Quebec's international activity is rooted firmly in these constitutional grounds. For more than forty-five years, Quebec has built a network of delegations abroad in regions that reflect its priorities and major interests. The Quebec Government has also entered into more than 550 international agreements, three hundred of which are still in effect today. In 1985, it solved another festering problem when Canadian Prime Minister Brian Mulroney and Quebec Premier Pierre-Marc Johnson agreed on an official status for Quebec that allowed the province to participate in the meetings and institutions of La Francophonie as an autonomous member. In addition, Quebec's National Assembly adopted legislation in 2002 that gave it the power to evaluate all international treaties signed by Canada in areas that fall under provincial jurisdiction and to vote upon their eventual enactment and implementation in Quebec.

While looking at these issues, a relatively new parameter must be considered, and that is the impact of globalization. Every day, new norms and standards are negotiated internationally in a wide range of areas, many of them specifically on matters that come under provincial control or shared jurisdiction. This is not unique to Canada – all federated entities have been required to address this issue in recent years, from Mexican states, to Bavarian and Austrian Länder, and even to US states. These subnational actors are fully aware that they must be equipped to deal effectively with the negative aspects of globalization, many of which can only be addressed locally, and that by the same token they must also be in a position to take full advantage of its many benefits. Quite simply, it is those very opportunities that define the new modernity, and Quebec, along with its many federated partners, just cannot take the risk of ignoring this reality. Nevertheless, many feel that while this argument might be logical and compelling, it is not enough to justify Quebec's presence in the international arena. There must be something more substantial, they argue, to justify Quebec's active presence in international affairs.

AN ANALYTICAL FRAMEWORK

There is a very rational argument that addresses this quandary, one that also lays the theoretical foundation for an active international role for Canadian provinces. This framework rests upon the many and diverse causes that motivate and guide the international activity of any state, and can be divided into two basic areas: preponderant interests and basic constraints. These two causes operate in opposite directions. The more a country can define its interests within a specific international field, the more likely it is to become involved in this area. Conversely, the more constraints there are on a country's international activity in a certain area, the less likely it is to take action on that front. This relationship between a state's international role and its interests and constraints can be illustrated by the following equation:

$$R \text{ (role)} = \frac{I \text{ (interests)}}{C \text{ (constraints)}}$$

These two factors are not constant. As a consequence, a reduction in constraints will lead quite logically to an increase in international activity, even if the level of interest remains substantially the same. It would then be said that a state takes advantage of a favourable context to become more actively involved in a particular domain. It may also occur that the level of both the interests and the constraints increase simultaneously, leading inevitably to a heightened degree of tension and friction between the parties involved. In fact, this portrays rather accurately the situation Quebec faced under the Martin Liberal Government in 2005: by influencing issue areas such as health and culture, globalization contributed to the rise of Quebec interests to be defended at the international level while; at the same time, Ottawa was raising the levels of constraints on Quebec's international presence. As we can see, the model offered here helps us better understand the clash we witnessed.

It is important at this point to make a functional distinction between interests and constraints. Although constraints may sometimes emanate from domestic causes – a scarcity of resources, for example – they generally come from outside the entity that wishes to become involved in international relations. It is more difficult, therefore, to exercise any real control over constraints. Interests, on the other hand, may be stimulated by external factors, but they are largely a matter of evaluation and perception, and arise from within the state itself. Consequently, they can be influenced much more directly by the state's political and administrative decision-makers.

The model outlined above refines our approach. It demonstrates that Quebec will vary the level of its international involvement in response to objective pressures, which are directly proportional to the growing volume of interests that need to be defended at the international level, and conversely proportional to constraints exercised against this will.

UNDERSTANDING INTERESTS

The next question flows directly from this primary conclusion, as we must first appraise whether these interests are growing or whether they are merely a convenient fabrication, a concocted body of rhetoric to serve the desires of a nationalist Quebec to become an international player for ideological reasons. In fact, we are back to our initial question: whether these interests are the mere whims of a province longing for recognition, a behaviour that could well penalize the other partners in the federation, or whether they do reflect a new international reality and translate into a necessity.

The first clue is offered to us by the changes that are characterizing our polity. Among the key changes, some go beyond diasporas and demography; they affect domestic politics and make domestic politics in turn influence, more than ever, foreign-policymaking. Here, we might first refer to the newest information and communication technologies. However, no matter how important this factor is in the conduct of international relations, it is difficult to agree that it has profoundly changed the *purpose* of the exercise. As well, an increasingly integrated economy is often cited as another example of change and it is considered by many to be reason enough for the provinces to become more directly involved in international affairs. However, it is important to understand that this phenomenon is merely the continuation of a process that began several centuries ago, which can be traced back to the time of the great explorations – and much earlier. Closer to home, Wilfrid Laurier campaigned in 1911 on a platform of reinstituting free trade with the United States, calling upon a model that had first been used in 1854 before finally being abandoned during the us Civil War. Mackenzie King signed a trade agreement with the United States in 1935 – and Brian Mulroney built a career upon taking the next step. Moreover, the most important impact an integrated economy has on polities and domestic policies affects labour conditions – that is, social norms – a factor that we will consider later. Again, as we can see, this factor, although hardly negligible, is in itself not prominent in advocating for a stronger international presence from Quebec.

To find a better answer, we have only to look back to the end of World War II. This period is characterized by the emergence of two phenomena that were actually rooted in separate causes and that evolved independently at first. They ultimately converged in a manner that had a lasting effect. Among their many impacts, they brought Quebec to develop new interests, leading to action on the international scene.

The first of these two phenomena was the establishment of social programs. They had been a relatively scarce commodity before 1945 but began to proliferate in many countries after the war as a direct result of the new wealth generated by the war economy. There was also a feeling that governments had to respond to the needs of the people and to do to whatever was necessary to prevent major crises like the Great Depression that had dominated the Western world throughout the 1930s. This was accompanied by a social revolution that eventually resulted in a new set of social norms and international standards, many of which were adopted at the international level – and with dizzying speed. The world had become a new place: there were significantly more women in the labour market, demobilized soldiers were returning home in huge numbers, and local economies were evolving faster than they could be understood. A host of new problems had to be solved, and in Canada most of these issues fell directly under provincial jurisdiction. Quebec was thrust into the process of dealing with these issues on a daily basis, its leaders forced to devise new approaches and novel techniques in order to accommodate the unprecedented demands of society. In the process, Quebec redefined the relationship with its people – and the Quiet Revolution was launched.

At the same time, we witnessed the second phenomenon as international institutions emerged. There had been previous attempts to establish such institutions following World War I, when US President Woodrow Wilson convinced world leaders that this approach could well eliminate wars in the future. But the embryonic League of Nations did not survive, in part because the principal protagonist could not elicit the support of his own people. The US was still strongly isolationist, and Americans rejected the idea sacrificing a portion of their sovereignty to be a member of a supranational organization.

After World War II, the situation was ripe for more permanent change. With the establishment of the United Nations, the reconstruction of Europe as per the vision of Jean Monet and Robert Schumann, the rebirth of the Commonwealth, the emergence of La Francophonie, and the liberating headiness of decolonization, international institutions assumed a new role on the world scene. Their mission was clear from the outset, and they continue to do their work to this day. They were there to set norms and to establish common benchmarks, initially in relation to security (UN, NATO) and the economy (the Bretton Woods institutions), which were the long-established domains of international relations – and finally in a host of other important areas as well, including social programs.

This is where the two important engines of the twentieth century finally met: as most countries either created their own social programs or modified existing ones, international institutions were just blossoming. It was inevitable that international institutions would ultimately turn to social programs, defining with their members a new set of norms that all could strive to achieve. This is how "the world in Canada" phenomenon started to take shape.

It soon became clear that these international standards were being negotiated in fields that fell, in most cases, under the decentralized jurisdiction of federated entities, and not that of the central government, which nevertheless remained the sole actor with a voice in the international arena. In concrete terms, this means that even if they do not enjoy formal international recognition, federated entities, which often have the exclusive constitutional responsibility for those important areas, must be able to react, adapt, and redefine their own standards and programs in order to meet the newly established international values. Typically, this means that legislation must be amended and regulations modified, sometimes substantially. In so doing, federated governments have to alter the expression of a social consensus. In other words, they have to intervene in what can be considered as an integral part of their own social fabric.

The options that arise are then easy to define: when states are called on to act as a result of the new international rules, they can sit idle, waiting for these standards to be established and then react to them after the fact, even if this involves changes imposed on their social consensus; or they can try influencing the crafting of these new values upstream, so that these norms to be established reflect their ideals and their identity. Of course, federated entities that do not wish to remain reactive need the tools to intervene before international standards are set; otherwise, they might see their specificity be washed away by the waves globalization brings to their shores.

Concretely, we can say that the increase in interests brought by a globalized world indeed creates an objective pressure in favour of Quebec's involvement on the international scene. This partial conclusion, however, needs to be confronted by other factors.

NATURE OF THE CONSTRAINTS

If interests have a guiding role in this issue, constraints have also come to play an important part in the process. As mentioned above, constraints often surface for domestic reasons and can usually be traced to the availability of resources. To overcome these constraints, the solution rests on the input of human, material, informational, financial, or functional resources. However, a state may not have access to them, or may prefer to invest them in other areas. The state, then, can generally exercise some control over this type of constraint. Most constraints, however, are imposed from the outside, and governments have little control over them.

When considering Quebec as an international actor, it is too easy to blame Ottawa for all of the external constraints. This allows no real understanding of the issues and is not particularly productive. It is true that blaming Ottawa can sometimes be politically useful for some, but it does not stand up under any meaningful analysis, since the constraints imposed by the federal government are secondary to those that emanate from the complexities of the international system itself. These can be traced directly to the Treaty of Westphalia (1648), which established an anarchical structure where nation-states became the only recognized players under international law. More importantly, all states that were then known were unitary: that is, they were organized under a single level of government.

In fact, it took close to another 140 years for the world to see its first federation when the USA was created at the end of the eighteenth century. Although this first federation has become very centralized today, it is no longer alone in the world. In fact, approximately 40 percent of the world's population now lives under a federated arrangement of some kind. After suffering setbacks in the early 1990s with the implosion of the USSR and Yugoslavia, the federal formula has regained popularity and has come to be seen once again as offering solutions to populations in countries torn apart by deeply rooted regional differences. Nevertheless, the international system still recognizes federated actors only when they have been granted legitimately the capacity to assume an international role of their own. This can be done in two different ways.

At present, international institutions function within the parameters established by their members, an important aspect that cannot be ignored. In large part, members have adopted the Westphalian system of recognition, whereby nation-states are known as the only legitimate international actors. This rule could certainly be changed if these institutions, perhaps inspired by the European Union, ever chose to develop a framework that recognizes multiple levels of autonomy for their members. It would then be possible for subnational states and regions to have a legitimate place at the table.

In order to reduce that particular form of constraint from within international institutions, it is possible to begin working toward a form of recognition that would finally allow a place at the table for federated entities that have the sole constitutional responsibility to act and legislate in the areas of interest to the institution. No federated entity can reach this goal by itself and the strategy of working with "like minded countries," one that is very dear to Ottawa, could finally be put to good use by Quebec; it would then operate in a joint effort with other federated entities willing to defend their interests upstream. Quebec and other similarly interested participants would then have direct access to the international institutions in those areas under their purview – and the question of "going through Ottawa" would no longer be an issue. However, no matter how good this solution may sound to some, it risks encountering a strong opposition coming from world actors who are not willing to share their clout and power.

We must therefore consider a second way to have the provinces' international action and presence be legitimized: it is by negotiating their recognition with Ottawa in a formula that could very well be accepted by the members of the major international institutions, as it is standard practice. Before this can be done, however, it is important that Quebec and other interested provinces devise a comprehensive definition of the areas for which they are responsible – and define their new role as the "partner" within a number of international agencies. After negotiating with the province, Canada must also recognize this new reality once and for all. Given the increasingly important role that is being played by these international institutions, it is no longer possible for Ottawa to include (or exclude) the provinces whenever they wish, a system highly dependant on the goodwill of the government of the day. It is essential that Quebec and the other provinces be allowed to defend their interests when the debates are actually occurring, and in order to do so they must rely on a stable and predictable framework that will not be at the mercy of political winds.

This information brings the third part to the answer this analysis is looking for. Of course, constraints do not justify the necessity of conducting international relations; nevertheless, they outline obstacles that exist on the way to exercising some influence on international vectors of change that will affect, sooner or later, federated entities' polities. To surmount these obstacles, federated entities have to internally contribute appropriate resources toward international questions; they can work collectively toward their recognition in international forums – which is at best hopeful; and, consequently, they also need to invest themselves federally in order to remove the systemic stumbling blocks identified above.

A UNIQUE CASE?

Most federated entities that take up the challenge of functioning as a credible international partner generally find that it is very demanding and have come to the conclusion that it can take a great deal of resources. A factor that maximizes the results from these efforts is the presence of international precedents, which can compensate, to some extent, for the lack of resources. In other words, groundbreaking initiatives are more costly than actions based on successful experiences, turned into accepted practices, by other players. And indeed, there are many examples of federated entities that are active and exert an influence within the international arena. A typology of these examples can be mapped out on a matrix that takes into account two main criteria. First, we need to know whether the entity intervenes directly on the international scene or whether it negotiates indirectly through the federal state. In addition, we have to determine whether the potential for action is framed within the country's constitution or whether is it has been determined through administrative arrangements. Table 1 offers a reading of this matrix and provides specific examples that correspond to the four possible combinations built from the criteria identified herein.

Belgium's federated entities serve as a fine example of autonomy.[6] The Belgian federal constitution explicitly allows regions and communities to exercise a direct influence on the international scene when the matters being discussed internationally fall under the jurisdiction of the federated entity. Paul-André Comeau has

Table 1
Types of arrangements that allow federated entities an international role

Frame Influence	Constitutional	Administrative
Direct	*Type: autonomy* *Example:* Belgium	*Type: emancipation* *Example:* Canada (La Francophonie)
Mediated	*Type: integration* *Examples:* Austria, Germany, South Africa, Switzerland	*Type: consensus* *Example:* Australia

shown that, in some instances, the federal government serves only as an observer, a situation that is very different from the one we know in Canada.

Canada, on the other hand, has given us the instance of an arrangement that favours emancipation. The formula used in La Francophonie allows for the full participation of federated entities, thanks to an administrative agreement between three interested provinces[7] and Ottawa. Although it is limited in scope, and applies to one specific forum, this administrative agreement grants these provinces a status of "participating government," a status defined within the organization's rules.

Does this mean that Quebec should then enter into other administrative agreements with Ottawa in order to be able to exercise direct influence within other international organizations? It must be noted that very few organizations can offer a status of "participating government" or its equivalent. Several organizations do offer an "associate membership," but federated entities that function in some circumstances as self-governing international actors are reluctant to accept this status, as they must recognize formally that they do not have control over their own international relations. For Quebec to accept this status, the government would have to abandon the position it has defended for more than forty years. A more suitable solution needs to be found.

Some federated entities choose not to exert influence directly when they get involved in the shaping of international norms and standards. They prefer to opt for an integrated action. In Austria, Germany, South Africa, and Switzerland, for example, federated states voice their needs at the federal level, a right that is constitutionally enshrined. This is done through the Bundesrat in Austria and Germany and through the National Council of Provinces in South Africa. It is through this process that German Länder were able to exert enough influence to incorporate the "subsidiarity principle" within the Treaty of Maastricht. Switzerland provides another excellent example of a highly organized system that allows formal input by its federated entities when defining foreign policy. Cantons make their needs known through the Conference of Canton Governments, where cross-border and trade issues are discussed – they are also present in the European Union and La Francophonie.

Finally, other federated states rely on a consensus based on an administrative frame, which allows them to exercise an indirect influence on international questions. The Australian constitution, for example, stipulates clearly that foreign policy falls under the federal government's exclusive responsibility. Over time, however, some Australian states became involved on the international scene in order to defend their interests, especially in matters dealing with trade and natural resources, the latter area being under their sole jurisdiction. A decision of the Australian High Court served to disrupt this system, and as a consequence Canberra might well have been required to legislate in areas that come under the jurisdiction of the federated state, which would also be unconstitutional. Given this constitutional deadlock, the governments agreed to enter into administrative agreements that will determine the action of each level of government.

As we can appreciate, Quebec's involvement in international affairs is not unique. More and more federated entities have a voice and exercise their influence in the international arena. Quebec's demands for a larger role in international affairs are not the expression of a whim; they reflect a reality of today's world and most federated entities are in the same position and are seeking ways to achieve this same goal. Given the importance of international institutions today, the real challenge is to find the correct formula.

OPTIONS

As outlined above, there already exists one formula – autonomy – based on an administrative framework that enables the Quebec Government to participate directly in La Francophonie. Unfortunately, this does not provide a solution that can be applied elsewhere, as most of the international organizations that interest Quebec do not recognize this formula. For instance, UNESCO would not recognize this type of arrangement for there are no such provisions in its charter. It would have to be amended for this to work – a proposition that is not at all realistic given the fact that two thirds of the members would have to support the amendment. By the same token, it is equally unrealistic to think of amending the Canadian Constitution at this point. Theoretically, the constitution could be modified to include new sections defining federal and provincial responsibilities in the international arena, but this is not a process to be embarked upon in the foreseeable future. Even short-term administrative agreements that appear to be the simplest to negotiate are not foolproof if they rest only on the goodwill of the actors of the day.

There is perhaps another option, a hybrid version of the administrative agreements that would grant Quebec long-term security within the Canadian delegation when direct influence is not possible due to institutional constraints. With this option, Quebec would be given autonomy or work from a consensus within its areas of jurisdiction and could intervene in those same areas in international institutions. This formula would provide Quebec with its own voice to exercise a mediated or, at times, direct influence; most importantly, this option would require no administrative or constitutional changes on the part of the institutions themselves. In addition, for both Quebec and Canada – and for any other province that wished to take part – the level of political uncertainty and continued tension would be lowered considerably by providing a predictable and stable framework from which to work. This solution does not call upon the actors to abandon their basic principles, now or in the future, and it would usher in a win-win situation.

SUMMARY

At the beginning of this paper, I asked whether it was really necessary for Quebec to be involved in the conduct of international relations, as some assert, or whether it was merely a whim and a political pretension, as others argue. It should be clear by now that the provinces have no choice but to be more involved in the international arena. In addition to the fact that international institutions are setting international norms and standards in a host of areas that fall under provincial jurisdiction, the wide-ranging demands that have come with globalization require that the provinces assume a direct role in debating the solutions – or they stand to lose the most. There are many benefits to the global world, but they will not come automatically. A modern Quebec must be prepared to respond to tomorrow's changes, and it can only do so if it is present when the pivotal issues that affect its future are being discussed. It is the government's responsibility to defend its people's values and identity. It is ultimately responsible to its people and must do what is necessary to be where needed to defend their interests. Quebec's involvement on the international scene is by no means idiosyncratic as it answers objective pressures, and this is not unique. It clearly can be portrayed as a necessary response to an evolving context.

For nearly forty-five years, Quebec has been trying to develop as a dynamic and modern society, one that is open to the world and that deals on a daily basis with the many challenges of the global reality. The response it offers has often been seen as a challenge to Canadian unity, especially by a federal government that works hard to preserve the international identity of the country, one which is recognized throughout the world – but one that is beset by a continuous onslaught from emerging middle powers seeking to get a piece of the shrinking pie.

One must come to realize, however, that Canada's place in the world will not be threatened by these requests coming out of Quebec. Indeed, years of neglect on the part of Ottawa have been much more damaging to Canada's prestige than forty-five years of constructive presence by Quebec. In reality, the obstinate refusal by Ottawa to reduce the constraints it imposes on provinces in the international arena is more likely to tarnish Canada's image, as the provinces will just not be able to deliver in the very programs that occupy such a large place internationally. Nor would it be very healthy for Canada to negotiate treaties in areas under provincial responsibility only to have them rejected by the provinces at the implementation stage. All parties need to be involved in the process, and it is time that Quebec City and Ottawa set a stable and predictable environment in the form of a long-term administrative agreement.

A last question awaits an answer: will the election of Stephen Harper, in part due to commitment toward such a solution, change the landscape? It remains to be seen if political will can succeed in overcoming bureaucratic constraints that are still blocking the road toward a solution.

NOTES

1 Which could be better understood in light of what both Chapnick (chapter 1 of this volume) and Michaud (2006) have analyzed.

2 The latest analysis of this evolution published in English is the one by Donaghy and Carter. For a more complete overview and an extensive topical bibliography, see Michaud (2004, 128).

3 From these readings, one can appreciate both sides of the coin from actors who were involved in the process.

4 "What falls under Quebec's jurisdiction at home, falls under Québec's jurisdiction everywhere" (our translation; Charest).

5 The only section that deals with international questions is s.132, and it adresses the obligation the Dominion has toward treaties signed by the Empire; however this section became irrelevant with the Statute of Westminster in 1931.

6 In other writings, I have used the term "emancipation" for this first type, and "autonomy" for the model inspired by Canada and Quebec in La Francophonie, which was confusing to some readers. Comments received following the publication made me reconsider my former use of terms, and I wish to thank those who provided me with this clarification.

7 Quebec, Ontario, and New Brunswick.

Conclusion:
Putting Canada's Diversity
into Canadian Foreign Policy

DAVID BERCUSON AND DAVID CARMENT

The "World in Canada" volume intended to find answers to the question: to what extent does Canada's ethnic, linguistic, and religiously diverse population impact Canadian foreign policy? A second and strongly related question was: just exactly how is foreign policy made in Canada anyway? Many of the authors in this volume addressed these questions directly or indirectly. Adam Chapnick examined the role of the prime minister in the process, using instances of decision-making that go as far back as the governments of William Lyon Mackenzie King. His conclusion is that a prime minister can indeed have a great impact on the policymaking process and may even be understood as the bridge between popular sentiment as the leader sees it and the final emanation of policy itself. Jack Granatstein has no doubt that ethnic diversity impacts policymaking, and most particularly the very different outlooks on world affairs that are apparently held by Quebecers as opposed to the ROC (Rest of Canada). He thinks governments pander too much to Quebec sentiment when making important policy decisions. David Haglund essentially agrees with this perspective, but frames the debate within the larger question of whether or not short-term needs to build power bases in Quebec necessarily adversely affect long-term strategic policy choices or whether the Quebec factor is in itself an essential variant of Canadian policymaking.

There is an *ipso facto* assumption, in these and the other chapters in this volume, that popular opinion plays – and must play – some role in the messy business of policymaking. There is a decided difference among authors here (and among others who have written on the subject) on what the role ought to be. What constitutes "legitimate" public opinion? Who decides where national interests lie, or where they ought to take us? Should such questions be determined by trying to read the public mind, whether via the latest poll, or via the keen political instinct of a man such as William Lyon Mackenzie King? This begs the question of what to do when the public mind isn't so easily read, or changes over the course of time, or even what role a prime minister should legitimately play in trying to lead public opinion. It also leaves unanswered the legitimacy of what some here have called "special pleading." Generally speaking diplomats in Canada differ little from diplomats in the US, Britain, and elsewhere in arguing that a nation's interests cannot be served by arbitrarily bending to the will of this special interest group or that. Indeed "special pleading" – whether by Jews about Israel, or Arabs about Palestine, or Irish about Northern Ireland, or Haitians about Haiti – is almost universally viewed by the policymaking community as ultimately damaging to national interests. All the authors here agree to some degree with that proposition. All would accept some part of the notion that, at some point, special interests may actually damage the national interest in making their case for or against Israel, for or against intervention in Haiti, etc.

At the same time virtually no one would argue that Canadian national interests can be determined in some formulaic way primarily by the cabinet and the diplomats (with perhaps some bit of spice added to the mix by an academic or two). How then are national interests discerned and what role is legitimate not only for "special interests" but for another of the bugaboos of policymakers – partisan politics?

Everyone can agree that a foreign policy that runs strongly counter to public opinion is not sustainable in the long run. If nothing else, the public will eventually have its say in an election and even though Canadian elections don't often resonate with the ebb and flow of passionately held views on foreign policy, that in itself says that Canadians don't much care about foreign policy to begin with. Between elections they may seem to claim that a government is too pro-Israel, or too anti-Israel, especially when TV screens show mounting violence and brutality in that region, but traditionally they will vote for the government that can shorten waiting times for hip-replacement surgery, no matter where it stands on the Israel question.

How, then, should public opinion shape foreign policy? Can it? It would be convenient if a consistent national consensus were to emerge on most international issues, yet it is rare. Most Canadians may agree that nuclear arms proliferation is undesirable, or that terrorism is evil or that the Canadian Forces should be sent to help the victims of a catastrophic tsunami in Southeast Asia, but how many will agree that Canada should send troops to intervene in a civil war in that same region, let alone agree on which side? That is where consensus breaks down. That is why relying on national consensus can precipitate paralysis that can, in fact, undermine national interests. The simple fact is that consensus is only one factor determining national interests. There can be many more factors and some of them might well undermine consensus.

One of the reasons why the legitimacy of so-called special-pleading by "special interests" is so frowned upon by both academics and policymakers in Canada is that it is a process that, on the face of it, takes place outside government in such a way as to put pressure on government to do that which it might not ordinarily do. If, however, the arguments made by different special interests were to be advanced within Parliament, by MPs representing the views of their constituents, such activity could in no way be thought of as bringing pressure on government from without; however, although Canada is a fully functioning liberal democracy, Parliamentarians are virtually excluded from the policymaking process. As Chapnick shows, there is no single answer to the question of whether or not the prime minister "controls" that process, but one thing is certain – Parliament has virtually no impact on that process at all. Virtually every foreign-policy decision that Canadian Governments make is made exclusive of Parliament. Individual MPs have but a miniscule impact on the process. Although it can certainly be argued that the "special pleading" of interests groups ought not to have too great an impact on policy, that argument is plain silly if it is directed at Parliament as a whole. Put simply, Parliament is not a special-interest group. It is the cockpit of our democracy. So how can it be legitimately excluded from the policymaking process?

There are few foreign policy decisions that a Canadian Government can make that are as significant as sending Canadian troops into harm's way. Yet historically such decisions have almost always been made at the executive level with little or no participation by Parliament. The latest instance of such a decision came on 17 May 2006, when the House of Commons approved by a small margin an extension of a significant deployment of Canadian troops abroad that had already begun. The Canadian mission to move its troops from the Afghanistan capital of Kabul to the "wild west" of southern Kandahar was, in fact, first announced to Canadians in May 2005 by the Liberal Government of the day. It was the first significant step of that government's newly unveiled International Policy Statement (IPS). Introduced the previous month, the IPS consisted of five documents under a single heading. The first of those documents was a general introduction to the new policy direction issued over the signature of Prime Minister Paul Martin. The other documents were prepared by the ministers of national defence, foreign affairs, international development, and international trade. The IPS was, in effect, the government's long awaited White Paper on defence and diplomacy, designed to update the 1994 Defence White Paper and the 1995 Foreign Policy statement. It was also the basis of the "Whole of Government" approach to international affairs stressing "Defence, Diplomacy and Development – the 3Ds" as the future of Canada's foreign endeavours.

The Canadian shift away from a peace support deployment in Kabul, first undertaken in late 2003, to the far more dangerous and contested region around Kandahar, was specifically designed to meet the "3D" challenge. In Kandahar a Canadian Provincial Reconstruction team (PRT) composed almost exclusively of military personnel was tasked to help the locals in and around Kandahar City rebuild their infrastructure. At the same time, a team of civilian diplomats under the leadership of Foreign Affairs Officer Glynn Berry was supposed to work with municipal and provincial officials to help them rebuild civil institutions. The RCMP and other Canadian police representatives were given the job of working with the Afghan police to train new recruits while Canadian International Development Agency (CIDA) workers were to direct and administer Canadian aid dollars. Non-governmental aid agencies were invited to work alongside the governmental personnel, though very few took up the offer. The entire mission was to be guarded by a contingent of soldiers whose two-fold task was to provide static defense for the recovery work and also to reach out into the countryside outside Kandahar to disrupt Taliban operations before they might rally against the PRT and its civilian counterparts.

The International Policy Statement that was the foundation of the Canadian deployment to Kandahar was not laid before Parliament, let alone approved by it. Further, the deployment itself was, in time honoured fashion, not approved by Parliament either. It was, instead, discussed in the House of Commons in Committee of the Whole on 15 November 2005 as a "take note" debate on a motion that "this committee take note of Canada's military mission in Afghanistan," and nothing more. In this way MPs were given an opportunity to "take note" of the mission – discuss it, debate it, put their views about it on the record – but not to actually decide upon it. That was, and is, the nature of a "take note" debate.

The 17 May 2006 vote in the Commons, called by the new Conservative Government after a great deal of foot dragging, was not a vote to approve the mission already ongoing. It was, instead, a vote to extend the mission by one year until February 2009. It was a very close vote indeed. The government achieved its mandate by a vote of only 149 to 145 with the support of thirty Liberals, including Acting Leader of the Opposition Bill Graham. The NDP and the Bloc were solidly opposed to the extension. But given that the very same Liberal Party had only a year before decided to accept the mission, why was the vote so close? The explanation is that all the parties in the Commons were "playing politics" with the deployment. The new Conservative Government, elected in January, had said repeatedly as late as the end of March 2006 that there would be no vote on the Kandahar mission. The decision to deploy to Kandahar had already been taken by the previous government, the Conservatives pointed out, they had no argument with that decision, and had supported it the previous year, so another debate would be pointless and might undermine the morale of the troops. But then the Conservatives changed their mind and decided to allow a "take note" debate. That was held on 10 April as MPs discussed a mission they had already discussed the previous November. Then, a little over a month later, the government decided to hold a vote to seek Parliamentary approval not just for the mission itself (retroactively, of course) but also for a one year extension of the existing mission. The government gave the opposition just thirty-six hours notice of that vote, claiming that the issues had already been extensively discussed. The mission had certainly been discussed extensively, but not the extension for one year that would call for two additional troop rotations to Afghanistan (each rotation is for six months).

The Bloc Québécois played to its anti-war base in Quebec. It seized on the already mounting casualty rate (Captain Nichola Goddard had been killed only a few hours prior to the debate, the first Canadian woman ever to be killed in action) to denounce the mission as not in keeping with what it called Canadian peacekeeping tradition. The Bloc had supported the original Canadian deployment to Afghanistan in 2002 – right in the wake of the 9/11 attacks – when Canadians were dispatched to Kandahar to fight – not to do peacekeeping – under United States command. The New Democrats had not previously opposed the new Kandahar mission *per se*, nor had they yet adopted their current position of demanding an immediate withdrawal from Afghanistan. But they too announced their opposition to both the mission and its extension. No doubt they reasoned that their decision would put the onus on the Liberals – or at least some of them – to support the government in sufficient numbers to see the resolution pass, or see the mission cancelled. They and the Liberals are locked in a perpetual struggle (going on since the founding of the NDP's predecessor, the CCF, in 1933) to demonstrate who can outdo whom in trying to attract moderate left-wing voters in Canada. A split in Liberal ranks could only help them.

The Liberals were in a tight position. They had presumably been fully aware of the risks of the mission when they had committed the country to it in May 2005. In fact, the initial announcement of that mission was followed by a cross-country tour by then Minister of National Defence Bill Graham, in which he and Chief of the Defence Staff General Rick Hillier had warned Canadians that this new deployment would involve combat, would be dangerous, and would likely bring casualties. Unlike the NDP and the Bloc, the Liberals had to think about the consequences to Canada if the commitment they had made – and which the Tories were merely following up on – was allowed to die. They had to think about it because some day, sooner or later, they will govern again. Had the motion been defeated and the mission cancelled because they had done a 180 degree turn-about in one year, no Canadian commitment to NATO or anyone else would ever again be taken seriously again. Washington, already unhappy with Canadian positions on Iraq and missile defense, would have been positively livid. So the Grits decided to release their members from caucus discipline, no doubt aware that some, at least, would vote with the government.

No one knows whether the government's slim victory was carefully calculated beforehand by Mr Graham and Mr Harper – i.e., if they agreed on how many Liberals would vote with the government to ensure passage of the motion, but it is clear that Mr Graham and Mr Harper both achieved a result they could live with. During the debate most Liberals focused their ire on the procedure, rather than the mission – the thirty-six hours that the government had allowed for the debate – and made their point while the Tories got the approval they were seeking. The Liberals also escaped pushing the nation into an election less than a half a year after they were chastised by the voters.

Many Canadians decry this sort of "playing politics" with a serious combat mission that is taking Canadian lives and see it as evidence that Parliament is simply too partisan a place to handle matters of life and death. But democracies at war are still democracies, and partisan politics have entered into virtually every factor of virtually every war that Canada has been involved in from the Boer War to the current mission in Afghanistan. Perhaps the problem isn't that there is too much partisan politics involved in key foreign-policy decisions in Canada, but that there has traditionally been too little.

Partisan politics is the currency of representative democracy. In the years since the Second World War, and especially with the adoption of the Charter of Rights and Freedoms, Canadians have built a democracy that is as vibrant, alive, and open as any on Earth. Canadians may once have been a rather dreary political lot, respectful to a fault of both government institutions and politicians, but no more. All the better. Canada is now a free market of ideas, a system wherein politicians do their level best to get the drop on their protagonists. Sometimes good taste is overly sacrificed, but sometimes all the heat really does give way to illumination. In any case, the public is being exposed to all manner of viewpoints on all manner of public policy topics as never before and the nation's foreign policy is a perfectly apt topic for the ebb and flow of political argument. If political parties openly and publicly disagree about appropriate courses of action for the nation to take, citizens can at least attempt to make informed choices about how to best serve national interests and how best to protect and project national values. In such a debate, the so-called "special interests" have as much right to be heard as anyone. Indeed, their arguments become part of the mixture out of which policy will emerge. Partisan politics does not deny the possibility of making informed decisions, it expedites it. And for partisan politics to influence policy, the cockpit of partisan politics – the House of Commons – ought to be integrally involved in all key decisions affecting Canadian foreign and defence policy.

That has rarely been the case in the past. Consider the very basic decision of entering war. Canada was a colony at the outbreak of the Boer War and the First World War. There was no vote in Parliament on any declaration of war because Canada was constitutionally at war when Britain went to war. At the outbreak of the Second World War Parliament met after Britain had declared war on Germany and issued a separate Canadian declaration of war on 10 September 1939. Before the vote, both the 1st and 2nd Canadian Infantry Divisions had already been mobilized, the Royal Canadian Navy had been placed on a war footing, and the first RCN-escorted convoy had departed Halifax for the UK (the merchant vessels therein having been placed under the jurisdiction of the navy on 26 August.)

But that was the last time a Canadian Parliament voted to send troops into harm's way. When the Liberal Government of Prime Minister Louis St Laurent sent the Canadian military to Korea no votes were held. The war began with an invasion of South Korea by North Korea on 26 June 1950. On 30 June Ottawa ordered three destroyers to Korean waters to aid whatever UN efforts might be mounted to blockade the north by sea. As North Korean forces swept aside their southern opponents, Ottawa dispatched an air transport squadron on 19 July to assist the United States' airlift from the west coast to Japan. Finally, on 7 August, under steadily increasing pressure from the public, the UN, and both the United States and Britain, the Cabinet decided to send a brigade group – about eight thousand persons – to fight alongside other UN contingents to turn back the invasion. The Cabinet meeting was actually held in Mr St Laurent's private railway car as it was riding back to Ottawa from the Toronto funeral of Mackenzie King. All these decisions were conveyed by orders in council. A Parliamentary debate on the Korean war was held in early September, but no formal vote on the Korean deployment was ever held.

All overseas deployments of ground troops or naval and air units to NATO or to the large number of "classical" peacekeeping operations conducted during the Cold War were also carried out by order in council. In the lead-up to Operation Desert Shield / Desert Storm in the late summer and fall of 1990 and early 1991, Prime Minister Brian Mulroney committed troops, naval units, and fighter aircraft without Parliamentary approval. A debate was held over several days in the last half of January 1991 – after the deployments had been announced and after most of the Canadian contingent had arrived in theatre – but no formal vote was held. In 1994 Prime Minister Jean Chrétien's government introduced the concept of the "take note" debate to discuss the extension of the peacekeeping mission that Canada had already agreed to (and was already participating in) in Croatia and Bosnia. The original concept of these "take note" debates was that MPs would be given an opportunity to make their views known to the government "before the government makes a decision." But that has never happened. For example, the procedure was used – again after the fact – to "take note" of Canada's deployment of fighter-bomber aircraft to Aviano, Italy, in late 1998. But no approval was sought by the government prior to the commitment of those aircraft to the bombing of Kosovo and Serbia in spring 1999.

"Take note" debates were the symptom, not the cause, of Parliament's virtual exclusion not only from decisions to commit troops but from virtually any oversight role in foreign or defense matters under governments both Liberal and Conservative. For all intents and purposes Canadian foreign and defense policy is still decided by the prime minister (sometimes also with cabinet participation) and almost always divorced from effective parliamentary scrutiny. Important international treaties have been signed, troops have been sent to wars, support to certain international causes has been withheld or given at the behest of the prime minister. The foreign affairs and defense committees in the Commons could hold hearings, call witnesses, or make recommendations, but nothing they recommend is legally binding on the prime minister. And, of course, the party members on those committees rarely act independently of their caucuses or leaders. This situation is both constitutionally valid and in accordance with historical practice, but it was and is most certainly not in accordance with the spirit of the democracy Canada has become.

The situation is especially unpalatable for members of the Canadian Forces who are subject to an unlimited liability when they take the Queen's shilling. Canadian Forces personnel, both regulars and reservists in uniform, know that as a part of their service, they may be ordered into harm's way and, indeed, placed in situations in which they may well lose their lives as part of the services they are called on to perform by the government. That is their fundamental duty. That duty separates them from all other Canadians citizens, including police and firefighters. The job of a soldier of a democracy is the lawful and ordered application of lethal force when ordered to do so by the government that represents the people of Canada. Under current practice, what guaranty is there that the government will not unnecessarily risk the lives of those who have put their lives in its care, not only through action, but also through inaction, delay, obfuscation, or other forms of governmental irresponsibility? Soldiers have no unions, no labour relations boards, no human-rights commissions to take up their cases. Who protects the men and women in uniform? Right now, it is the very same people who make the decision to deploy in the first place – the executive. Who, then, defends the defenders of Canada?

The lives of Canadian diplomats are rarely at stake as a result of government policy, but the well-being and good fortune of millions of Canadians can be at stake whenever crucial foreign policy decisions are made. A nation that is as dependent on international trade as is Canada is particularly vulnerable to the perditions of foreign governments that may retaliate for some perceived Canadian diplomatic transgression or arbitrary trade measure. Canada's interests are no less at stake in the daily process of diplomacy than in war, but again those interests are interpreted and pursued only by the executive branch of government and, more often than not, by the prime minister.

In any broadly based democracy built upon the immigration of millions of people from hundreds of different backgrounds, with at least five distinct geographic regions, the question of who wields the greatest impact on policymaking will always be asked. Usually, depending on the issue, someone will always point to this group or that, to this region or that, and claim undue influence in policy-making. The argument is inevitable. But no one can question that all Canadians will have an effective say, one way or the other, through the voting process, as to what the domestic spending prior-ities will be, or how crime will be attacked, or how many immigrants is optimal for the nation. And yet nobody (except for a very few) will have an effective voice in whether or not Canada ought to have a free trade agreement with Brazil or send troops to Darfur.

Canada ought to have a foreign-policymaking process that pro-duces the largest possible degree of consensus. Prime ministers can have a truly canny sense of consensus, or they can use polls, but the national interest will surely best be served if they are forced by law, by convention, or by the constitution, to seek Parliamentary ap-proval for all treaties and other significant international agree-ments. Then, at least, debates about foreign policy will not be empty and essentially meaningless and politicians will know that they will assume an important part of the responsibility for making decisions. Parliament, which, for better or worse, reflects Canada's diverse population with all its "special interests," should be a neces-sary part of the policymaking process. In that way, our "world within Canada" will become an integral and legitimate part of the shaping of Canadian foreign policy.

Bibliography

CHAPTER ONE

Brecher, Michael, and Jonathan Wilkenfeld (2000). *A Study of Crisis*. Ann Arbor: University of Michigan Press.

Cabinet War Committee (1943). Minutes of Meeting, 31 August. Library and Archives Canada, *Privy Council Office Papers*, RG2, 7c, vol. 13.

Chan, Steve, and Donald A. Sylvan (1984). "Foreign Policy Decision Making: An Overview." *Foreign Policy Decision Making: Perception, Cognition, and Artificial Intelligence*, Sylvan and Chan, eds. New York: Praeger, 1–19.

Chapnick, Adam (2000). "The Canadian Middle Power Myth." *International Journal*, vol. 55, no. 2, 188–206.

Chapnick, Adam (2005a). *The Middle Power Project: Canada and the Founding of the United Nations*. Vancouver: University of British Columbia Press.

Chapnick, Adam (2005b). "Peace, Order, and Good Government: The 'Conservative' Tradition in Canadian Foreign Policy." *International Journal*, vol. 60, no. 3, 635–50.

Cohen, Andrew. "A Foreign Policy, Martin Style." *Ottawa Citizen*, 20 July 2004, A12.

Cooper, Andrew Fenton (2004). *Tests of Global Governance: Canadian Diplomacy and United Nations World Conferences*. Tokyo: United Nations University Press.

Dyson, Stephen Benedict (2006). "Personality and Foreign Policy: Tony Blair's Iraq Decisions." *Foreign Policy Analysis*, vol. 2, no. 3, 289–306.

Eayrs, James (1961). *The Art of the Possible: Government and Foreign Policy in Canada*. Toronto: University of Toronto Press.

Edinger, Lewis J. (1967). "Editor's Introduction." *Political Leadership in Industrialized Societies: Studies in Comparative Analysis*, Edinger, ed. New York: John Wiley & Sons, 1–25.

Farrell, R. Barry (1969). *The Making of Canadian Foreign Policy.* Scarborough: Prentice Hall.

Fletcher, Frederick J. ([1971] 1977). "The Prime Minister as Persuader." *Apex of Power: The Prime Minister and Political Leadership in Canada,* 2nd ed., Thomas A. Hockin, ed. Scarborough: Prentice Hall, 86–111.

Gecelovsky, Paul (2007). "Of Legacies and Lightning Bolts: The Prime Minister and Canadian Foreign Policy." *Readings in Canadian Foreign Policy: Classic Debates and New Ideas,* Patrick James, Nelson Michaud, and Marc J. O'Reilly, eds. Don Mills: Oxford University Press, 196–205.

Granatstein, J.L., and Robert Bothwell (1990). *Pirouette: Pierre Trudeau and Canadian Foreign Policy.* Toronto: University of Toronto Press.

Greenstein, Fred I. (1967). "The Impact of Personality on Politics: An Attempt to Clear Away Underbrush." *American Political Science Review,* vol. 61, no. 3, 629–41.

Harper, Tim. "Tough Wording Stays ... Thanks to Canada." *Toronto Star,* 15 September 2005, A6.

Harper, Tim. "Harper's Latin American Challenge." *Toronto Star,* 30 January 2006, A1.

Hermann, Margaret (1980). "Explaining Foreign Policy Behavior Using the Personal Characteristics of Political Leaders." *International Studies Quarterly,* vol. 24, no. 1, 7–46.

Hermann, Margaret (1984). "Personality and Foreign Policy Decision Making: A Study of 53 Heads of Government." *Foreign Policy Decision Making: Perception, Cognition, and Artificial Intelligence,* Sylvan and Chan, eds. New York: Praeger, 53–80.

Hermann, Margaret (2003). "Assessing Leadership Style: Trait Analysis." *The Psychological Assessment of Political Leaders,* Jerrold M. Post, ed. Ann Arbor: University of Michigan Press, 375–86.

Hilliker, John and Donald Barry (1995). *Canada's Department of External Affairs,* vol. 2, *Coming of Age, 1946–1968.* Montreal and Kingston: McGill-Queen's University Press.

Hockin, Thomas A. ([1971] 1977). "The Prime Minister and Political Leadership: An Introduction to Some Constraints and Imperatives." *Apex of Power: The Prime Minister and Political Leadership in Canada,* 2nd ed., Thomas A. Hockin, ed. Scarborough: Prentice Hall, 2–21.

Hogg, William (2004). "Plus Ça Change: Continuity, Change, and Culture in Foreign Policy White Papers." *International Journal,* vol. 59, no. 3, 521–36.

Hook, Sidney ([1943] 1962). *The Hero in History: A Study in Limitation and Possibility.* Boston: Beacon Press.

Hudson, Valerie M. (2005). "Foreign Policy Analysis: Actor-Specific Theory and the Ground of International Relations." *Foreign Policy Analysis*, vol. 1, no. 1, 1–30.

Janigan, Mary. "Martin: I Don't Like It." *Maclean's*, 25 April 2005, 18.

Keller, Jonathan M. (2005). "Leadership Style, Regime Type, and Foreign Policy Crisis Behavior: A Contingent Monadic Peace?" *International Studies Quarterly*, vol. 49, 205–31.

King, William Lyon Mackenzie ([1918] 1973). *Industry and Humanity*. Toronto: University of Toronto Press.

King, William Lyon Mackenzie (1943). Speech to Parliament, 9 July. In Canada, House of Commons, *Debates*. Vol. 238.

King, William Lyon Mackenzie (1944). Speech to Parliament, 4 August. In Canada, House of Commons, *Debates*. Vol. 244.

King, William Lyon Mackenzie (1945a). Speech to Parliament, 20 March. In Canada, House of Commons, *Debates*. Vol. 245.

King, William Lyon Mackenzie (1945b). Speech to Second Plenary Session of the United Nations Conference on International Organization, 27 April. *Documents of the United Nations Conference on International Organization, San Francisco, 1945*, vol. 1, *General*. London and New York: United Nations Information Organizations.

Lyon, Peyton V. ([1971] 1977). "Prime Minister Diefenbaker and the Cuban Missile Crisis." *Apex of Power: The Prime Minister and Political Leadership in Canada*, 2nd ed., Thomas A. Hockin, ed. Scarborough: Prentice Hall, 294–306.

Malone, David (2001). "Foreign Policy Reviews Reconsidered." *International Journal*, vol. 56, no. 4, 555–78.

Michaud, Nelson (2006). "The Prime Minister, the PMO, and PCO: Makers of Canadian Foreign Policy?" *Handbook of Canadian Foreign Policy*, Patrick James, Nelson Michaud, and Marc J. O'Reilly, eds. Lanham, MD: Lexington Books, 21–48.

Morrison, David R. (1988). *Aid and Ebb Tide: A History of CIDA and Canadian Development Assistance*. Waterloo: Wilfrid Laurier University Press.

Nossal, Kim Richard ([1985] 1997). *The Politics of Canadian Foreign Policy*, 3rd ed. Scarborough: Prentice Hall.

Pal, Leslie A. (1988). "Hands at the Helm? Leadership and Public Policy." *Prime Ministers and Premiers: Political Leadership and Public Policy in Canada*, Pal and David Taras, eds. Scarborough: Prentice Hall, 16–26.

Pearson, Lester B. (1945). Broadcast over CBC Network, 29 April. In Library and Archives Canada, W.L.M. King Papers, MG26 J4, vol. 340, file 3674.

Pearson, Lester B. (1969). *Partners in Development: Report of the Commission on International Development*. London: Pall Mall Press.

Pickersgill, J.W., and D.F. Forster, eds. (1970). *The Mackenzie King Record*. Vol. 4. *1947–1948*. Toronto and Buffalo: University of Toronto Press.

POLLARA (2006). "Canadians' Expectations for Stephen Harper's Foreign Policy." February. www.ciia.org.

Ravenhill, John (1998). "Cycles of Middle Power Activism: Constraint and Choice in Australian and Canadian Foreign Policies." *Australian Journal of International Affairs*, vol. 52, no. 3, 309–27.

Richardson, James L. (1994). *Crisis Diplomacy: The Great Powers Since the Mid-Nineteenth Century*. Cambridge, UK: Cambridge University Press.

Stairs, Denis (1982). "The Political Culture of Canadian Foreign Policy." *Canadian Journal of Political Science*, vol. 15, no. 4, 667–90.

Stairs, Denis (2001). "Architects or Engineers? The Conservatives and Foreign Policy." *Diplomatic Departures: The Conservative Era in Canadian Foreign Policy, 1984–93*, Nelson Michaud and Kim Richard Nossal, eds. Vancouver and Toronto: University of British Columbia Press, 25–42.

Thordarson, Bruce (1976). "Posture and Policy: Leadership in Canada's External Affairs." *International Journal*, vol. 31, no. 4, 666–91.

Travers, James. "Graham Still in the Picture." *Toronto Star*, 22 July 2004, A21.

CHAPTER TWO

Abu-Laban, Yasmeen (1998). "Welcome/STAY OUT: The Contradiction of Canadian Integration and Immigration Policies at the Millennium." *Canadian Ethnic Studies*, vol. 3, no. 3, 190–211.

Bell, Stewart (2002). "Blood Money: International Terrorist Fundraising in Canada." *Canada Among Nations 2002: A Fading Power*, Norman Hillmer and Maureen Appel Molot, eds. Don Mills, Ontario: Oxford University Press, 172–90.

Black, Jerome (2000a). "Minority Representation in the Canadian Parliament Following the 1997 Election: Patterns of Continuity and Change." Presented at the Fourth National Metropolis Conference. Toronto, March.

Black, Jerome (2000b). "Ethnoracial Minorities in the Canadian House of Commons: The Case of the 36th Parliament." *Canadian Ethnic Studies*, vol. 32, no. 2, 105–14.

Black, Jerome (2000c). "Entering the Political Elite in Canada: The Case of Minority Women as Parliamentary Candidates and MPs." *Canadian Review of Sociology and Anthropology*, vol. 37, no. 2, 143–66.

Black, Jerome (2002). "Ethnoracial Minorities in the House of Commons: An Update on the 37th Parliament." *Canadian Parliamentary Review*, vol. 25, no. 1, 24–8.

Cameron, Maxwell A., J. Robert Lawson, and Brian W. Tomlin, eds. (1998). *To Walk Without Fear: The Global Movement to Ban Landmines.* Toronto: Oxford University Press.

Canadian Jewish Congress (2005). "CJC Pacific Region and Darfur Association call on Prime Minister to keep his commitments." *News Releases*, 27 January 2005: www.cjc.ca.

CBC News. "PM offers $170 M, 100 troops to Sudan." 12 May 2005: www.cbc.ca/story/canada/national2005/05/12/darfur-canada050512.html?print.

Citizenship and Immigration (2005). "Who Is a Business Immigrant." www.cic.gc.

Citizenship and Immigration (2005a). "Facts and Figures 2004: Immigration Overview: Permanent and Temporary Residents." Ottawa: www.cic.gc.ca/english/pub/facts2004/index.html.

Citizenship and Immigration (2005b). "Becoming a Canadian Citizen." Ottawa: www.cic.gc.ca/english/citizen/becoming-howto.html.

Citizenship and Immigration (2006). "What is the Business Immigration Program?" Ottawa: www.cic.gc.ca/english/business/index.html.

Council on American-Islamic Relations Canada (2001). "Muslims Must Immediately Urge Parliamentary Committee to Amend Bill C-36." *CAIR-CAN Action Alert.* Ottawa: www.caircan.ca.

Council on American-Islamic Relations Canada (2005). "Demand Prime Minister Appoint Investigation into Torture of Canadian Muslims Abroad." *CAIR-CAN Action Alert.* Ottawa: www.caircan.ca.

English, John (1998). "The Member of Parliament and Foreign Policy." *Canada Among Nations 1998: Leadership and Dialogue,* Fen Osler Hampson and Maureen Appel Molot, eds. Toronto: Oxford University, 69–80.

Industry Canada (2003). "Canadian Imports (Exports) Year Annual Trend 1990–2002." Ottawa: strategis.gc.ca.

Kitchen, Veronica (2001). "From Rhetoric to Reality: Canada, the United States, and the Ottawa Process to Ban landmines." *International Journal*, vol. 57, no. 1, 37–55.

Kobayashi, Audrey (2000). "Advocacy from the Margins: The Role of Minority Ethnocultural Associations in Affecting Public Policy in Canada." *The Nonprofit Sector in Canada: Roles and Relationships,* Keith G. Banting, ed. Kingston: McGill-Queen's University Press, 229–66.

Lapp, Miriam (1999). "Ethnic Group Leaders and the Mobilization of Voter Turnout: Evidence from Five Montreal Communities." *Canadian Ethnic Studies*, vol. 31, 17–42.

Macdonald, Nikki (2005). "Women Beneath the Electoral Barrier." *Electoral Insight*, January: www.elections.ca.

Neufeld, Mark (1999). "Democratization in/of Canadian Foreign Policy: Critical Reflections." *Studies in Political Economy*, vol. 58, Spring, 97–119.

Nossal, Kim Richard (1995). "The Democratization of Canadian Foreign Policy: The Elusive Ideal." *Canada Among Nations 1995: Democracy and Foreign Policy*, Maxwell A. Cameron and Maureen Appel Molot, eds. Ottawa: Carleton University, 29–43.

Panetta, Alexander. "Ottawa Plans to Boost Immigrant Intake." *London Free Press*, 24 September 2005, A7.

Parliament (2004). "Members of the House of Commons, 1867 to Date: Born Outside Canada." Ottawa: www.parl.gc.ca.

Parliament (2005). "38th Parliament, Members of the House of Commons." (October 25) and "Members of the House of Commons, 1867 to Date: Born Outside Canada." Ottawa: www.parl.gc.ca.

Pratt, Cranford (1996). "Competing Perspectives on Canadian Development Assistance Policies." *International Journal*, vol. 51, no. 2, 235–58.

Prime Minister's Office (2002). "Address by Prime Minister Jean Chrétien on the Occasion of the United Nations General Assembly High-Level Plenary Debate on the New Partnership for Africa's Development." New York: pm.gc.ca.

Pross, A. Paul (1986). *Group Politics and Public Policy*. Toronto: Oxford University Press.

Riddell-Dixon, Elizabeth (1985). *The Domestic Mosaic: Interest Groups and Canadian Foreign Policy*. Toronto: Canadian Institute of International Affairs.

Riddell-Dixon, Elizabeth (2001). *Canada and the Beijing Conference on Women: Governmental Politics and NGO Participation*. Vancouver: University of British Columbia Press.

Saloojee, Anver (2002). "Inclusion and Exclusion: A Framework of Analysis for Understanding Political Participation by Members of Racialized and Newcomer Communities." Presented to the Sixth National Metropolis Conference. Toronto, March.

Statistics Canada (2003). "Canada's Ethnocultural Portrait: The Changing Mosaic." Ottawa: www12.statcan.ca.

Statistics Canada (2005a). "Study: Canada's Trade and Investment with China." *The Daily*, 16 June 2005: www.statcan.ca.

Statistics Canada (2005b). "The Daily: Demographic Statistics." Ottawa: www.statcan.ca.

Subcommittee on International Trade, Trade Disputes and Investment (2003). Standing Committee on Foreign Affairs and International Trade, "Presentation by Mitch Kowalski, Vice-President, Hong Kong-Canada Business Association." Ottawa, 26 February.

United Nations (2005). Office for the Coordination of Humanitarian Affairs. "Sudan: Annan Calls for Support to AU Mission in Darfur." New York: www.irinnews.org/print.asp?ReportID'47315.

Whitworth, Sandra (1995). "Women, and Gender, in the Foreign Policy Review Process." *Canada Among Nations 1995: Democracy and Foreign Policy,* Maxwell A. Cameron and Maureen Appel Molot, eds. Ottawa: Carleton University, 83–98.

CHAPTER THREE

Amnesty International. "Jamaica." www.amnesty.org.

Anderson-Manley, Beverley. "Facing the Monster." *Jamaica Gleaner,* 9 January 2006: www.jamaica-gleaner.com/gleaner/20060109/cleisure/cleisure4.html.

Associated Haitian Press (2004). "Haiti: Electoral Council Member's Past Connection to Drug Trafficking Alleged."

Associated Press (2004). "Ex-Haitian Police Director Added to Drug Indictment of Former High-Ranking Officials." 29 August.

Barrera, Alexa, Sonia Bouffard, Andrew Harrington and Per Unheim (2006). "Jamaica: A Risk Assessment Brief." Country Indicators for Foreign Policy: www.carleton.ca/cifp/docs/brief_jamaica.pdf.

Blair, Leonardo. "Jamaican Diaspora Disturbed: Vexed and Vocal." *Enterprise Reporter,* 26 June 2005: www.jamaica-gleaner.com/gleaner/20050626/lead/lead1.html.

Borger, Julian. "Army Ordered to Wage War on Kingston's Gangs." *The Guardian,* 14 July 1999: www.guardian.co.uk/Archive/Article/0,4273,3883091,00.html

British Broadcasting Corporation, "Spanish Town New 'Murder Capital,'" 9 September 2004: news.bbc.co.uk/2/hi/americas/3635426.stm

British Broadcasting Corporation Monitoring Service, "Haitian Ex-Soldiers Arrest Two Policemen Carrying Drugs." 2004.

British Broadcasting Corporation Monitoring Service, "Highlights of Signal FM Radio News." 2004.

Caistor, Nick. "Haiti's Drug Money Scourge." *British Broadcasting Corporation News*, 19 March 2004: news.bbc.co.uk/1/hi/world/americas/3524444.stm.

Canadian Council for International Cooperation (2006). "A CCIC Review of the 2006–07 Part III Estimates CIDA Report on Plans and Priorities." Ottawa.

Canadian Foundation for the Americas (2005). "Latin American and Caribbean Diaspora Group Meeting Report." Proclamation from the Latin American and Caribbean Diaspora Group Meeting, 26 October 2005. Ottawa: www.focal.orgCaymen Net News, 9 February 2006: www.caymannetnews.com/2006/02/1025/jamaican/dis.shtml.

Canadian International Development Agency (2004). "Strategic Approach: Haiti." Ottawa: www.acdi-cida.gc.ca/CIDAWEB/acdicida.nsf/En/NIC-223124433-NTE#11.

Canadian International Development Agency (2005). "CIDA Announces New Development Partners: Developing Countries Where Canada Can Make a Difference." News release. 19 April: www.acdi-cida.gc.ca/CIDAWEB/acdicida.nsf/En/JER-324115437-MU7.

Canadian International Development Agency (2006). "Report on Plans and Priorities 2006–2007." Section I: Departmental Overview. 28 November: www.tbs-sct.gc.ca/rpp/0607/cida-acdi/cida-acdi01_e.asp#s1.1.

Caribbean Media Corporation News Agency. "Jamaica's Ruling Party to Elect New Leader on 25 February." Accessed on 25 January 2006.

Caribbean Media Corporation News Agency. "Gunrunning to Haiti through Jamaica." 3 August 2005. Archived in Haiti Democracy Project: Haitipolicy.org/content/3162.htm?PHPSESSID=c4d02e6e91fb32eba811dc39b135feod.

Carment, David, Stewart Prest and Samy Yiagadeesen (2006). "Assessing the Fragility of Small Island Developing States." *Building the Economic Resilience of Fragile States*, Lino Briguglio, Gordon Cordina, and Ellawony J. Kisanga, eds. Malta: Formatek Publishing: www.carleton.ca/cifp/docs/CIFP_SIDS_chapterper cent 207_febo6.pdf.

Central Intelligence Agency (2006). *The World Factbook: Haiti.*

Centre pour l'Ethique et l'Intégrité Publique et Privée (2004). "Enquete sur l'Intégrité: L'État des lieu de la corruption en Haïti (2003)."

Citizenship and Immigration Canada (2000). "Recent Immigrants in the Montreal Metropolitan Area: A Comparative Portrait Based on the 1996 Census." May 2000.

Citizenship and Immigration Canada (2002). "Facts and Figures 2002."

Citizenship and Immigration Canada (2003). "Immigrate to Canada." May 2000: www.cic.gc.ca/english/immigrate/index.html.

Citizenship and Immigration Canada (2005). "Facts and Figures: Immigration Overview 2005." Ottawa.

Country Indicators for Foreign Policy. *Country Indicators Database.*

Dade, Carlo, Luz Rodriguez-Novoa, and Jennifer Domise (2005). "Canada – Caribbean Diasporas and Development Conference Series Report." Proclamation of Canada – Caribbean Diasporas and Development Conference, 30 and 31 May. Toronto and Montreal.

Dade, Carlo (2006). "Survey of Remittance Recipients in Four Parishes in Jamaica: Analysis of Data." Canadian Foundation for the Americas: www.focal.ca/projects/ privatesector/diasporas/publications_e.asp.

de Pierrebourg, Fabrice, and Jérôme Dussault, "Les Gangs de rue à Laval." *Journal de Montréal,* 2 October 2003: www2.canoe.com/infos/societe/ archives/2003/10/20031002–075310.html.

Delva, Joseph Guyler. « Kidnappings, Violent Crime Surge in Haiti." Reuters, 27 November 2006: today.reuters.com/News/CrisesArticle. aspx?storyId=N27175023&WTmodLoc=IntNewsHome_C4_Crises-4.

Docquier, Frédéric, and Abdeslam Marfouk (2006). "International Migration by Education Attainment, 1990–2000." *International Migration, Remittances and the Brain Drain,* Çaglar Özden and Maurice Schiff, eds. Washington, DC: World Bank.

Drug Enforcement Agency (2003). "Drug Intelligence Brief: The Drug Trade in the Caribbean, A Threat Assessment." September. www.usdoj.gov/dea/pubs/intel/03014/03014.html. (Accessed 27 November 2004.)

Erikson, Daniel, and Adam Minson (2005). "The Caribbean: Democracy Adrift?" *Journal of Democracy,* vol. 16, no. 4: muse.jhu.edu/journals/ journal_of_democracy/vo16/16.4erikson.pdf.

Gutierrez, Lino (2002). "State Department Policy Statement: Haiti and Development Assistance." US Department of State, Remarks delivered to the Inter-American Dialogue Conference, Washington, DC, 22 May: www.state.gov/p/wha/rls/rm/10416.htm.

Headley, Bernard. "Looking at Deportees (Part I) – 'They Were No Angels,'" *Jamaica Gleaner,* 26 February 2006: www.jamaica-gleaner.com/ gleaner/20060226/focus/focus5.html.

Howlett, Michael, and M. Ramesh (2003). *Studying Public Policy: Policy Cycles and Policy Subsystems.* Toronto: Oxford University Press.

Hudson, Valerie, and Andrea den Boer (2004). *Bare Branches: The Security Implications of Asia's Surplus Male Population.* Cambridge, Massachusetts: Massachusetts Institute of Technology Press.

Industry Canada (2003). "Canadian Imports (Exports) Year Annual Trend 1990–2002." Ottawa: strategis.gc.ca.

Inter-American Commission on Human Rights (2005). "Haiti: Failed Jus-
    tice or Rule of Law? Challenges Facing Haiti and the International Com-
    munity." Organization of American States.
Inter-American Development Bank and the Multilateral Investment Fund
    (2004). "Remittance to Latin America and the Caribbean."
Inter-American Foundation (2001). "Approaches to Increasing the Pro-
    ductive Value of Remittances." Papers presented at a conference held at
    the World Bank. 19 March. Washington, DC.
International Bank for Reconstruction and Development (2006). "Global
    Economic Prospects." Washington, DC: World Bank.
International Crisis Group (2006). "Haiti after the Elections, Challenges
    for Preval's First 100 Days." Latin America/Caribbean Briefing 10.
International Crisis Group (2006). "Haiti: Security and the Reintegration
    of the State." www.crisisgroup.org/home/index.cfm?id=4475&l=1.
International Mission for Monitoring Haitian Elections (2006). "Supplemen-
    tary Report on the February 7, 2006, Elections." www.mieeh-immhe.ca/
    sup_report_e.html.
Jamaica Diaspora Online Forum. "Jamaican Diaspora Must Open Their
    Eyes to Jamaica's Realities." jamaicandiaspora.org/forum/index.php?
    board=1;action=display;threadid=46;start=0.
Jamaica Gleaner (2002). "Phillips calls in PSOJ – Private Sector to Bridge
    Gap between Parties, Police." 27 March: www.pnpjamaica.com/
    innewsmarch27a.htm.
Jamaica Gleaner (2004). "US Study Finds Strong Deportee-Crime Links." 3 Oc-
    tober: www.jamaica-gleaner.com/gleaner/20041003/lead/lead3.html.
Jamaica Gleaner (2006). "'Blood Lane' – Guns, Drugs, Deportees and a Cry
    for Help." 12 February: www.jamaica-gleaner.com/gleaner/20060212/
    news/news2.html
Jamaica Gleaner (2006). "Booted from the Lands of Opportunity … – De-
    portees a Criminal Link."12 February: www.jamaica-gleaner.com/
    gleaner/20060212/news/news3.html.
Jamaica Gleaner (2006). "The Utility of Political Jam Sessions." 23 November:
    www.jamaica-gleaner.com/gleaner/20061123/cleisure/cleisure1.html.
Jamaica Impact Inc. "JAMPACT." www.jampact.org.
Jamaica Ministry of Finance and Planning, Debt Management Unit. "Ob-
    jectives." www.mof.gov.jm/dmu/about/objectives.htm. Accessed in
    March 2007.
Jamaica Ministry of Finance and Planning. "Total Public Debt and Indica-
    tor,   1990/91-2004/05."   www.mof.gov.jm/dmu/download/2005/
    pubdebt/pd0506fy.pdf

Jamaica Ministry of Land and Environment (2003). "Jamaica National Assessment Report of the Barbados Programme of Action."

Jamaican Constabulary Force. "'Operation Kingfish': About Operation Kingfish." www.jamaicapolice.org.jm/kingfish/home.htm.

Jamaican Diaspora Foundation. www.diaspora.org.jm/content/home/default1.asp

Kerr, Hon. Justice James (1997). "Behind Jamaica's Garrisons." Report of the National Committee on Political Tribalism.

Khan, Irene (2006). "Haiti: Open Letter to the President of the Republic of Haiti." web.amnesty.org/library/Index/ENGAMR360112006?open&of=ENG-382.

Lak, Daniel (2004). "Problem of Haiti's Gun Culture." British Broadcasting Corporation, 11 March: news.bbc.co.uk/1/hi/world/americas/3500290.stm.

Lapointe, Michelle (2004). "Diasporas in Caribbean Development." Rapporteur's Report, Inter-American Dialogue and the World Bank, August.

Market Research Services Ltd. (2005). "A Survey of the Remittance Market in Jamaica." FOCAL, PowerPoint Presentation for the Canada-Caribbean Diasporas and Development Conference Series, 30–31 May, Toronto and Montreal: www.focal.ca/projects/privatesector/diasporas/Anderson.ppt.

Mascoll, Philip (2001). "The Guns of Jamaica." Toronto Star, 24 July. Archived in Media Awareness Project: www.mapinc.org/drugnews/v01/n1335/a05.html

Metropolis (2003). "Labour Market Outcomes for Immigrants." Conversation Series, December: www.canada.metropolis.net/research-policy/conversation/ conversation_report_15.pdf.

Milford, J. (1997). "DEA Congressional Testimony before the House International Relations Committee Regarding Haiti." Drug Enforcement Agency, 9 December.

Mozingo, Joe (2005). "Jamaicans Are Living in Fear as Homicide Rate Skyrockets." The Miami Herald, 7 July: www.miami.com/mld/miamiherald/12072505.htm.

National Public Radio (2004). "Haiti's Role in Drug Trafficking."

Newland, Kathleen, and Erin Patrick (2004). "Beyond Remittances: The Role of Diaspora in Poverty Reduction in their Countries of Origin." Migration Policy Institute: www.eldis.org/static/DOC17672.htm.

Oliver, Mark. "Violence in Jamaica: Gun Battles Between Law Enforcers and Gangs in Kingston Have Left at Least 22 People Dead in the Past Three Days." The Guardian, 11 July 2001: www.guardian.co.uk/print/0,3858,4219933-103701,00.html.

Organization for Economic Co-operation and Development (2005). "Total Population by Nationality and Country of Birth (detailed countries)." www.oecd.org/document/51/0,2340,en_2649_201185_34063091_1_1_1_1,00.html.

Orozco, Manuel (2002). "Remitting Back Home and Supporting the Homeland: The Guyanese Community in the U.S." Washington, DC: Inter-American Dialogue.

Radio Jamaica. "Haitian Interior Minister Freed of Murder Charges." www.radiojamaica.com/news/story.php?category=6&story=25600/

Schifferes, Steve (2004). "Haïti: An economic basket-case." British Broadcasting Corporation News Online, 1 March: news.bbc.co.uk/1/hi/business/3522155.stm.

Seiveright, Delano (2005). www.jamaicans.com/articles/primecomments/jamaicanrealities.shtml.

Sheil, Ross (2006). "Guns Found at Kingston's Port." *Jamaica Gleaner*, 6 May: www.jamaica-gleaner.com/gleaner/20060506/lead/lead4.html.

Simmons, Alan, Dwaine Plaza, and Victor Piché (2005). "The Remittance Sending Practices of Haitians and Jamaicans in Canada." CERLAC Report.

Sinclair, Glenroy (2003). "Haiti Drug Link – Cops Say Fake Fishermen Smuggling Arms, Aliens." *Jamaica Gleaner*, 9 September. Archived on Hartford Web Publishing: www.hartford-hwp.com/archives/43a/452.html

The Statistical Institute of Jamaica. "Main Labour Force Indicators 2002–2005." www.statinja.com/stats.html#3.

Statistics Canada (2001). "Canada's Ethnocultural Portrait." www12.statcan.ca/english/census01/products/analytic/companion/etoimm/canada.cfm#immigrants_increasingly_asia.

Transparency International (2004). "TI Report on Jamaica calls for party finance reform and tighter clampdown on corruption in public procurement." www.transparency.org/news_room/latest_news/press_releases/2004/2004_08_10_nis_jamaica.

Transparency International (2004/05). "Corruption Perceptions Index." www.transparency.org/surveys/index.html

United Nations Development Programme (2004). "Rapport National sur les Objectifs du Millénaire pour le Développement (2004): Une Vision Commune du Développement Humain Durable." mirror.undp.org/Haïti/OMD/.

United Press International (2004). "Drug Trafficker Gets 11 Years in Haiti."

United States State Department (2001). "Jamaica: Country Reports on Human Rights Practices." www.state.gov/g/drl/rls/hrrpt/2000/wha/805.htm.

University for Peace (2006). *Final Report*, Expert Forum on Capacity Building for Peace and Development, Roles of Diaspora, Toronto, 19–20 October: www.toronto.upeace.org/diaspora/index.html.

Ventura, Arnoldo (2005). "Bridging the Technological Divide between and Within Countries – The Jamaican Approach." Kingston, Jamaica. UNCSTD Panel, Rabat, Morocco 11–12 November: www.unctad.org/sections/dite_dir/docs/dite_pcbb_stdev0016_en.pdf.

Verma, Sonia (2004). "Aid in Haiti a "Logistical Nightmare,'" *Toronto Star*, 25 September.

Vertovec, Steven (2005). *The Political Importance of Diasporas*. Washington, DC: Migration Policy Institute Report: www.migrationinformation.org/feature/print.cfm?id=313.

Vigil, Micheal (2000). "DEA Congressional Testimony before the Subcommittee on Criminal Justice, Drug Policy and Human Resources." Drug Enforcement Agency: www.usdoj.gov/dea/pubs/cngrtest/ct041200.htm (accessed 10 September 2004; note: no longer available online).

Voice of America (2004). "American Airlines Official in Haiti Indicted on Drug Smuggling Charges." 16 October.

World Bank (2006a). Global Economic Prospects, The International Bank for Reconstruction and Development.

World Bank (2006b). World Development Indicators, GDP growth per capita, accessed 19 June 2006.

Zhang, Kenny (2006). "Recognizing the Canadian Diaspora." *Canada Asia Commentary*, no. 41 Asia Pacific Foundation of Canada.

CHAPTER FOUR

Globe and Mail (2005). "Canadian Attitudes Harden on Immigration." 12 August.

Granatstein, J.L. and J.M. Hitsman (1977). *Broken Promises: A History of Conscription in Canada*. Toronto: Oxford University Press.

Granatstein, J.L. (1981). *A Man of Influence: Norman A. Robertson and Canadian Statecraft, 1929–68*. Ottawa: Deneau.

Granatstein, J.L. and Norman Hillmer (1999). *Prime Ministers: Ranking Canada's Leaders*. Toronto: Harper Collins.

Granatstein, J.L. (2004). *Who Killed the Canadian Military?* Toronto: Harper Collins.

Haglund, David (2005). "Does Quebec have an 'Obsession Anti-Américaine'?" Unpublished paper.

Ibbitson, John (2005). "She Is the New Canada." *Globe and Mail,* 5 August.

Innovative Research Group (2004). *Visions of Canadian Foreign Policy.* Survey sponsored by the Canadian Defence and Foreign Affairs Institute and the Dominion Institute: www.cdfai.org/PDF/DCI_CDFAI_report_formatted_V5.pdf.

Ivison, John. "'Pro-Israel' federal advisor must go, Elmasry says." *National Post,* 17 August 2005.

Kashmeri, Zuhair (1991). *The Gulf Within: Canadian Arabs, Racism and the Gulf War.* Toronto: James Lorimer.

The Nation (2005). "Terror's Greatest Recruiting Tool." 29 August.

New York Times Magazine (2005). "An Islamic Alienation." 14 August.

Off, Carol (2004). *The Ghosts of Medak Pocket: The Story of Canada's Secret War.* Canada: Random House.

Ottawa Citizen, 31 October 2005.

Rioux, Jean-Sébastien (2005). "Two Solitudes: Quebeckers' Attitudes Regarding Canadian Security and Defence Policy." *Canadian Defence & Foreign Affairs Institute Research Paper Series,* vol. 1, no. 1, 4–36: www.cdfai.org/currentpublications.htm.

Travers, James (2005). "Underscoring a Message of Zero Tolerance." *Toronto Star,* 14 July.

CHAPTER FIVE

Adams, Michael (2005). "Bash Thy Neighbour." *Globe and Mail,* 19 October, A21.

Allison, Graham (2005). "Is Nuclear Terrorism a Threat to Canada's National Security?" *International Journal,* vol. 60, Summer, 713–22.

Appleby, Timothy and Colin Freeze (2006). "Plot Targeted Peace Tower." *Globe and Mail,* 5 June, A1, A4.

Bell, Stewart (2005). *The Martyr's Oath: The Apprenticeship of a Homegrown Terrorist.* Toronto: John Wiley & Sons.

Cline, Ray S. (1977). *World Power Assessment 1977: A Calculus of Strategic Drift.* Boulder: Westview.

Collacott, Martin (2006). *Canada's Inadequate Response to Terrorism: The Need for Policy Reform.* Vancouver: Fraser Institute Digital Publication.

Cooper, Robert (2004). *The Breaking of Nations: Order and Chaos in the Twenty-First Century.* Toronto: McClelland and Stewart.

De Conde, Alexander (1992). *Ethnicity, Race, and American Foreign Policy: A History.* Boston: Northeastern University Press.

den Tandt, Michael (2005). "Foreign Policy Initiatives Will Help Woo Quebeckers, Pettigrew Says." *Globe and Mail,* 22 October, A11.

Dittmer, Lowell (1977). "Political Culture and Political Symbolism." *World Politics,* vol. 29, July, 552–83.

Dunsky, Dan (2005/06). "Canada's Three Solitudes." *National Interest,* no. 82, Winter, 94–9.

Elkins, David J., and Richard E. B. Simeon (1979). "A Cause in Search of Its Effect, or What Does Political Culture Explain?" *Comparative Politics,* vol. 11, July, 127–45.

Fortmann, Michel, and David G. Haglund (2002). "Canada and the Issue of Homeland Security: Does the 'Kingston Dispensation' Still Hold?" *Canadian Military Journal,* vol. 3 (Spring), 17–22.

Freeze, Colin (2005). "The Khadr Effect." *Globe and Mail,* 3 October, A10.

Granatstein, Jack (2005). "Quebecers Are at the Helm." *Ottawa Citizen,* 1 November, A15.

Haglund, David G. (2004). "What Good Is Strategic Culture? A Modest Defence of an Immodest Concept." *International Journal,* vol. 59, Summer, 479–502.

Harris, John F. (1997). "On Tape, Chretien Slights Clinton." *International Herald Tribune,* 11 July, 7.

Innovative Research Group (2004). *Visions of Canadian Foreign Policy.* Survey sponsored by the Canadian Defence and Foreign Affairs Institute and the Dominion Institute: www.cdfai.org/PDF/DCI_CDFAI_ report_formatted_V5.pdf.

Jenkins, Brian (1969). *Fenians and Anglo-American Relations during Reconstruction.* Ithaca: Cornell University Press.

Lacorne, Denis (1997). *La Crise de l'identité américaine: Du melting-pot au multiculturalisme.* Paris: Fayard.

Lamonde, Yvan (2001). *Allégeances et dépendances: L'histoire d'une ambivalence identitaire.* Quebec: Éditions Nota Bene.

Lane, Ruth (1992). "Political Culture: Residual Category or General Theory?" *Comparative Political Studies,* vol. 25, October, 362–87.

LeBlanc, Daniel and Gloria Galloway (2005). "Washington Scolds Ottawa." *Globe and Mail,* 14 December, A1, A12.

Martin, Pierre (2005). "All Quebec's Fault, Again? Quebec Public Opinion and Canada's Rejection of Missile Defence." *Policy Options,* vol. 26, May, 41–4.

Mearsheimer, John, and Stephen Walt (2006). "The Israel Lobby." *London Review of Books*, vol. 28, March.

Murphy, Rex (2005). "The Elephant Speaks to the Mouse." *Globe and Mail*, 24 September, D6–7.

Naím, Moisés (2003). "The Perils of Lite Anti-Americanism." *Foreign Policy*, vol. 136, May/June, 95–6.

Rioux, Jean-Sébastien (2005). "Two Solitudes: Quebecers' Attitudes Regarding Canadian Security and Defence Policy." Calgary: Canadian Defence and Foreign Affairs Institute.

Roussel, Stéphane and Charles-Alexandre Théorêt (2004). "A 'Distinct Strategy'? The Use of Canadian Strategic Culture by the Sovereigntist Movement in Quebec, 1968–1996." *International Journal*, vol. 59, Summer, 557–77.

Schlesinger, Arthur M. Jr (1998). *The Disuniting of America: Reflections on a Multicultural Society.* New York: W.W. Norton.

Simpson, Jeffrey (2006). "Mr. Ignatieff's Repeated Errors in Judgment." *Globe and Mail*, 28 October, A25.

Smith, Tony (2000). *Foreign Attachments: The Power of Ethnic Groups in the Making of American Foreign Policy.* Cambridge: Harvard University Press.

Sutherland, R. J. (1962). "Canada's Long Term Strategic Situation." *International Journal*, vol. 17, Summer, 199–201.

CHAPTER SIX

Barratt, Bethany (2006). "Canadian Foreign Policy and International Human Rights." *Handbook of Canadian Foreign Policy*, Patrick James, Nelson Michaud, and Marc O'Reilly, eds. Lanham: Lexington Books.

Bruneau, Michel, ed. (1995). *Diasporas.* Reclus: Montpellier.

Canadian Arab Federation. www.caf.ca.

Canadian Islamic Congress. www.canadianislamiccongress.com or www.muslimcanadiancongress.org/.

Canadian Islamic Congress (2004). *Elections 2004: Towards Informed and Committed Voting. A Research Report on Grading Federal MPs 2000–2004*: www.canadianislamiccongress.com/election2004/Election2004.pdf.

Coward, Harold, John R. Hinnells, and Raymond Brady Williams, eds (2000). *The South Asian Religious Diaspora in Britain, Canada, and the United States.* Albany, NY: State University of New York Press.

Foreign Affairs and International Trade Canada. www.dfait-maeci.gc.ca/middle_east/menu-fr.asp.

Government of Canada (2006). Canada-Afghanistan Relations: www.
canada-afghanistan.gc.ca/background-en.asp.

Government of Canada (2004). Federal Budget.

Heritage Canada. Official Languages. www.patrimoinecanadien.gc.ca/
progs/lo-ol/pubs/census2001/5_e.cfm.

Islam Memo. www.islammemo.cc/west/one_news.asp?IDnews=20.

Pipes, Daniel (2003). "[Fixing] Islam's Image Problems." *New York Post*,
29 July: www.danielpipes.org/article/1179.

Legault, Albert (2005). *Sada Al Machrek,* no. 180.

O'Reilly, Marc J. (2006). "Canadian Foreign Policy in the Middle East: Reflexive Multilateralism in an Evolving World." *Handbook of Canadian Foreign Policy,* Patrick James, Nelson Michaud, and Marc O'Reilly, eds.
Lanham: Lexington Books.

Sallot, Jeff. "Influence of Muslim voters is Growing." *Globe and Mail,* 19 December 2005.

Shain, Yossi and Aharon Barth (2003). "Diasporas and International Relations Theory." *International Organization,* vol. 57, no. 3, 449–79.

Sheffer, G., ed. (1986). *Modern Diasporas in International Politics.* New York:
St Martin's Press.

Statistics Canada, *Recensement de 2001: serie « analyses" Les Religions au Canada.*
www12.statcan.ca/francais/census01/Products/Analytic/companion/rel/
pdf/96F0030XIF2001015.pdf.

CHAPTER SEVEN

Alexander, Cynthia, and Leslie A. Pal (1998). *Digital Democracy: Policy and
Politics in the Wired World.* Toronto: Oxford University Press.

Ayres, Jeffrey M. "Civil Society Participation in Canadian Foreign Policy."
Handbook of Canadian Foreign Policy, Patrick James, Nelson Michaud and
Patrick O'Reilly, eds. Lanham: Lexington Books, 491–512.

Birkland, Thomas A. (1997). *After Disaster: Agenda Setting, Public Policy and
Focusing Events* Washington, DC: Georgetown University Press.

Canadian International Development Agency (2003/04). *Statistical Report
on Official Development Assistance.* Ottawa.

Canadian Ports Magazine (2002).

Connolly, William E. (1969). *The Bias of Pluralism.* New York: Atherton
Press.

Cooper, Andrew (1997). *Canadian Foreign Policy: Old Habits and New Directions.* Toronto: Prentice Hall Canada.

Dahl, Robert (1956). *A Preface to Democratic Theory*. Chicago: University of Chicago Press.

Dahl, Robert (1985). *A Preface to Economic Democracy*. Berkeley, CA: University of California Press.

Department of Foreign Affairs and International Trade (2003). *Dialogue on Foreign Policy Report to Canadians*. Ottawa.

Department of Foreign Affairs and International Trade (2005). *International Policy Statement: A Role of Pride and Influence in the World*. Ottawa.

Delvoie, Louis A. (2000). "Canada and International Security Operations: The Search for Policy Rationales." *Canadian Military Journal*, vol. 2, no. 1, 13–24.

Doran, Charles F. (1984). *Forgotten Partnership: U.S.-Canada Relations Today*. Baltimore: Johns Hopkins University Press.

Government of Canada (2004). *National Security Policy: Securing a Free and Open Society*.

Government of Canada (2005). *Canada's International Policy Statement: A Role of Pride and Influence in the World*.

Haas, Ernst B. (1958). *The Uniting of Europe: Political, Social, and Economic Forces, 1950–1957*. Stanford: Stanford University Press.

Hagan, Joe D. (1993). *Political Opposition and Foreign Policy in Comparative Perspective*. Boulder: Lynne Rienner.

Hagan, Joe D. (1995). "Domestic Political Explanations in the Analysis of Foreign Policy." *Foreign Policy Analysis: Continuity and Change in Its Second Generation*, Laura Neack, Jeanne A.K. Hey and Patrick J. Haney, eds. Englewood Cliffs: Prentice-Hall, 117–43.

Holsti, K. J. (1991). *Change in the International System: Essays on the Theory and Practice of International Relations*. Aldershot: Edward Elgar.

Hudson, Valerie, and Christopher S. Vore (1995). "Foreign Policy Analysis Yesterday, Today, and Tomorrow." *Mershon International Studies Review*, vol. 39, October 1995, 209–38.

Hughes, Barry (1978). *The Domestic Context of American Foreign Policy*. San Francisco: W.H. Freeman and Company.

Ignatieff, Michael. "To Be Realists and Demand the Impossible: Balancing Foreign and Domestic Policy." *Policy Options*, vol. 26, no. 7, September 2005, 5–7.

Immergut, Ellen M. (1998). "Theoretical Core of the New Institutionalism." *Politics and Society*, vol. 26, no. 1, 5–34.

Innovative Research Group (2004). *Visions of Canadian Foreign Policy*. Survey sponsored by the Canadian Defence and Foreign Affairs Institute and the Dominion Institute: www.cdfai.org/PDF/DCI_CDFAI_ report_ formatted_V5.pdf.

Innovative Research Group (2005). *The World in Canada: Demographics and Diversity in Canadian Foreign Policy.* Report prepared for the Canadian Defence and Foreign Affairs Institute. Toronto.

Ipsos-Reid (2005). *Canadian Views on Canada's Roll in International Affairs.* Report prepared for the University of Ottawa. Vancouver.

Keohane, Robert and Joseph Nye (1989). *Power and Interdependence* 2nd ed. Glenview: Scott, Foresman.

Kratochwil, Friedrich (1993). "The Embarrassment of Changes: Neo-Realism as the Science of Realpolitik without Politics." *Review of International Studies,* 19 January, 63–80.

Lee, Steven (1998). "Beyond Consultations: Public Contributions to Making Foreign Policy." *Canada Among Nations 1998: Leadership and Dialogue,* Fen Osler Hampson and Maureen Appel Molot, eds. Don Mills: Oxford University Press.

Liberal Party of Canada (1993). *Liberal Foreign Policy Handbook.* Ottawa.

Liberal Party of Canada (1993). *Creating Opportunity: The Liberal Plan for Canada.* Ottawa.

London, Kurt (1965). *The Making of Foreign Policy East and West.* New York: J.B. Lippincott Company.

MacDonald, Ryan, and John Hoddinott (2004). "Determinants of Canadian Bilateral Aid Allocations: Humanitarian, Commercial or Political?" *Canadian Journal of Economics,* vol. 37, no. 2, 294–312.

Maoz, Zeev (1996). *Domestic Sources of Global Change.* Ann Arbor: University of Michigan Press.

March, James G., and Johan P. Olsen, eds. (1998). "The Institutional Dynamics of International Political Orders." *International Organization,* vol. 52, no. 4, 943–69.

Miliband, Ralph (1977). *Marxism and Politics.* Oxford: Oxford University Press.

Milner, Helen (1992). "International Theories of Cooperation Among Nations: Strengths and Weaknesses." *World Politics,* vol. 44, no. 3, 466–96.

Noël, Alain, Jean-Phillippe Thérien, and Sébastien Dallaire (2004). "Divided over Internationalism: The Canadian Public and Development Assistance." *Canadian Public Policy,* vol. 30, no. 1, 29–46.

Nossal, Kim Richard (1988). "Mixed Motives Revisited: Canada's Interest in Development Assistance." *Canadian Journal of Political Science,* vol. 21, 35–56.

Nossal, Kim Richard (1995). "The Democratization of Canadian Foreign Policy: The Elusive Ideal." *Canada Among Nations 1995,* Maureen Appel Molot and M.A. Cameron, eds. Montreal and Kingston: McGill-Queen's University Press, 29–44.

Nye, Joseph S. Jr. (2002). "The American National Interest and Global Public Goods." *International Affairs*, vol. 78, no. 2, 233–44.

O'Reilly, John E. (1999). *American Public Opinion and U.S. Foreign Policy*. Chicago: Chicago Council on Foreign Relations.

Piper, Don C., and Ronald J. Terchek, eds. (1983). *Interaction: Foreign Policy and Public Policy*. Washington: American Enterprise for Public Policy Research.

POLLARA (2004). *Canadian's Attitudes Toward Foreign Policy*. Report prepared for The Canadian Institute of International Affairs. Toronto.

Privy Council Office (2004). "Securing an Open Society: Canada's National Security Policy." Canada: Her Majesty the Queen in Right of Canada.

Rioux, Jean-Sébastien (2006). "Canadian Official Development Assistance Policy." *Handbook of Canadian Foreign Policy*, Patrick James, Nelson Michaud and Patrick O'Reilly, eds. Lanham: Lexington Books, 209–33.

Risse-Kappen, Thomas (1991). "Public Opinion, Domestic Structure, and Foreign Policy in Liberal Democracies." *World Politics*, vol. 43, 479–512.

Rosenau, James (1967). *Domestic Sources of Foreign Policy*. New York: The Free Press.

Rosenau, James (1997). *Along the Domestic-Foreign Frontier: Exploring Governance in a Turbulent World*. Cambridge: Cambridge University Press.

Rousseau, Jean-Jacques (1987). *On the Social Contract*. In *The Basic Political Writings*. Hackett Classics Series no. 47. Indianapolis: Hackett Publishing Co.

Simmons, Beth A. (1994). *Who Adjusts? Domestic Sources of Foreign Economic Policy During the Interwar Years*. Princeton: Princeton University Press.

Smillie, Ian (1998). *Relief and Development: The Struggle for Synergy*. Providence: Watson Institute Occasional Paper #33.

Smith, Steve (1987). "Paradigm Dominance in International Relations: The Development of International Relations as a Social Science." *Millennium: Journal of International Studies*, vol. 16, no. 2, 189–206.

Sokolsky, Joel. J. (2004). "Realism Canadian Style: National Security Policy and the Chrétien Legacy." *Policy Matters*, vol. 5, no. 2 .

Spicer, Keith (1966). *A Samaritan State? External Aid in Canada's Foreign Policy*. Toronto: University Press.

Thelen, Kathleen, and Sven Steinmo (1992). "Historical Institutionalism in Comparative Perspective." *Structuring Politics: Historical Institutionalism in Comparative Analysis*, Sven Steinmo, Kathleen Thelen and Frank Longstreth, eds. Cambridge: Cambridge University Press, 1–32.

Thérien, Jean-Philippe (1989). "Le Canada et le régime international de l'aide." *Études Internationales*, vol. 20, 311–40.

Thérien, Jean-Philippe, and Alain Noël (1994). "Welfare Institutions and Foreign Aid." *Canadian Journal of Political Science*, vol. 27, no. 3, 529–58.

Thérien, Jean-Philippe and Alain Noël (2000). "Political Parties and Foreign Aid." *American Political Science Review*, vol. 94, no. 1, 151–62.

Triantis, S.G. (1971). "Canada's Interest in Foreign Aid." *World Politics*, vol. 24, 1–18.

Waltz, Kenneth W. (1954). *Man, the State and War: A Theoretical Analysis*. New York: Columbia University Press.

Welsh, Jennifer (2004). *At Home in the World: Canada's Global Vision for the 21st Century*. Toronto: Harper Collins Publishers.

CHAPTER EIGHT

Adams, Michael (2003). *Fire and Ice: The United States, Canada, and the Myth of Converging Values*. Toronto: Penguin Canada.

Adams, Michael. "Canada-U.S. Relations: Bash Thy Neighbour." *The Globe and Mail*, 19 October 2005, A21.

Boucher, Christian (2004). "Canada-US Values: Distinct, Inevitably Carbon Copy, or Narcissism of Small Differences?" *North American Linkages*, vol. 7, no. 1: policyresearch.gc.ca/page.asp?pagenm=v7nl_art_08

Bricker, Darrell and Edward Greenspon (2001). *Searching for Certainty: Inside the New Canadian Mindset*. Random House Canada.

Cellucci, Paul (2005). *Unquiet Diplomacy*. Toronto: Key Porter Books.

Centre for Research and Information on Canada (2003). "Canada and the United States: An Evolving Partnership." *The CRIC Papers*.

Continuum Research (2003). "Diverging Paths – Common Goals." Willson House, Meech Lake: 12 September. Presentation.

Ekos Research Associates (2005). "Decision-Maker Survey: Canada and the U.S." *Rethinking North American Integration*.

Environics Research Group (2004). Survey.

GPC Research (2004). Powerpoint presentation to the Department of Foreign Affairs and International Trade. Ottawa.

Innovative Research Group (2005). *The World in Canada: Demographics and Diversity in Canadian Foreign Policy*. Report prepared for the Canadian Defence and Foreign Affairs Institute. Toronto.

Parkin, Andrew (2003). "Pro-Canadian, Anti-American or Anti-War? Canadian Public Opinion on the Eve of War." *Policy Options*.

The Pew Research Center for the People and the Press (2004). "Americans and Canadians: The North American Not-so-odd Couple." people-press.org/commentary/display.php3?AnalysisID=80.

Rioux, Jean-Sebastien (2005). "Two Solitudes: Quebecers' Attitudes Regarding Canadian Security and Defence Policy." *Canadian Defence and Foreign Affairs Institute*: www.cdfai.org/PDF/Two%20Solitudes.pdf.

Roussel, Stéphane, and Charles-Alexandre Théorêt (2004). "A 'Distinct Strategy'? The Use of Canadian Strategic Culture by the Sovereigntist Movement in Quebec, 1968–1996." *International Journal*, vol. 59, Summer, 557–77.

CHAPTER NINE

Bachand, Claude (2004). *Débats de la Chambre des communes du Canada*, 37e législature, 3e session, 19 February: www.parl.gc.ca/37/3/parlbus/chambus/house/debates/014_2004-02-19/HAN014-F.htm#SOBQ-.

Berger, François (1990). "La Crise amérindienne: les choses auraient été différentes dans un Québec souverain – Lucien Bouchard." *La Presse*, 15 September, A8.

Bland, Douglas L., and Roy Rempel (2004). "A Vigilant Parliament: Building Competence for Effective Parliamentary Oversight of National Defence and the Canadian Armed Forces." *Policy Matters*, vol. 5, no. 1.

Bloc québécois (1997). *Plate-forme électorale. Version intégrale.* Montreal.

Bloc québécois (1999). "La fermeture des frontières du Kosovo fait des Kosovars des prisonniers chez eux." *Communiqué du Bloc québécois*, 9 April.

Bloc québécois (2005). *Imaginer le Québec souverain.* Proposition principale.

Bloc québécois (2006). *Le Bloc québécois dit non à la militarisation de l'espace.* www.blocquebecois.org/fr/Dossiers/Bouclier/bouclier.asp.

Bouchard, Lucien (1994a). *Débats de la Chambre des communes du Canada*, 35e législature, 1ère session, 25 January: www.parl.gc.ca/english/hansard/previous/007_94-01-25/007TOCF.html.

Bouchard, Lucien (1994b). *Débats de la Chambre des communes du Canada*, 35e législature, 1ère session, 21 April: www.parl.gc.ca/english/hansard/previous/054_94-04-21/054PB1F.html#LASITUATIONENBOSNIE.

Buzzetti, Hélène, and Manon Cornellier (2001). "Attaque contre les États-Unis. Consterné, Chrétien offre l'aide du Canada." *Le Devoir*, 12 September, A4.

Buzzetti, Hélène. "Canada-États-Unis, même combat." *Le Devoir*, 18 January 2002, A1.

Buzzetti, Hélène. "Le Canada n'a pas à jouer les arbitres. Un haut fonctionnaire des Affaires étrangères rejette la proposition bloquiste," *Le Devoir*, 17 September 2002, A3.

Chambre des Communes (2002a), "Rapport dissident du Bloc québécois concernant le rapport final du Comité permanent de la défense nationale et des anciens combattants sur l'état de préparation des Forces armées canadiennes." *Faire face à nos responsabilités. Rapport du Comité permanent de la défense nationale et des anciens combattants.* Ottawa.

Chambre des Communes (2002b). "Le Comité ouvre des perspectives intéressantes, mais ne va pas assez loin pour les mettre de l'avant. Opinion dissidente du Bloc québécois au rapport sur l'intégration continentale." *Partenaires en Amérique du Nord: Cultiver les relations du Canada avec les États-Unis et le Mexique. Rapport du Comité permanent des affaires étrangères et du commerce internationale.* Ottawa, 349–55.

Charbonneau, Jean-Pierre, and Gilbert Paquette (1978). *L'Option.* Montreal: Éditions de l'Homme.

Confédération des syndicats nationaux (1995). *Un choix clair pour la CSN: La souveraineté du Québec.*

Coulon, Jocelyn (1992). *La dernière croisade. La guerre du Golfe et le rôle caché du Canada.* Montreal: Méridien.

Coulon, Jocelyn (1994). "La défense canadienne mise au pas." *Le Devoir,* 2 November.

Dion, Jean (1994). "Les Libéraux divisés, l'opposition unie." *Le Devoir,* 27 January, A1.

Duceppe, Gilles (2001). *Débats de la Chambre des communes du Canada,* 37e législature, 1ère session, 17 September, www.parl.gc.ca/37/1/parlbus/chambus/house/debates/079_2001-09-17/HAN079-F.htm#OOB-47884.

Duceppe, Gilles (2003). *Débats de la Chambre des communes,* 37e législature, 2e session, 20 March, www.parl.gc.ca/37/2/parlbus/chambus/house/debates/074_2003-03-20/HAN074-F.htm#SOBQ-.

Fortmann, Michel, and Gordon Mace (1993). "Le Bloc québécois et la politique étrangère." *La politique étrangère canadienne,* vol. 1, no. 3, 109–12.

Gauthier, Gilles (1995). "Un contrat de 2 milliards à l'Ontario." *La Presse,* 17 August, B1.

Granatstein, Jack (2005). "Quebecers Are at the Helm. It Is Bad For National Unity to Have Quebec Setting the Agenda on the War in Iraq or a Missile-Defence Program." *The Ottawa Citizen,* 1 November, A15.

Haglund, David, and Stéphane Roussel (2004). "Escott Reid, the North Atlantic Treaty, and Canadian Strategic Culture." *Escott Reid: Diplomat & Scholar,* Greg Donaghy and Stéphane Roussel, eds. Montreal: McGill-Queen's.

Haglund, David (2005). *Does Quebec Have an 'Obsession Anti-Américaine'?*
    Montreal: McGill University. Unpublished paper.

Jacob, Jean-Marc (1995). *Débats de la Chambre des communes du Canada,*
    35ᵉ législature, 1ère session, 4 December: www.parl.gc.ca/english/
    hansard/previous/270_95-12-04/270GO1F.html#LESBALKANS.

Jockel, Joseph T. (1980). "Un Québec souverain et la Défense de
    l'Amérique du Nord contre une attaque nucléaire." *Études internation-
    ales*, vol. 11, no. 2, 303–16.

Jockel, Joseph T. (1995). "Washington and 'An Act Respecting the Sover-
    eign Quebec'." *Decision Quebec Series Study 1*. Washington: Center for
    Strategic & International Studies.

Lessard, Denis (1991). "Des péquistes veulent rappeler à Parizeau la voca-
    tion pacifiste du parti." *La Presse*, 25 January, B1.

Lortie, Marie-Claude, and Gilles Paquin (1991). "Le début des combats
    met fin au débat des députés à Ottawa." *La Presse*, 17 January A5.

Massie, Justin, and Stéphane Roussel (2005). "Le Dilemme canadien face
    à la guerre en Irak (ou de l'art d'étirer un élastique sans le rompre)."
    Diplomaties en guerre. Sept États face à la crise irakienne, Alex Macleod, ed.
    Montreal: Athéna, 74–5.

Nossal, Kim R. (1997). *The Politics of Canadian Foreign Policy*. Scarborough:
    Prentice-Hall.

Parliament of Canada (1994a). "Rapport dissident des députés du Bloc
    québécois membres du Comité mixte spécial sur la révision de la politique
    de défense du Canada." *La sécurité dans un monde en évolution. Rapport du
    Comité mixte spécial sur la politique de défense du Canada*. Ottawa: Service des
    publications, Direction des publications parlementaires, 79–102.

Parliament of Canada (1994b). "Pour une autre politique étrangère. Rap-
    port dissident des députés du Bloc québécois." *La politique étrangère du
    Canada. Rapport du Comité mixte spécial du Sénat et de la Chambre des com-
    munes chargé de l'examen de la politique étrangère du Canada: Opinions dissi-
    dentes et annexes*. Ottawa, Services des publications, Direction des
    publications parlementaires, 1–28 November.

Rempel, Roy (2002). *The Chatter Box. An Insider's Account of the Irrelevance of
    Parliament in the Making of Canadian Foreign and Defence Policy*. Toronto:
    Breakout Educational Network.

Roussel, Stéphane, and Chantal Robichaud (2001). "L'élargissement vir-
    tuel: Un Québec souverain face à l'OTAN (1968–1995)." *Les cahiers d'his-
    toire*, vol. 20, no. 2, 147–93.

Roussel, Stéphane, and Charles-Alexandre Théorêt (2004). "A 'Distinct
    Strategy'? The Use of Canadian Strategic Culture by the Sovereignist

Movement in Quebec, 1968–1996." *International Journal*, vol. 59, no. 3, 557–77.

Roussel, Stéphane (2006). "Une culture stratégique en évolution. La société québécoise et le mouvement souverainiste face aux questions de défense et de sécurité militaire." *Histoire des relations internationales du Québec*, Stéphane Paquin, Louise Beaudoin and Robert Comeau, eds. Unpublished paper.

Le Soleil (1996). "Révélations du bloquiste Jean-Marc Jacob: Des officiers prêts à créer un état-major québécois. Le ministère de la Défense aurait même étudié la possible mise en place d'une armée québécoise en cas de victoire du oui." 15 March, A9.

Le Soleil (1999). "Québec, l'ennemi à abattre. Un exercice militaire durant lequel l'armée fait la guerre aux forces indépendantistes." 11 January, A1.

Tramier, Sylviane. "Quelle politique étrangère?: Les questions internationales sont à peu près absentes de la campagne électorale." *Le Devoir*, 12 October 1993, A1.

Tremblay, Jeanne-d'Arc, ed. (1988). *La défense du Québec et la famille Tremblay*. Montreal: Fides.

Young, Huguette (1996). "Ottawa approuve la riposte américaine à l'Irak." *Le Devoir*, 4 September, A5.

Young, Huguette. "Débat sur la crise de l'Irak aux Communes." *Le Droit*, 10 February 1998, 18.

CHAPTER TEN

Aird, Robert (2005). *André Patry et la présence du Québec dans le monde*. Montreal: vlb éditeur.

Charest, Jean (2004). *Allocution du premier ministre du Québec à l'ÉNAP*. www.premier.gouv.qc.ca/general/discours/archives_discours/2004/fevrier/dis20040225.htm.

Comeau, Paul-André. *Régionalisation et relations internationales en Europe* in Robert Bernier. Quebec: Presses de l'Université du Québec. Unpublished paper.

Donaghy, Craig, and Neal Carter (2006). "'There Are No Half-Countries': Canada, La Francophonie, and the Projection of Canadian Biculturalism, 1960–2002." *Handbook of Canadian Foreign Policy*, Pat James, Nelson Michaud and Marc O'Reilly, eds. Lanham: Lexington Books, 133–64.

Government of Canada (2005). *A Role of Pride and Influence in the World*. Canada's International Policy Statement: Diplomacy. www.dfait-maeci.gc.ca/cip-pic/ips/ips-diplomacy9-fr.asp.

Harper, Stephen (2005). *Allocution prononcée devant la Chambre de commerce de Québec.* 19 December.

Martin, Paul, Jr (2004). Discours du Premier ministre Paul Martin devant la Chambre de commerce de Laval, 19 May: www.pm.gc.ca/fra/news.asp?category=2&id=207.

Martin, Paul, Sr (1985). *A Very Public Life: So Many Worlds.* Toronto: Deneau.

Michaud, Nelson (2004). "Le Québec dans le monde: faut-il redessiner les fondements de son action?" *L'État québécois au XXIème siècle*, Robert Bernier, ed. Quebec: Presses de l'Université du Québec.

Michaud, Nelson (2006). "The Prime Minister, PMO, and PCO: Makers of Canadian Foreign Policy?" *Handbook of Canadian Foreign Policy*, Pat James, Nelson Michaud and Marc O'Reilly, eds. Lanham: Lexington Books, 21–48.

Ministère des Relations internationales (2005). *L'action internationale du Québec. Le Québec dans les forums internationaux.* www.mri.gouv.qc.ca/fr/pdf/action_internationale1.pdf.

Morin, Claude (1987). *L'Art de l'impossible.* Montreal: Boréal.

Quebec Legislative Assembly (1967). *Débats de l'Assemblée législative du Québec*, vol. 5, no. 49, 13 April.

Contributors

DAVID BERCUSON earned his Ph.D. in History in 1971 at the University of Toronto. He has published on a wide range of topics specializing in modern Canadian politics, Canadian defense and foreign policy, and Canadian military history. Dr Bercuson's most recent book, co-authored with Dr Herwig, is *One Christmas in Washington: Churchill, Roosevelt and the Making of the Grand Alliance.* Dr Bercuson is also director of programs at the Canadian Defence and Foreign Affairs Institute, member of the Board of Governors of Royal Military College, and a member of the Advisory Council on National Security.

DAVID CARMENT is professor of International Affairs at the Norman Paterson School of International Affairs, Carleton University and fellow of the Canadian Defence and Foreign Affairs Institute (CDFAI). He is listed in the Who's Who in International Affairs. In addition Carment is the principal investigator for the Country Indicators for Foreign Policy project (CIFP). He has served as director of the Centre for Security and Defence Studies at Carleton University and is the recipient of a Carleton Graduate Student's teaching excellence award, Carleton University's research achievement award, and the Petro-Canada Young Innovator Award.

ADAM CHAPNICK is a Social Sciences and Humanities Research Council Postdoctoral Fellow in the Department of History at the University of Toronto. He is the deputy chair, Department of Command, Leadership, and Management and assistant professor, Department of defence Studies, Canadian Forces College. He is the author of *The Middle Power Project: Canada and the Founding of the United Nations* (UBC Press 2005) as well as a number of articles on Canadian foreign policy, Canadian-US relations, and the United Nations. He is currently writing a biography of the former Canadian diplomat and commentator John Holmes.

J.L. GRANATSTEIN, OC, is Distinguished Research Professor of History Emeritus at York University. He is chair of the Advisory Council of the Canadian Defence and Foreign Affairs Institute and writes widely on defense and foreign policy.

DAVID HAGLUND is the Sir Edward Peacock Professor of Political Studies at Queen's University (Kingston, Ontario). From 1985 to 1995, and again from 1996 to 2002, he served as director of the Queen's Centre for International Relations. He has held visiting professorships in France and Germany, as well as at the McGill Institute for the Study of Canada, where he held the Seagram Chair in 2004–05. His research focuses on transatlantic security, and on Canadian and American foreign and security policy. He is co-editor of the *International Journal*.

ANDREW HARRINGTON is an MA candidate at the Norman Paterson School of International Affairs and a law student at University of Ottawa. His research focuses on early warning, diaspora criminal organizations, and conflict prevention in East Timor.

TODD HATALEY completed his Ph.D. at Queen's University in Kingston, Ontario. His current research focuses on the management of international boundaries, transnational crime, and issues in Canadian foreign policy. He is currently a member of the Royal Canadian Mounted Police.

CHRISTIAN LEUPRECHT is assistant professor in the Department of Political Science and the Division of Continuing Studies at the Royal Military College of Canada. He is cross-appointed to the Department of Political Studies at Queen's University where he is also a research associate at the Institute of Intergovernmental Relations and a fellow at the Queen's Centre for International Relations. He holds degrees from the University of Toronto, the Institut d'Études Politiques de Grenoble, and Queen's University. His publications and research focus on political demography, liberal-democratic and constitutional governance and theory, ethnopolitical and internecine conflict and violence, military sociology, and federalism and federal governance, with a particular interest in the study of politics and government in Canada, Germany, and small-island developing states. His books include *Canada: The State of the Federation 2004: Municipal-Federal-Provincial Relations* (with Robert

Young; Montreal and Kingston: McGill-Queen's University Press, 2006) and *Comparative Multilevel Governance* (with Harvey Lazar; Montreal and Kingston: McGill-Queen's University Press, 2007).

NELSON MICHAUD (Ph.D. Laval) is associate professor of Political Science and International Relations, chair of the Groupe d'études, de recherche et de formation internationales (GERFI), and chair of the Laboratoire d'étude sur les politiques publiques et la mondialisation at the École nationale d'administration publique; he is fellow of the Canadian Defence and Foreign Affairs Institute, researcher-member of the Institut Québécois des Hautes Études Internationales, associate researcher at the Centre d'études interaméricaines, and research fellow at the Centre for foreign policy studies (Dalhousie University). He has taught at Dalhousie and Laval Universities and has been invited as a guest professor at the Canadian Royal Military College.

EVAN H. POTTER is an assistant professor in the Department of Communications at the University of Ottawa, where he teaches international and strategic communications. He is the editor of *Cyber-Diplomacy: Making Foreign Policy in the 21st Century* (2002) and is currently completing a study on Canada's public diplomacy

STEWART PREST is a graduate of the Norman Paterson School of International Affairs and senior analyst for Country Indicators for Foreign Policy at Carleton. His current research includes work on governance monitoring and failed states. He has written extensively on the Haitian criminal diaspora, risk analysis, and conflict monitoring for the Canadian Government.

ELIZABETH RIDDELL-DIXON is a professor of International Relations and former chair of the Department of Political Science at the University of Western Ontario. Her publications include *Canada and the Beijing Conference on Women: Governmental Politics and NGO Participation* (Vancouver: University of British Columbia Press, 2001); *The State of the United Nations, 1993: North-South Perspectives* (Providence, RI: Academic Council on the United Nations System, Brown University, 1993); *International Relations in the Post-Cold War Era* (Toronto: Nelson Canada, 1993); *Canada and the International Seabed: Domestic Determinants and External Constraints* (Montreal: McGill-Queen's, 1989); and *The Domestic Mosaic: Interest Groups and Canadian Foreign Policy.* (Toronto: Canadian Institute of International Affairs, 1985). She is currently vice-president of the board of directors of the London Museum of Ontario Archaeology. Previously she has served on the executive and board of directors of the Canadian Political Science Association (2004–06), as co-director of the Summer Workshop Program for the Academic Council on the United Nations System (2004); and on the board of directors of the Lester B. Pearson Canadian International Peacekeeping Centre (1998–2003).

STÉPHANE ROUSSEL is currently assistant professor, Department of Political Science, Université du Québec à Montréal (UQAM) where he holds the Canada Research Chair in Canadian Foreign and Defence Policy. From 2000 to 2002, he was professor at Glendon College (York University) in Toronto, where he taught international relations and security studies. He was previously lecturer and visiting professor, Department of Political Science, Université de Montréal. He is a graduate of Université de Montréal (Ph.D., 1999).

PER UNHEIM is an MA candidate at Norman Paterson School of International Affairs. His research focuses on corporate social responsibility, diaspora remittances, and conflict analysis.

Index